Transforming Leadership Pathways for Humanities Professionals in Higher Education

NAVIGATING CAREERS IN HIGHER EDUCATION

The success of diverse faculty entering institutions of higher education is shaped by varying factors at both the individual and institutional levels. Gender, race, class, ethnicity, and immigrant generation as well as their intersections and interplay influence experiences and aspirations of faculty members and administrators. Women have earned half or more of all doctoral degrees for almost a decade yet remain disproportionately underrepresented in tenured and leadership positions throughout academia.

The Navigating Careers in Higher Education series utilizes an intersectional lens to examine and understand how faculty members and administrators navigate careers and their aspirations to succeed. The series includes edited collections and monographs that adopt an interdisciplinary, empirical approach that has theoretical, pedagogical, or policy impacts in addition to enabling individuals to navigate their own careers. Books may adopt a US or a global focus, and topics may include addressing sexism, homophobia, racism, and ethnocentrism; the role of higher education institutions; the effects of growing non-tenure-track faculty; the challenge of research agenda that may be perceived as controversial; maintaining a life-work balance; and entering leadership positions. Additional topics related to careers in higher education are also welcome.

Series editors

Mangala Subramaniam, Series Editor
Professor and Butler Chair and Director, Susan Bulkeley Butler Center
for Leadership Excellence, Purdue University

M. Cristina Alcalde, Series Coeditor
Vice President for Institutional Diversity and Inclusion and Professor, Global
and Intercultural Studies, Miami University

Other titles in this series

Dismantling Institutional Whiteness:
Emerging Forms of Leadership in Higher Education
M. Cristina Alcalde and Mangala Subramaniam (Eds.)

Transforming Leadership Pathways for Humanities Professionals in Higher Education

Edited by
Roze Hentschell and
Catherine E. Thomas

Purdue University Press • West Lafayette, Indiana

Cataloging-in-Publication Data is on file at the Library of Congress.

978-1-61249-824-9 (hardback)
978-1-61249-825-6 (paperback)
978-1-61249-826-3 (epub)
978-1-61249-827-0 (epdf)

Cover images: foreground, mycola/iStock via Getty Images; background texture, Anastasiia_Guseva/iStock via Getty Images

For the leaders who mentored and inspired us, the colleagues who walk beside us on our leadership pathways, and our students, the leaders of the future.

CONTENTS

ACKNOWLEDGMENTS

THIS VOLUME IS THE RESULT OF MANY YEARS OF CONVERSATIONS WITH COLLEAGUES AT CON-ferences, in formal and less formal settings. We would like to acknowledge the participants of the 2018 Ohio Valley Shakespeare Conference roundtable session "Shakespeare's Administrators," which Catherine facilitated, and the 2021 Shakespeare Association of America Forum on Administration, which we jointly facilitated. While the project has grown to encompass a much wider group of humanities professionals engaged in higher education leadership work, we appreciate the ideas and collegiality that our early modernist colleagues initially provided. We are especially grateful to this volume's contributors, who thoughtfully and openly offered their stories and shared with the academic community a more representative account of the diverse leadership pathways and challenges in higher education. Enormous thanks as well to our fabulous editorial assistant, Sadie Kinney-McGrath. This volume is better for your keen eyes and terrific organizational skills.

We also would like to acknowledge the institutions that offered learning opportunities as we developed as faculty members and administrators: University of California at Santa Barbara, William Paterson University in New Jersey, Colorado State University, Pennsylvania State University, College of Charleston, Georgia Gwinnett College, and Georgia Institute of Technology. In particular, we'd like to thank our mentors who took the time and energy to pour into us, to show by direction and example how to be successful in navigating change and the throes of university life. Catherine would like to thank Drs. Kent Cartwright, Charles Rutherford, Maynard (Sandy) Mack Jr., Susan Lanser, Linda Woodbridge, Garrett Sullivan, Laura Knoppers, Amy McCandless, Patricia Ward, Scott Peeples, Justin Jernigan, and Teresa Winterhalter. Roze would like to thank Drs. Patricia Fumerton, the late Richard Helgerson, Bruce Ronda, Louann Reid, Alex Bernasek, Ben Withers, Sue James, Mary Pedersen, Kelly Long, Rick Miranda, Tony Frank and her University of California San Diego mentors Becky Petitt, John Moore, James Soto Antony, and Elizabeth Simmons.

While there are multitudes of colleagues who became friends (each other included!) who have sustained us in our careers, we would like to acknowledge several who walk the higher ed leadership pathways with us and who have provided particular support and inspiration. Roze would like to thank Ryan Claycomb, Catherine DiCesare, and Ria Vigil, the many College of Liberal Arts department chairs with whom she has worked over her years as associate dean, and the phenomenal Dean's Office, especially Sadie Kinney-McGrath, Magdeline Hall, Beth Etter, Kelsey Schultz, Elizabeth Terry-Emmot, Cole Wise, Tonya Malik-Carson, Wes Scharf, and Colleen Weitzel. I simply could not be half as effective without your amazing work and support. Catherine would like to thank Greg Colón Semenza, Niamh O'Leary, P. Dustin Stegner, Nicole Jacobs, Jennifer Feather, Michelle Dowd, Cara Delay, Sandra Slater, J. Michael Duvall, Karen Jackson, Rachel Bowser, Rolando Marquez, and two amazing leaders who left the world too soon, Alison Piepmeier and Conseula Francis. You all have taught us so much and helped us in times of light and shadow. Thank you, sincerely.

Finally, none of this work would be possible without our families, the sine qua non of our lives, and the balancing forces who keep us (moderately) sane. To Robert and Beverly Thomas, thank you for showing me [Catherine] what strong, compassionate leadership means and for living that example for your colleagues and our family. To my brother, LTC Joshua Thomas, thank you for your service to our country and for commiserating over common leadership challenges, despite our different career environments. To my husband, Bill, and son, Owen, thank you for your patience during stressful times and for your enduring love and confidence in me. I am blessed to have this life with you. Roze would like to thank her mother, Celia Hillings, and siblings, Felicia Bond, Paul Bond, and Celia Hoffman who support me in all things and never let me forget I'm the youngest child, no matter the title in front of my name. To my children, Eleanor and Felix, and my husband, Tom: I know my professional choices have made our lives complicated and somewhat chaotic. Thanks for sitting down for dinner (most nights) and reminding me that whatever drama comes my way at work, or how heavy the world seems, there is good reason for hope, levity, geography quizzes, and cats.

INTRODUCTION

Other Duties as Assigned, or Desired

ROZE HENTSCHELL AND CATHERINE E. THOMAS

The popular Twitter account Associate Deans (@ass_deans, over 127,000 followers as of this writing) is dedicated to "making fun of middle management in college and universities." The profile picture for the account is of Imelda Staunton in her role as Dolores Umbridge, the abusive, despotic Headmistress of Hogwarts School of Witchcraft and Wizardry in two of the *Harry Potter* films. In short order, Umbridge moves up the ranks from an ineffective professor of Defense Against the Dark Arts, to headmistress of Hogwarts (replacing a beloved, aging headmaster who was forced out), to Hogwarts High Inquisitor, a new senior leadership position created just for her. Delightfully ridiculous as she is, it is easy to satirize Umbridge's career trajectory from professor to administrator to an executive position no one has heard of and no one knew was necessary. The account is particularly harsh in its satirical portrayal of the role of humanities faculty in a science, technology, engineering, and mathematics (STEM)–focused higher ed landscape. In one stinging tweet, the author says, "We appreciate the humanities faculty are unhappy with the college restructuring toward STEM. However, we are not sure that striking and refusing to do a job the board wants eliminated is good strategy. But, hey, go for it!"[1] Umbridge, and the Twitter page, present the narrative of leadership in higher education as a story of academic administrators who are at best hypocritical and power hungry and at worst a bit evil.

We might take some lessons from Umbridge: learning the culture of your institution when you arrive is critical; replacing a well-loved administrator will be challenging; ignoring faculty governance by issuing "educational decrees" may be unpopular. But the Twitter account's point hits hard: if you are an ass dean, even one who hails from the ranks of humanities faculty, there must be a little bit of Dolores Umbridge in you. Indeed, a move into administration is often met with colleagues' jeers of "going to the dark side?" and mixed-bag wishes of "congratulations and sympathies."[2] Leadership positions are often disparaged as roles that no one in their right mind should want to pursue. For those in the humanities, this can be even more acute, since many of our disciplines have taught us to be suspicious of hierarchies, power, and privilege.

What both popular culture and some elements of faculty culture may be missing, however, is the transformational potential of administrative roles in higher education. Not all leadership roles are created equal, nor do they require identical skills, mindsets, or orientations, nor do they have the same scope of influence. While there are core competencies that can help a leader be successful, there is administrative diversity that can accommodate a range of interests and individualities. A program coordinator or director role overseeing study abroad, a minor, or a first-year experience curriculum is differently positioned than a department chair or dean. A faculty affiliate position supporting colleagues in developing service-learning experiences for students is different work than coordinating a writing program. And the problem-solving, budget-juggling, and people-managing work of a department chair is different in scope and relation than a dean's, which is different than a provost's. And that is just the point.

Often, we think very narrowly about what administration can offer and who can and should occupy such positions. Depending on our relationships and experiences with the people in those roles, we may have assumptions about what those roles represent, whether positive, negative, or something in between. While it remains true that not everyone who becomes an administrator may wish to serve as one, at least as a destination, or considers the work professionally sustaining, many others just might find it to be a positive professional pathway—one filled with satisfaction, growth, opportunities, and, yes, *joy*. If you are currently in an administrative role and wish there were more spaces to talk honestly about what it is like, if you're wondering what leadership is like "on the inside" or are considering a move into administration (the "admin-curious"), or if you are just interested in learning more about different leadership careers in higher education—this book is for you.

In this volume, we explore the professional transition to administration and several critical issues that surround that decision. The purpose is to provide our audience of administrators or admin-curious individuals with stories with which they may identify and with practical advice for navigating this new life. Just as there are many different leadership roles in the higher ed landscape, so too are there many pathways in and out of those roles—some by choice, some by necessity, some by serendipity. The collection takes up these issues from a variety of vantage points. The chapters consider administrative life at a range of institutional types and give voice to individuals in an array of leadership roles, occupying different ranks and academic statuses, and holding diverse personal identities and values.

Transforming Leadership Pathways examines the ways in which humanities-trained professionals are particularly suited for and often find themselves in leadership roles in higher ed. Many humanities teacher-scholars inhabit these roles, and it is worth exploring why. This collection of thirteen essays investigates how humanities professionals grapple with the opportunities and challenges of leadership positions and connect them to their teaching and research endeavors. It makes space for serious conversation about the multiple roles humanities specialists play and offers strategies for professional growth, sustenance, and satisfaction. The collection also considers the relationship between our disciplinary areas of study, our academic training, the skill sets and habits of mind we have cultivated, and the lives we inhabit and aspire to. These essays address diverse types of institutions and leadership positions and speak to the lived experience in them.

While we emphasize that a leadership path in higher education can be a welcome and positive professional move for many humanities professionals, our volume also acknowledges the issues that arise when faculty take on administrative positions while otherwise marginalized on campus, either by virtue of faculty status, rank, or personal identities. The goals of this collection are to demystify and normalize the path into higher education administration and to demonstrate that, rather than lacking the skills that stereotypically are associated with academic leadership (deep knowledge of budgets, affirmation of exclusive, hierarchical power systems, and an endorsement of neoliberal institutions that have become ever more corporate in structures and practices), humanities scholars are uniquely qualified for administrative roles. Empathetic, deeply analytical, attuned to historical context, and trained in communication, teachers and scholars who hail from humanities disciplines often find themselves well suited to the demands of complex academic leadership in twenty-first-century colleges and universities.

We see this volume adding a new perspective to the existing literature on higher ed leadership. Many books addressing college and university administration presuppose the reader is employed at a research or four-year institution and are usually authored by individuals from such institutions. Likewise, the definition of leadership roles in many texts seems to focus on executive leadership roles and imagine an administrator who has progressed through a career in a traditional manner (tenure-track faculty, to department chair, to dean, and beyond). Some titles include C. K. Gunsalus's *The College Administrator's Survival Guide*, George Justice's *How to Be a Dean*, and Thomas McDaniel's *The New Dean's Survival Guide: Advice from an Academic Leader*. These books assume that you have made, embraced even, the transition into a leadership role and have practical and important advice on how to lead effectively at a time when higher education confronts many challenges. For example, Jeffrey Buller's *The Essential Department Chair* and its companion volume *The Essential Dean or Provost* provide expansive guidance on these roles' relationships and duties within the college/university, from identifying, soliciting, and managing resources; to managing annual course rotations, curricular development, and budgeting; to tackling tasks like hiring, firing, mentoring, developing, and evaluating faculty on local and campus-wide scales. Similarly, Daniel Grassian's *An Insider's Guide to University Administration* offers an honest glimpse into areas of administration that academic leaders will need to know but are often least prepared for. In addition to delineating leadership styles, Grassian discusses university finances, strategic planning, and navigating minefields of campus free speech and faculty grievances.

There are, of course, books that speak to the challenges of leadership pathways. In *Reframing Academic Leadership*, Joan V. Gallos and Lee G.

Bolman acknowledge the "accidental" path that some academic leaders take, as well as the lack of training they receive, and focus on the positive aspects and rewards of academic leadership. A central claim is that "thinking and learning are at the heart of effective leadership," and the book provides pragmatic advice on a range of issues administrators are likely to face and takes seriously self-care as a strategy for success.[3] Some other positive trends in the literature of higher ed administration include work focused on leadership vis-à-vis diversity and inclusion. The essays in Adrianna Kezar and Julie Posselt's *Higher Administration for Social Justice and Equity* demonstrate how to incorporate equitable and justice-minded practices into the daily activities and responsibilities of campus leaders. The emphasis on practical, day-to-day strategies fits within the how-to leadership subgenre discussed earlier, but the call to address inclusive work practices illuminates the growth areas the academy has yet to embrace fully.

A focus on gender and higher ed administration is the hallmark of Karen Longman and Susan Madsen's collection *Women and Leadership in Higher Education*, which highlights the increasingly diverse cohort of college administrators and admin-curious individuals. It explores key issues around women in higher education: to what degree and in what ways women occupy leadership roles, avenues for professional development, women's experiences and takeaways from holding various positions, and future directions for women in higher ed administration. And M. Cristina Alcade and Mangala Subramaniam's collection *Dismantling Institutional Whiteness: Emerging Forms of Leadership in Higher Education* shines a light on the historical makeup of higher ed leaders as predominantly white and male-identified and underscores that when women of color enter leadership positions, colleges and universities can begin to unsettle their own systemic, institutional racism. The essays, however, also reveal that leadership often "carries professional and personal costs" for women of color.[4] These volumes' more intersectional approach to engaging questions around higher ed leadership aligns with the goals of *Transforming Leadership Pathways*, particularly as our contributors represent a variety of institution types, subject positions, and orientations toward the work.

Often, texts in this genre assume an audience that identifies with and embraces the role of administrator. They tend not to acknowledge the varied paths to those roles and the complex personal and professional transformations that need to happen in order to get to the place of sitting comfortably in them. Semenza and Sullivan's *How to Build a Life in the Humanities: Meditations on the Academic Work-Life Balance* (2015) is a notable exception. Their volume explores different dimensions of life as an academic faculty member, focusing primarily on the personal considerations that attend such a career pathway. It takes seriously the "life" aspects of work-life balance. *Transforming Leadership Pathways* closes the gap between the traditional how-to orientation of the higher ed leadership genre and *How to Build's* gathering of personal accounts of negotiating work and other important aspects of life as a humanities professional. This collection presents a range of perspectives on administrative roles, leadership challenges, and diverse ways people move in (and out) of such positions. It also represents voices from a diverse portfolio of occupational subject positions and institution types, both highlighting and celebrating that leadership looks and feels different across the academy. Its orientation is positive but realistic about the opportunities that administration provides for professional development and career longevity, as well as the trials and complications that can arise along the way.

CHARTING LEADERSHIP PATHWAYS

Faculty who emerge in academic leadership positions usually enter academia with a different vision of their professional path, one involving a tenure-track position, a healthy balance of teaching and research, and professional and financial support for one's work.[5] If one has attained these, then the road to tenure or academic advancement is one where individuals have little reason to pay attention to the administrative goings-on at their institutions. Following a "traditional" path toward tenure means six or more years in graduate school and another six or so years building one's scholarly reputation and teaching dossier, with some service to the department and profession sprinkled in. We are neither encouraged to do nor rewarded for doing much more than that. Most of us lack the specific skills to do the complex and usually unsung tasks of administration because we have never been taught how or why we should. Ironically, many people who head into administration are *only* able to do so because of the years they have put into their scholarship. Often, full professor is a preferred qualification for a senior leadership position. And, of course, at many institutions, one only becomes a full professor after many years and an investment in the scholarly work that is rewarded with that rank. Some administrators will happily switch gears and leave their life as a scholar behind. But many will not. And those who decide that they have invested too much in their research and publication agenda to abandon it are faced with the unpleasant reality that their life as an administrator will leave very little time for the work that they have devoted their career to cultivating.

On the other hand, department reorganizations, market forces, and labor shifts at many institutions mean that nontenured and non-tenure-track faculty increasingly find themselves in administrative roles. As William Bowen and Eugene Tobin note, while in 1969 78 percent of university faculty held tenure or tenure-track positions, by 2009, that number dropped to only 33 percent. Furthermore, the number of part-time, non-tenure-track faculty has exponentially scaled up.[6] This means that a number of administrators find themselves in the unique, challenging, and sometimes uncomfortable position of having to supervise or direct their colleagues, some of whom will occupy higher faculty ranks and more culturally powerful positions. Many do this with higher teaching loads and lower salaries than their coworkers. In addition, while they are managing significant administrative work and negotiating complex professional relationships, they also may be pursuing tenure or a more secure position that requires extensive teaching, research, and (other) service. The issue of work-work balance is even more intense as a result. While our collection demonstrates that leadership roles can be incredibly generative professionally and personally, provide financial security, and open new career pathways, we do not wish to elide the very real and often troubling material conditions that undergird the constitution of the professorial and administrative ranks. As several of our contributors show, it can be done and be done well, but it requires the nimble, creative thinking, and integrative orientation that many humanities disciplines cultivate.

It is well known that faculty who attain leadership positions rarely receive adequate, or any, professional development for their new roles. Most of our training is on-the-job experience that we somehow managed to do well enough to be considered competent and trustworthy. Indeed, administrators seldom receive formal training because their institutions do not provide the infrastructure to support those who want to move into and thrive in these roles. Supervisor training, conflict management, fundraising, knowledge of budgets, university policies, procedures, infrastructure, and organizational development are often the skills most necessary for administrators, but we usually learn them while in the role. As a result, colleges and universities have a small pool of people from which to hire administrators, whether those people are excellent or not.

This is a crucial opportunity for academic institutions. Some are beginning to recognize the need to cultivate leaders as they consider planning for the future. The well-established mentorship model in academia continues to provide helpful one-to-one coaching on the ins and outs of the administrative world of the university. However, leadership mentoring is not always embedded into the infrastructure of institutions, so ensuring availability, consistency, sustainability, and quality of support is difficult. It is also not clear that all individuals gain equal or equitable access to leadership mentors in roles that may have the influence to catalyze their careers. Therefore, mentorship as a sole mechanism for professional development can have an uneven impact. Scaffolding efforts and being more intentional about providing them can better reach more "admin-curious" faculty and promote a healthy, inclusive culture around administrative work.

Among the promising shifts that signal a greater desire to "develop a bench" for campus administrative roles are leadership programs and academies, providing funding to send faculty to leadership networking and development events, and campus workshops and programming aimed at developing leadership skills. Another ongoing set of opportunities—albeit ones that are more selective and oriented around further developing existing campus leaders—are offered by higher education professional development organizations. These include local, networking-based groups like Georgia Association for Women in Higher Education and national programs such as the Higher Education Resource Services Leadership Network, the Harvard Institutes for Higher Education, and American Council on Education Fellows program. Involving and supporting interested faculty and lower- to mid-level administrators in such opportunities is a worthwhile investment in individuals, the campus community, and the life of the institution. As with the mentoring of students, reaching out to colleagues to encourage them to apply for these opportunities because they have the potential to be strong leaders—and ensuring that you will support them if they do—can go a long way in motivating good people to pursue leadership roles.

Potential allies in this work are professional disciplinary organizations. These groups should—if they are not already doing so—acknowledge the complex, compartmentalized lives that their members have and do more to support the various professional pathways that those in the humanities have taken. For example, the Shakespeare Association of America (SAA) recently began offering a series of professionalization sessions at their annual meetings. Including topics such as preparing articles for publication, teaching Shakespeare within the general education curriculum, and exploring administrative career pathways, this series recognizes that its members serve in a variety of institutions and job types and do diverse types of professional work. Seminars and workshops like "Shakespeare and Women's Leadership," part of SAA's 2022 conference, also signal a greater awareness of this fact and a responsiveness to their membership's needs and multivalent interests. When more disciplinary organizations in the humanities embrace leadership development as a valued element of their members' careers, attitudes toward and academic culture around higher ed administration will grow more positive as well.

As the academy begins to shift away from older models of colleges and universities that inculcate systems of privilege and benefit the fortunate few who proceed on a "traditional" track from graduate school to tenure track then tenured professor, higher-level administrators should in tandem reflect on and define clear leadership pathways and preparation for those within their institutions. In other fields, professional development and leadership coaching are expected. It is common to coach staff for administrative advancement where there is interest and aptitude and to provide resources to support that track. It also is rare that one holds a single job or stays at a single organization for an entire career. Shifts within and among organizations are common. Higher education is still coming into the twenty-first century; while it is adopting increasingly a market-based orientation to hiring and student services, it still clings to structures and policies that may not fully serve its faculty, staff, and students. Honestly and critically interrogating the systems, structures, and policies that govern faculty advancement and leadership pathways will result in a more inclusive and equitable workplace where expectations and compensation are transparently just. In that model, leadership roles are not perceived as part of an exclusive "dark side" conspiracy to preserve individual and institutional power, but rather they become viable, respected, and well-supported career avenues for individuals to pursue and in which to become change agents for the greater benefit of all.

MANAGING ALL THE THINGS

When we transition into these positions it often seems easier to compartmentalize our professional selves to handle the competing activities we are engaged in simultaneously. There is the self that has training as a teacher and a scholar. This self identifies as a faculty member, as part of a group of intellectuals who are decidedly resistant to the officiousness and perceived aggrandizement of the administration. This self relishes complexity of conversation and is innately averse to spreadsheets and annual reports. This self often is siloed from the workings of the university since what matters to her is creating knowledge and educating students who find themselves in our orbit. This self says, "Yes, and ..." because there is always time for more permutations of an idea.

Then there is the administrative self, whether that be program coordinator or director, chair, associate dean, dean, provost, or something else. This self is pragmatic. She needs to understand the structures of a university to do her job well; her life is filled with bullet points, spreadsheets, meetings, and checklists. This self may find that she needs to learn additional skills and fields of knowledge to perform all aspects of her work successfully. She may be motivated or required to build new relationships across campus and work closely with staff members who may possess different academic cultural values or orientations on how things get done. This self knows that there will be new levels of policy, procedure, and interrelationships to master and that they require extra time, energy, and proclivity to embrace.

Like many others entering leadership roles, I [Catherine] experienced some professional identity shifts when I first joined the student success team at my previous institution, which has spurred ongoing reflection. My colleagues knew I taught, but I was on a largely staff-based team. Alternately, while I attended department meetings and joined a department committee to get to know my faculty peers and contribute to the life of my discipline, there were several occasions when those colleagues looked at me in surprise. They were unaware of my areas of expertise, that I had a long-standing faculty career at a previous institution, that I had taught and published on a variety of subjects, that I had done administrative work before, that I worked a twelve-month schedule. Such moments reminded me that I was both *them* and *not-them*. Some of this was explained by having worked at a different institution prior to joining that one, but much of the disjunction was because I held an administrative role that set me outside of the daily rhythms of department life. Another question that arose quickly was how I should be evaluated as an administrative faculty member. I was both staff and faculty in the roles I held and the work I did.

This situation brings to light some questions—both practical and philosophical—about the faculty administrator. How will your professional evaluation(s) work? Who will complete them and provide feedback, and when? What box do you check on institutional surveys and other forms—faculty or staff? (There never seems to be a "both" option.) What LISTSERVs are you a member of? What information are you privy to? At which events are you welcome and which would be awkward to attend because of perceived power differentials or the changed nature of the relationship? The list goes on and on. The ground often shifts, and one may not realize it until one is walking across it and trying to figure out how to inhabit this new identity. While time and familiarity with one's role, colleagues, and institution can ameliorate some of the tensions, other aspects of faculty-administrator roles remain structurally liminal.

Regardless of one's professional pathway into and level of preparation for higher education leadership, very few of our roles are singly focused. Rather, they are divided into percentages that seemingly have little overlap. How then might one successfully juggle a multi-faceted professional life and achieve some semblance of a work-work balance? For one thing, one must redefine "balance." If one's administrative position is officially described as 75 percent administration and 25 percent teaching, for example, and scholarly or creative work is not evaluated in the annual review process, one must seriously consider the time spent on those pursuits or the personal and professional value attached to them. There are only so many hours in the day and so much energy to go around. Faculty are taught the primacy of caring for their students' learning needs and publishing what needs to get published to receive tenure and promotion (or their equivalent, at non-tenure-granting institutions). And many of us still derive satisfaction from engaging with our disciplines through conference-going or publication. While academic leaders take a variety of approaches, what is universal is the need to make personal choices—often difficult and mercenary ones—about what that work balance looks like and where priorities will be assigned. It is worth noting that priorities also will shift, sometimes daily, so time management, organizational skills, and honest self-reflection are necessary. This is to say nothing of the impact holding a higher leadership role can have on the time and energies available for caregiving, maintaining domestic partnerships, friendships, and other relationships, or participating in volunteer work and hobbies. While here we focus on frequently competing professional selves, we also acknowledge that our personal lives and obligations play a crucial role in how we navigate our professional lives.

In my [Catherine's] case, I take a two-pronged approach to work-work juggling. First, to whatever extent I can, I try to align my pedagogical work as a faculty member with my administrative work as a staff member. For example, I often have taught a first-year composition or first-year seminar course in a learning community, programs I coordinated or assisted with. At Georgia Gwinnett College, I served on the collegewide Curriculum and Assessment Advisory Committees and the English department's Transitional Studies Committee, all of which tie into the curriculum I supported and assessed. Second, I have tried to think through how my love of and background in early modern studies could possibly mesh with efforts we are making in student success initiatives. This resulted in an article on using Shakespeare reading groups to support growth mindset and self-efficacy development in first-generation college students and a seminar paper on using an intrusive advising model to think through early modern notions of good counsel. While admittedly it is not always possible to align one's research interests with current duties and work orientation, possessing a growth mindset and seeking points of intersection or topic-adjacent ideas can lead to some interesting research avenues. In addition, while it can be a steep learning curve, adopting new scholarly pursuits that *do* align with one's current position can diversify a research portfolio, strengthening one's marketability and value to the institution. Doing so also may open doors to other leadership opportunities.

In contrast, my [Roze's] scholarship and teaching on early modern literature and culture have not overlapped at all with my work as an associate dean for academic programs at an R1 institution (defined as 70 percent administration and 30 percent scholarship/teaching). Teaching preparation, class time, and grading simply cannot be ignored, so that time is often prioritized. What has changed is the time to continually propose new classes, read the latest scholarship in preparation for class, and deeply reflect on my discipline. I must trust that a career spent teaching and researching has afforded me the ability to do a respectable job delivering content, but one that might look different than it did earlier in my career. Part of my administrative portfolio is supporting instruction, so that work has allowed me to continue to learn and grow in best practices of inclusive pedagogy and good classroom management. Teaching still brings me immense joy and satisfaction, and if I can manage my own expectations, it often feels like a "break" from my administrative duties, is a professional activity that is still legible to my campus partners, and a space where I can incorporate new learning on pedagogy.

On the other hand, the scholarly "profile" I have attained comes with the institutional or personal expectation that I will not abandon the work that got me here. Research and publishing continue to be part of my professional life, but it is almost always done in small chunks of time and in the predawn hours, not while "on the clock" (having one's work bound by the eight to five workday is one of the first culture shocks of becoming an administrator). The key to my progress has been in participating in writing groups with campus colleagues and in virtual writing productivity platforms to keep my work habitual and to hold me accountable. Having a busy workday means that I must manage my time efficiently. While I have trained myself to work well this way, I sometimes find myself questioning the value of my scholarly work. While the work of academic administration operates on a specific time line, often with quick turnaround, the pace of academic (and especially archival humanities) research and publishing is comparatively slow. This dichotomous sense of time further polarizes how I view my own efforts. Seeing the positive and comparatively swift effect of administrative work can be thrilling for those of us who are uncertain whether our published writing has made any impact at all. In other words, while I have figured out how to navigate the workday balance, I continue to grapple with the relative value of my academic contributions and rewards. Admitting this is both painful and liberating.

The creation of this volume serves as a good example of work-work balance best practices. Finding allies—people with whom to work or keep you accountable, who share not only your passions and goals but also a similar work ethic and energy level—creates an important support system. Reflection on your goals and the project can also prove fruitful in helping you organize your time and efforts. What is in your favor and where are the strength areas that will push things forward? What tasks need more attention, time, or energy to be successful? What opportunities do you have to leverage existing knowledge and resources? How will this project advance your various interests? And what people, processes, or other demands might threaten your achievement of the goal? "Threat" need not be sinister but rather something that takes time and energy away from reaching the finish line.

Consistent progress on scholarly projects relies upon regular commitments of time. Setting up a calendar with benchmarks for completing different components of the article, book, or presentation will keep the work on schedule and manageable in its scope. Establishing and *holding* regular time for these tasks on the calendar (in whatever denominations you can) will assist in protecting it against all odds. Being mindful to allot time and tasks based on what suits one's energies and availability can also make the juggling smoother and less stressful. For example, one could squeeze in some research in the afternoon before the day's wrap-up but might need uninterrupted time early in the morning to write original content. We have found that letting go of perfectionistic tendencies and just *doing* the things, even if they are messy or inchoate at first, creates momentum. As the proverb goes, don't let the best be the enemy of the good.

Work-work balance therefore need not be a competitive binary between administrative and other types of academic work. Rather, we contend, leadership roles encourage growth and cross-training. For example, when I [Catherine] came to Georgia Gwinnett College, a relatively new institution, my accumulated experience and love for creating curricula, programs, and events were incredibly useful. I was given the freedom to collaborate with campus partners and build lasting infrastructure and curricular opportunities. This was exciting to me because my efforts were making a real, measurable difference. In addition, while I had been advising and supporting students and faculty in various ways prior to taking an associate dean role, I had the invigorating opportunity to embrace a new disciplinary field—transitional studies. The learning curve was steep, but as a new full professor, this was a welcome challenge to learn something new and broaden my research and praxis horizons. Likewise, I [Roze] had served as a faculty mentor to colleagues, but when I took on an administrative role, I found myself *supervising* staff for the first time. Through overseeing staff whose educational background, professional training, and job were quite distinct from my own, I have come to see that my role as a supportive mentor transcends the job description. Working with staff has given me a much better understanding of the complexities of the personnel at an institution and how my faculty research and teaching position fits into the larger landscape.

As these examples show, work-work balance can be framed as both a creative challenge and a pragmatic one, which makes all the difference in terms of professional sustainability. One learns very quickly what is most important to them—in terms of work tasks that must be done on a set time line and other types of work that are valued and energizing. It is important to note that administrative responsibilities and tasks are not always at odds or the enemy of other important efforts like teaching, service, and research. Administrative work can be inspiring and meaningful and have a tangible impact on students, colleagues, and the institution. Leadership roles can hone who you are and what you contribute to the life of the mind *and* the life of the institution. One's work life is likely to be enriched in ways that both are and are not anticipated. Leadership positions are gateways to new learning and ongoing professional development.

Why focus on *humanities* professionals in our discussion of leadership pathways in higher education? Aside from noticing that there are many administrators with humanities training across the academy, we contend that there are several reasons this group is particularly suited to and gravitates toward leadership work.[7] First, the disciplinary practices humanities professionals engage in align with core foundational skills and questions that create proclivity for leadership roles. For example, individuals trained in humanities are facile with the reading, analysis, and production of texts for different audiences. Following the argument that almost anything can be a text, scholars in these disciplines can bring to bear their skills in reading colleagues' reactions in a meeting for a campus initiative, producing effective messaging to different constituents, and unpacking opaque policy language to understand its historical context, as well as its impetus, and communicate that to others.

Second, many disciplines under this umbrella are focused on the study of the human experience—its history, constructive nature, evolution, cultural lenses, and implications. The humanities help us understand people, systems, and culture. The questions asked and activities engaged in encourage self-reflection and foster adaptability. Through studying both historically and culturally inflected texts, as well as lived experiences, these disciplines allow practitioners to understand and effectively build relationships, an aspect crucial to successful leadership. They both teach and cultivate empathy. At minimum, humanities scholars are expected to embrace the problematic nature of complex issues, to realize that there may be several answers, and even several good answers, to the same question, as well as anticipate counterarguments. This is not to say that administrators who come from other disciplines do not see things in a multivalent way, but the leap may be less far for those in the humanities because our disciplines require us to think this way.

While not all graduates of humanities programs will embody these traits, many will possess some or all of them, and those are particularly useful when situated in an administrative role, whether at the lower level of the academic hierarchy, at the very top, or somewhere in between.

Professing the humanities crafts one into an agile leader—in the sense of being nimble, flexible, and responsive and in the model of the recent "agile coaching" movement.[8] These types of administrators are quick but accurate assessors, effective change navigators, collaborative leaders, creative thinkers, team-building aficionados, and goal-focused problem solvers. The chapters in *Transforming Leadership Pathways* aptly illustrate how these qualities manifested when our contributors responded to different challenges, structures, and circumstances on their leadership pathways.

CHAPTER OVERVIEW

The chapters in part 1 of our collection, "Leadership Pathways," investigate the skills, perspective, and self-awareness required to thrive in academic leadership positions. In so doing, the authors acknowledge the situatedness of leadership and the cultural and social factors at play in inhabiting these positions. The authors demystify pathways and processes and offer concrete examples of self-aware successes. In "What It Takes: How to Develop Academic Leadership," Darryl Dickson-Carr argues against the idea that only a select few faculty are suited to leadership roles. He asserts that such a narrative tends to perpetuate a system in which knowledge and agency are concentrated in a small group, thereby disenfranchising and infantilizing the majority of faculty. In addition, much of the work that allows colleges and universities to function frequently falls on women and people of color, creating tiers of privilege that mirror labor caste systems outside the academy. Dickson-Carr outlines what faculty should know and do to be fully engaged department, college, or university citizens capable of moving into leadership positions and providing visions for their units and their institutions that will allow their colleagues to thrive. Dickson-Carr, writing from the perspective of a department chair, offers a profile of a competent faculty leader at work, from daily operations to grander views of a department's, college's, or university's future. Most pointedly, the chapter argues that relative "sanity" is not the precursor to leadership; rather, mentoring, professionalization, strategic planning, and simple goal setting map the path to robust leadership and shared governance.

Philip Robinson-Self, associate professor of learning and teaching at BPP University, UK, brings forward the research in the science of teaching and learning in "The Politics, Practice, and Poetics of Teaching Leadership." Robinson-Self discusses the evolving role in higher education of teaching leadership through the lens of poetics of leadership practices. Leadership is a complex and contested issue in higher education, and the notion of leadership can sit particularly uncomfortably alongside the traditionally democratic and collegiate forms of discourse common to arts and humanities subjects. Moreover, social, political, and public health pressures have come to the fore in the academy, and the economic ripples of these pressures are often felt, particularly in the humanities. Robinson-Self asserts that the humanities also offer us paths forward in terms of teaching us how to deconstruct and interrogate processes of leadership; how to lead in authentic, moral, value-driven ways; and hence offers alternative paradigms for leadership models. The articulation of the critically complex, the problematic, and the subjective is one of the signature intellectual joys of the humanities, and it is precisely suited to understanding ways forward in the leadership of teaching.

A tenet of this collection is that context matters, and leadership can look quite distinct from institution to institution. In "Academic Duck-Rabbit: Faculty Leadership at the Smaller College or University," Emily Ruth Isaacson, director of the Integrated Studies General Education Program and Life of the Mind Honors Program and English department chair, asserts that the faculty leader or administrator at the small school must learn not only to be a generalist in the classroom, but also a generalist in service to the institution. The small college setting also requires faculty leaders to engage with this service in many ways throughout their careers. While some of these roles are clear in their positioning between faculty and administration, many roles on smaller campuses fall somewhere in between the two, creating a tension between the faculty role and the administrative role, and further creating the potential for conflict with fellow faculty members, who often become friends. While every institution will have its peculiarities of organizational structure, Isaacson draws a set of conclusions about what can help at any small institution: a tolerance for ambiguity, a commitment to relationship building across campus, an ability to view the larger institutional picture without ego, a capacious curiosity for the work being done across campus, and a commitment to the institutional mission of the student-centered small college.

Writing from the vantage points of multiple leadership positions and institutions in higher education, Genesea M. Carter, Aurora Matzke, and Bonnie Vidrine-Isbell's chapter, "Navigating Networks and Systems: Practicing Care, Clarifying Boundaries, and Reclaiming Self in Higher Education Administration," discusses how systems and networks act like agentive beings, imposing influence on the work of academic leaders. The authors (associate director of composition, senior associate provost, and director of English language program, respectively) provide targeted examples from their own faculty administrative positions to help readers see how systems and networks shape the opportunities and challenges of leadership roles. Finally, Carter, Matzke, and Vidrine-Isbell offer recommendations for readers to practice recognizing the disembodiment of themselves and others, balancing work with self-care, and reclaiming the embodied nature of educational administration. They believe it is necessary to strive for a healthy, sustainable relationship between the lives individuals inhabit and aspire to as faculty, administrators, and human beings.

The chapters in part 2, "Interdisciplinarity and Innovation in Higher Education Administration," consider the role of inter- or antidisciplinarity in engendering leadership opportunities for humanities professionals. Administrative positions focused on overseeing collaboration and innovation in teaching and learning across disciplines are well suited for humanities professionals, who, especially in the last generations, have disrupted traditional scholarly boundaries. Overseeing such initiatives requires deft ability to communicate why and how these collaborations work well and how they move an institution forward and are beneficial for students and faculty alike. In his chapter "Administering Antidisciplinarity: Navigating a Diverse Career Path from Theory to Institutional Practice," Associate Dean Ryan Claycomb considers how his early days as an academic located in the humanities, although writing and teaching through an avowedly "antidisciplinary" lens, shaped his later administrative career. Occupying a range of academic roles that had varying degrees of power taught him to see how infrastructural disciplinarity may be a way to contain some resistant forms of knowledge but also of protecting them, frequently in bureaucratic ways. Claycomb considers that career path: informed by critical theory and reflection but built with an eye toward effecting positive, practical, and rewarding changes around how we make and sustain knowledge.

Laurie Ellinghausen's chapter, "'We Know What We Are, but Know Not What We May Be': Academic Innovation and the Reinvention of Professional Identities," argues for an approach to academic innovation that derives from humanist thought—specifically, from humanist views of the disciplines as fostering personal growth and expansion, as well as civic participation. "Innovation" has become a mainstay of many strategic plans in higher education, resulting in appointments, including her own as associate vice provost for academic innovation, dedicated to the creation of academic programming that connects students to the workforce and promotes social and economic equity. However, the current ubiquity of "innovation" in higher education has invited skepticism, as have curricular approaches that purport to shoehorn "the arts" into a technical and business-oriented career preparation model. While acknowledging those critiques, Ellinghausen proposes that academic innovation offers a greater benefit, one germane to the growth and expansion of professional identities in higher education.

The section's final chapter, Anne-Marie E. Walkowicz's "Administering Instructional Reform: Interdisciplinary Learning and the Humanities Profession," examines the opportunity interdisciplinary education offers faculty trained in the humanities to connect their research endeavors to their roles as administrators. Walkowicz discusses the value of undergraduate interdisciplinary education and explains why humanities professionals are uniquely trained to develop and administer interdisciplinary curricula. Using her role as coordinator of interdisciplinary studies and her institution as a case study, Walkowicz argues that interdisciplinary education prepares students for the workforce by engaging them in learning experiences focused on using multiple disciplinary lenses to bring evidence-based reasoning to complex problems.

The authors in part 3, "Leadership, Equity, and Social Justice," examine what it means to emerge as a campus leader when one's personal and professional identities are not traditionally privileged. They explore the challenges of occupying leadership roles from these subject positions but also discuss how their strengths and skill sets have enabled them to be successful. The chapters explain the value of leadership mentoring and illustrate how resilience, persistence, and flexibility have aided the authors in navigating complex institutional landscapes. In Chyna N. Crawford's chapter, "Leading While Young, Black, and on the Tenure Track," she outlines the research suggesting that Black women faculty, and often administrators, are not only undervalued, but are also positioned at a distinct disadvantage of having to traverse their race as well as their gender; they have lower rates of retention, tenure, and promotion, and may have their expertise questioned. Crawford addresses the specific barriers that Black women who are appointed to leadership roles before they are granted tenure encounter. Faculty who accept this opportunity often do so at great threat to themselves and their professions. Drawing on experiences as chair and associate professor, Crawford discusses the challenges and rewards of holding administrative positions while on the tenure track and argues for the integral role of mentoring. Finally, she offers recommendations for the success of Black women who are currently pursuing tenure or who may choose to enter leadership roles.

A discussion of the precarious position of untenured leaders is extended in Kristina Quynn's chapter, where she interrogates the increasingly common scenario of leadership roles inhabited by people off the tenure track. In "Leading through Precarity: A Tale of (Un)Sustainable Professional Advancement," she examines the variety of professional experiences on her pathway to assistant dean of graduate studies and director of a professional campus writing program. Quynn reflects on the nature of leadership and professional advancement available to contingent faculty in contemporary higher education. She then brings together the literature on academic productivity with analyses of contingency and the corporatization of higher education to detail the often hidden, unspoken, and shame-filled workloads of those who pursue leadership roles off the tenure track. Hers is a narrative of professional transformation, critique, and devotion, which reflects on how to build much-needed pathways for faculty advancement and professionalization while fostering a culture of sustainable success to model and serve the needs of all on campus.

Engaging also with the issues around administrative work while holding intersectional identities, Rowena M. Tomaneng illustrates the ways in which leadership roles can be harnessed to amplify social justice work in both the community and the academy. In "Ito Ang Kwento Ko: Pinayist

Pedagogy/Praxis and Community College Leadership," she discusses her lived experience as a community college president whose leadership, teaching, and service are guided by social justice and equity frameworks. Tomaneng explains how her pathway into leadership includes an academic progression and self-actualization process heavily influenced by community engagement, advocacy work, and grassroots organizing. She then outlines several frameworks that have meaningfully shaped her praxis as an equity-minded educational leader: *Pinayist* pedagogy/praxis and social movement theory. Pinayist pedagogical/praxis approach is deeply rooted in both critical and ethnic studies pedagogies in addition to transnational feminism. Development of self-agency is grounded in decolonizing praxis for restoration of humanity, Pilipina women's knowledge production, community dialogue, and commitment to action. Social movement theory has shaped Tomaneng's social justice lens and strengthened her commitment to creating civic pathways in the three California community college institutions she has served and led in the past twenty-five years.

The chapters in part 4, "Community, Communication, and Calling," highlight the crucial roles that collaborative decision-making, transparent communication, and self-awareness play in effective twenty-first-century higher education leadership. To promote shared governance and foster trust within diverse institutional and local communities, an academic administrator must build consensus and operate from places of shared value. However, leaders must also be self-aware and self-reflective about their strengths, growth areas, and callings for the work. These chapters provide models of how to do these types of work, to benefit students, colleagues, the institution, and the self.

Emily J. Morgan's chapter, "Collaborative, Introverted Leadership: Engaging Your Stakeholders to Move a Program Forward," introduces collaborative leadership as a means of rallying one's stakeholders to build a productive program or department. Morgan discusses her experiences using this model as director of dance for several years. With faculty colleagues and students, and higher administration's approval, they generated a new mission statement, vision statement, and program learning objectives. She successfully proposed a new degree program, significantly altered an existing one, and is in the process of adding a new concentration. Drawing on both research and her own experiences, she offers strategies for using collaborative leadership to facilitate big- and small-picture thinking in one's own program, department, or college. By engaging one's stakeholders, collaborative leadership can empower one's community, create a better opportunity for substantial results, and help a program move forward in the best possible direction.

The relationship between executive academic leadership responsibilities and humanistic training is explored by Michael Austin in "Communication and Crisis Management: A Case Study and a Cautionary Tale." In this chapter, Austin draws on his own experiences as executive vice president and provost during the early days of the 2020 COVID-19 pandemic to talk about the value that training in the humanities can offer academic administrators who must build and use communication networks in crisis situations. He cautions administrators not to mistake frequent or elegant communication for an effective communication strategy, and he discusses both the failures and the successes of his communication during the global pandemic. The chapter concludes that, while communication strategies are important, and very much a part of a humanities education, the core philosophies behind a humanistic education are even more important. Communication fails when it is transactional and occurs between institutional categories. It succeeds when it is grounded in genuine human interaction of the sort that the study of humanities is based upon. While communication strategies can be taught fairly quickly, a humanities education also conveys a deep understanding of why communication is important and the human dimensions of a crisis.

Sean Benson, professor of English, concludes our collection with an important perspective: that of a faculty member who served in and then decided to step away from academic leadership. In "Vocation and the Drudgery I Love," Benson recounts his journey into and ultimately out of administration. Benson focuses first on his experience as a dual teacher/administrator, mentoring students and colleagues in and out of the classroom while also taking on other managerial tasks. He encountered moments of professional dissonance, though, which compelled him to reflect on his values, priorities, and desires for his career. While Benson was leading a reading group on vocation, Martin Luther's understanding of calling helped him to think about aligning his abilities with the needs of others. Benson contends that choosing to pursue administration over teaching and writing is a trade-off, one that potential administrators are wise to consider closely before taking the plunge. Benson's account of disaffection with administrative service is an important one to tell, as not everyone who enters administration will find it precisely what they envisioned. Administrative work clarified what he was good at and felt fulfilled in—"called" to do—and directed him to a professorship where his skills and abilities were a perfect fit for the nonadministrative job he took at another institution.

What the collection of writings in *Transforming Leadership Pathways* offers then is a critically minded look at the lived experience of twenty-first-century higher education leaders. From exploration of pathways into and out of such roles, to examination of how institution type and diverse levels of administrative participation shape the experience, to reflection on how identity, power, and privilege intersect, inhibit, and enable one to be successful, these are the stories of the 99 percent, our colleagues in arms. These authors offer different perspectives on leadership that are empowering and hopeful but at the same time honest about trade-offs and challenges that attend such career pathways. They also highlight how being a humanities-trained professional equips them to analyze, synthesize, collaborate, flex, and succeed in leadership work. Our intent is to give space to these voices and to create a new narrative around higher ed administration. This narrative acknowledges the potential "dark side" elements of academic leadership but also demonstrates its potential to actualize real, positive change in the lives of students, faculty and staff, and the larger community. Becoming a leader in academia encourages self-reflection, requires grit and persistence, and builds new skill sets and relationships that are enriching to one's personal and professional growth. May we eschew the stereotype of Umbridge and instead embrace our inner Dumbledores and McGonagalls, leading with courage, compassion, and commitment to a brighter future for all.

NOTES

1. Associate Deans, "We appreciate the humanities faculty are unhappy with the college restructuring toward STEM,"Twitter, May 25, 2021, 8:13 p.m., https://twitter.com/ass_deans/status/1397269587700457476.

2. For an essay addressing the typical reaction to those who choose higher ed administration, see George Justice and Carolyn Dever, "Beyond the Dark Side," *Inside Higher Ed*, May 16, 2019, https://www.insidehighered.com/advice/2019/05/16/practical-advice-faculty-members-considering-joining-administration-opinion.

3. Joan V. Gallos and Lee G. Bolman, *Reframing Academic Leadership*, 2nd ed. (Hoboken, NJ: Jossey-Bass, 2021), xiii.

4. M. Cristina Alcalde and Mangala Subramaniam, "Introduction: Gendering and Racializing Contemporary Leadership in Higher Education," in *Dismantling Institutional Whiteness: Emerging Forms of Leadership in Higher Education*, eds. M. Cristina Alcalde and Mangala Subramaniam (West Lafayette, IN: Purdue University Press, 2023), 1.

5. As Kevin Dettmar puts it, "No one completes a Ph.D. (as opposed to an Ed.D.) in order to enter campus administration." Kevin J. H. Dettmar, "Don't Cry for Me, Academia!," *The Chronicle of Higher Education*, June 27, 2016, https://www.chronicle.com/article/dont-cry-for-me-academia/.

6. William G. Bowen and Eugene M. Tobin, *Locus of Authority: The Evolution of Faculty Roles in the Governance of Higher Education* (Princeton, NJ: Princeton University Press, 2015), 152.

7. While our project is to stress the ways in which humanities professionals are characteristically well suited to leadership work, it is also worth acknowledging that many may pursue administration because of the tangible financial benefits. Humanities professors are among the lowest paid on most US campuses. This may not be the most altruistic reason to pursue a leadership position, but it is nonetheless a pragmatic and relevant one.

8. See Forbes Coaches Council, "What It Means to Be an 'Agile' Leader and Why It Matters," *Forbes*, June 24, 2021, https://www.forbes.com/sites/forbescoachescouncil/2021/06/24/what-it-means-to-be-an-agile-leader-and-why-it-matters/?sh=6e0b91d04d61.

BIBLIOGRAPHY

Alcalde, M. Cristina, and Mangala Subramaniam. "Introduction: Gendering and Racializing Contemporary Leadership in Higher Education." In *Dismantling Institutional Whiteness: Emerging Forms of Leadership in Higher Education*, edited by M. Cristina Alcalde and Mangala Subramania. West Lafayette, IN: Purdue University Press, 2023.

Associate Deans. "We appreciate the humanities faculty are unhappy with the college restructuring toward STEM." Twitter, May 25, 2021. https://twitter.com /ass_deans/status/1397269587700457476.

Bowen, William G., and Eugene M. Tobin. *Locus of Authority: The Evolution of Faculty Roles in the Governance of Higher Education*. Princeton, NJ: Princeton University Press, 2015.

Buller, Jeffrey L. *The Essential Dean or Provost: A Comprehensive Desk Reference*. 2nd ed. San Francisco: Jossey-Bass, 2015.

Buller, Jeffrey L. *The Essential Department Chair: A Comprehensive Desk Reference*. 2nd ed. San Francisco: Jossey-Bass, 2012.

Dettmar, Kevin J. H. "Don't Cry for Me, Academia!" *The Chronicle of Higher Education*, June 27, 2016. https://www.chronicle.com/article/dont-cry-for-me -academia/.

Forbes Coaches Council. "What It Means to Be an 'Agile' Leader and Why It Matters." *Forbes*, June 24, 2021. https://www.forbes.com/sites/forbescoaches council/2021/06/24/what-it-means-to-be-an-agile-leader-and-why-it-mat ters/?sh=6e0b91d04d61.

Gallos, Joan V., and Lee G. Bolman. *Reframing Academic Leadership*. 2nd ed. Hoboken, NJ: Jossey-Bass, 2021.

Grassian, Daniel. *An Insider's Guide to University Administration*. Baltimore, MD: Johns Hopkins University Press, 2020.

Gunsalus, C. K. *The College Administrator's Survival Guide*. 2nd ed. Cambridge, MA: Harvard University Press, 2021.

Justice, George. *How to Be a Dean*. Baltimore, MD: Johns Hopkins University Press, 2019.

Justice, George, and Carolyn Dever. "Beyond the Dark Side." *Inside Higher Ed*. May 16, 2019. https://www.insidehighered.com/advice/2019/05/16/practical -advice-faculty-members-considering-joining-administration-opinion.

Kezar, Adrianna, and Julie Posselt, eds. *Higher Administration for Social Justice and Equity: Critical Perspectives for Leadership.* New York: Routledge, 2020.

Longman, Karen, and Susan Madsen, eds. *Women and Leadership in Higher Education.* Charlotte, NC: Information Age Publishing, 2014.

McDaniel, Thomas. *The New Dean's Survival Guide: Advice from an Academic Leader.* Madison, WI: Magna Publications, 2019.

Semenza, Greg Colón, and Garrett A. Sullivan, Jr., eds. *How to Build a Life in the Humanities: Meditations on the Academic Work-Life Balance.* New York: Palgrave Macmillan, 2015.

PART 1
Leadership Pathways

1

WHAT IT TAKES

How to Develop Academic Leadership

DARRYL DICKSON-CARR

This chapter has a rather pressing goal: to encourage more academics to consider seriously taking on administrative roles that have the potential to transform the university. Academe is losing an enormous amount of institutional knowledge and useful experience as faculty from the first wave of the "baby boomer" generation reach retirement age. As we lose that population, we lose many who helped shape academic life by training graduate students, mentoring junior faculty, and serving in the various leadership roles that kept departments functioning and faculty governance alive. The COVID-19 pandemic has only accelerated these departures. While the knowledge these colleagues possess is often passed on to others, their ability and willingness to serve do not always transfer safely. For a variety of reasons, faculty may refuse outright to become the faculty senators, program directors, department chairs, associate deans, deans, and provosts that keep our embattled colleges and universities alive. After looking at the reasons faculty resist administrative paths, I argue that more of us could—and should—pursue them, with the right sort of mentoring and guidance. While that mentoring begins in graduate school, it can happen at any point in a productive career. Leadership is not just for an innately gifted (or stereotypically power hungry) class but for all who wish to engage in faculty governance and play active roles in guiding and changing the institutions where they work. Using my own experiences as but one guideline, I suggest ways faculty may be encouraged and prepared to enter administration, and why it makes all the difference. Without more faculty willing to engage in administrative work, such labor falls to a shrinking pool of people, thereby limiting new ideas, undermining faculty governance, and potentially burning out some of our brightest colleagues.

DR. FAUSTUS, I PRESUME?

Academics love dichotomies and melodrama. As much as we privilege nuance and subtlety in our analyses and spurn essentialism, rank-and-file faculty members also find great comfort in casting ourselves as the occasionally tragic heroes of extensive dramatic tableaux. Under eternal assault and torment from upper administration—the Faustian villains who sold their souls to chthonic beings in exchange for access to power, bloated staff, and astronomical salaries—faculty can never escape the endless, fruitless initiatives and shadow work they generate. These tableaux have been revised many times, with the latest version having the breathtaking title of *The Tragical History of the Neoliberal University* (composed ca. 1985, or whenever the Culture Wars began in earnest). It's a drama told in infinite acts, repeated ad nauseam, with the victims the faculty who sadly held onto their souls (read: their teaching and pure research), while venal colleagues hailed Satan and lost theirs.

At some point in American higher education's history, academics started taking Christopher Marlowe's *The Tragical History of the Life and Death of Dr. Faustus* (1588) and certain sections of Books III and IV of *Gulliver's Travels* (1726) a bit too seriously. Marlowe's classic tale recounts how Dr. Faustus, an arrogant, self-righteous theological scholar, engages in necromancy, pays homage to Lucifer, and sells his soul to gain knowledge, power, and access to sensual delights. In Book III of *Gulliver's Travels*, the eponymous hero travels to the Grand Academy of Lagado, where the pursuit of science—knowledge in all its forms—is lampooned as perverted and absurd. In Book IV, Gulliver tells his Master Houyhnhnm—leader of a land of rational horses—about the fraternity of attorneys, who are ever on the side of injustice, while judges are "Persons appointed to decide all Controversies of Property, as well as for the Tryal of Criminals;

and picked out from the most dexterous Lawyers who are grown old or lazy: And having been byassed by Necessity of favouring Fraud, Perjury and Oppression[, have refused to do] any thing unbecoming their Nature or their Office."[1] Where Faustus, Lagado's scholars, and English Judges go, so must administrators, who have sacrificed their scholarship, scholarly ethoi (if they ever had any), and their ability to deal squarely and honestly with the faculty at large.

Academics who have taken on leadership roles, both large and small, often encounter something quite different. And perhaps needless to say, in the previous paragraphs it would appear that I have set up a truly grand straw man, one meant to deride my fellow faculty. This is not quite true. Tales of busybody and occasionally venal administrators abound, and many of them are not only true but occasionally make Marlowe's and Swift's characters seem mild in comparison. Nearly every academic stands ready to recount—often accurately—the legend of the assistant vice president of creative groundskeeping who absconded with thousands of dollars misappropriated from the coffers intended for classroom instruction. But most administrative work is relatively mundane in nature and decidedly benign, frequently helpful or useful, and utterly necessary.

Nevertheless, it's easy to understand why the legends persist and grow, as faculty at many universities have watched the number of administrative positions proliferate, while full-time, tenure-track faculty lines have plummeted over the last forty years, replaced with contingent labor. None of this is disputable. From an academic system in which the overwhelming majority of faculty were on the tenure track, between 2008 and 2009 as well as 2018 and 2019, the percentage of faculty in non-tenure-track positions grew from 10.1 percent to 26.6 percent, with doctoral institutions seeing a jump from 8.7 percent to 27.1 percent.[2] At the same time, faculty, students, and alumni have watched as what appears to be "administrative bloat" has grown, which Johns Hopkins University political science professor Benjamin Ginsberg famously summarized as follows:

Every year, hosts of administrators and staffers are added to college and university payrolls, even as schools claim to be battling budget crises that are forcing them to reduce the size of their full-time faculties. As a result, universities are now filled with armies of functionaries—vice presidents, associate vice presidents, assistant vice presidents, provosts, associate provosts, vice provosts, assistant provosts, deans, deanlets, and deanlings, all of whom command staffers and assistants—who, more and more, direct the operations of every school.[3]

Naturally, Ginsberg calls for universities to reduce the size of their administrative staff to improve quality and reduce tuition.

Yet even this call for administrative austerity, which faculty echo on innumerable campuses, overestimates the cost and control for which administrators are responsible. Most faculty are keenly aware of what we broadly label "shadow work": small, annoying administrative tasks that faculty apparently did not have to do in the past, such as submitting their own travel and expense reports, regularly checking on students' progress, and—the bête noire—assessment, which lends a Kafkaesque feel to academic life. Didn't rank-and-file faculty pursue advanced degrees to enter the profession free of reports, endless data, and micromanaging hierarchies? The Matrix, it seems, has us.

But reducing academic leadership in today's college and university environment to narratives of misprision, misappropriation, venality, cooptation, nepotism, and incompetence carries certain risks. First and foremost, these narratives obscure the fact that, indeed, we do need functional, competent, and empathetic people to help craft policies and structures that allow us to teach, to conduct research, and to engage in the service needed for our departments, colleges, universities, and disciplines to grow and thrive. Universities and colleges need to be reaccredited. Programs need to be assessed. Donors need to be cultivated and asked for support. Students need to be recruited. Relationships with the local community need to be maintained. State legislatures, ever ready to cut funds to state universities, need to be lobbied effectively. While faculty can and should play roles in these efforts, it doesn't take much imagination to understand that most individuals should leave the daily grind to dedicated, full-time administrators. What are the odds, for example, that state legislators would welcome a fiery (or even mild) condemnation of the neoliberal university on the floor? Will accrediting bodies happily accept that they have no legitimate purpose and be told to butt out of college and university affairs?

Should faculty simply pull a general strike when assessment data are due? Shouldn't each department be able to funnel part of its budget to support a needy local charity? If these questions sound absurd or extreme, I assure the reader that I know faculty who have suggested or attempted all of the above. Pragmatism makes no pulse run faster, but it does keep departments out of receivership.

Second, the people who tend to work most fruitfully in leadership positions are often drawn directly from faculty ranks within institutions rather than from outside; those who know the institution and its history best may know how to address its most pressing concerns. As Ivy Kaplan writes, a number of factors have contributed to administrative growth in recent years, including "more diverse student bodies" that require "academic and social support services to serve these new student demographics adequately."[4] With Title IX enforcement becoming ever more complicated, as well as recent and imminent drops in student enrollment, we do need someone to manage mundane bureaucratic tasks, such as reading and understanding new regulations that govern universities, following through on faculty and student complaints about violations of their rights, and working out new strategies to improve retention and prevent institutions from being shuttered.[5]

Moreover, most growth in administrative staff occurs at lower levels, where faculty and students need the most assistance in an increasingly complex academic arena, full of Learning Management Systems such as Moodle, Canvas, Instructure, and D2L, to say nothing of travel and expense software, faculty, staff, and student service platforms, library databases, search engines, and so on. While faculty and students may be fully justified in voicing concerns about how these systems are chosen and implemented, especially when such decisions come without faculty input, the need for these systems and administrators who make the decisions implementing them cannot be disputed. *How high* those decisions are made, of course, remains an open question. During the COVID-19 pandemic, faculty across the United States often found they were not part of discussions regarding university responses, especially regarding policies and protocols on which student, staff, and faculty lives could depend. Their complaints had great merit. But should policy be made via consensus? Who bears responsibility for implementing policy? Who answers questions that students and their families might have? Who works with staff?

Third, these narratives risk keeping academics in perpetual and potentially futile "wars of maneuver" rather than "wars of position," following Antonio Gramsci's concepts. For Gramsci, wars of maneuver are attempts to upend the social and political order, almost invariably stifled or squelched to the extent that the prevailing hegemony is at the center of civil life. The more hegemony—analogous to what many of us now call the "neoliberal university"—is entrenched, the less likely a war of maneuver is to succeed.[6] Broadly speaking, the chances that academic structures will readily agree to their dismantling are slim to the point of being almost nonexistent. While we may easily argue that administrative structures have become bloated and should be streamlined, the basic structure is fully entrenched; a college or university needs a president/chancellor or similar figurehead, as well as a provost, various deans, and department chairs or heads responsible for making decisions, along with the staff needed to implement those decisions. Whether those provosts and deans always need the associate provosts, associate deans, assistant deans, and other jobs that have proliferated is certainly open for debate, but no one seriously argues that deans and provosts are unnecessary.

Instead, academics are most often engaged in wars of position that try to redefine how the officials who increasingly govern our academic life engage in their roles. How much agency, for example, does an associate dean have to create and implement policy, as opposed to departments and their chairs or heads? Where is the fulcrum of faculty governance? Most importantly, how do we ensure that those occupying these roles are prepared to be active, productive, and effective leaders?

In the remainder of this chapter, I want to examine some ways to navigate the paths to more effective leadership. I begin by looking back on some personal experiences to highlight the lessons—positive and negative—gained in each case to show how institutions might develop leaders. Naturally, I'm aware of several hazards here. I do not claim that extrapolating from my personal experiences leads to universally applicable solutions. Nor do I believe that I have necessarily been effective as chair of departmental committees, as a program director, or as a department chair. For every positive lesson obtained, I have managed to find a way to misread situations or have failed to grasp fully what happened until much later, as more information became available. Each of these instances was an opportunity to learn—the clichéd "teaching moment," if you will. But each moment deepened my understanding of why seemingly arbitrary rules and procedures are in place, as well as the fact that some of these same rules and procedures are in fact arbitrary and need revision or replacement. I have been fortunate enough to see how faculty in leadership roles developed the next generation of leaders' capabilities.

DATELINE: 1992

I obtained my PhD in English from the University of California, Santa Barbara (UCSB). After passing the program's comprehensive master's examination in the spring of 1992, I returned to regular studies, coursework, and teaching in the fall quarter. Soon after classes began, I received a letter from the chancellor—the late Dr. Barbara Uehling—indicating that I'd been nominated to be the graduate student representative on the search committee for a new vice chancellor for academic affairs, equivalent to a provost. To be honest, I was like most students, graduate and undergraduate, and didn't quite know what the vice chancellor for academic affairs did. I understood even less why or how I was nominated. I took the letter to my faculty mentor, whose eyes brightened as he explained that such a nomination was a sign that someone—most likely the director of graduate studies or another English Department member—thought that I was reliable and had good judgment. Although the chancellor's letter outlined in broad terms how long such an appointment would last, I called her office to discover how much time it might consume, to avoid interfering too much with my studies, and then accepted.

I soon received the full committee's roster. Although I don't remember the precise details, the committee comprised an undergraduate representative, at least two and perhaps three faculty members from each of the university's colleges, at least one faculty senate representative, and officials from administrative divisions who would need to work with the winning candidate. The committee chair was a senior English professor; the humanities, social sciences, the so-called hard sciences, and engineering were represented in roughly equal measure.

From the committee's first meeting, I began to grasp as I hadn't before how the university was organized, and how that organization inevitably set up divisions—administrative and political—between different units. After reviewing our charge with the chancellor, we then established normal ground rules of confidentiality and candor that all search committees need to have. From that point, the committee's internal wars of maneuver began, with representatives from the humanities and sciences alike letting their peers know that the successful candidate for the position needed to respect their disciplines, if not be from them. My fellow student representative and I declared that we wanted students' needs and interests protected in the end, along with the university's high academic standards. None of our initial establishing of bona fides was surprising in itself.

But after the position was advertised and applicants' cover letters and curricula vitae (CV) began to arrive, I began to notice how faculty would read the many lengthy and impressive CVs. Records I thought were impeccable were analyzed for any gaps in time or lapses in productivity. Awards were praised or dismissed; teaching records and graduate student supervision were subjected to occasional brutal assessments. Committee members investigated and discussed reputations, whether local, national, or international. Through it all, I witnessed how easy it was for a candidate to get close to being rejected for what was likely the birth of a child or following a spouse, unless and until another committee member pointed out that we could not discriminate against someone for supporting their personal or career choices. Such defenses kept more women and people of color in the pool until the late stages. This lesson was crucial. More on this to come.

In general, I drew several other important observations:

Faculty wanted stability and longevity in academic leadership.
Faculty wanted innovation but not at the expense of stability and clarity of vision.

Clarity of vision meant, ideally, that the successful candidate would not make drastic policy changes, or at least not make policy changes for their own sake.

On any large committee, alliances are formed, tested, occasionally broken, and reconstituted.

Institutional values—sometimes synonymous with a nebulous "fit" between candidate and job—could be used to keep or exclude candidates arbitrarily.

Confidentiality was exceedingly difficult to maintain.

No process, regardless of its complexity and safeguards, guarantees a particular outcome.

I must stress that our search yielded an excellent winning candidate, after attracting some rather renowned finalists. And while this graduate student representative's attempts to appreciate and negotiate different narratives were often clumsy, I still felt that my concerns were heard and respected. My fellow student representative and I weren't infantilized, nor were we treated with condescension, for the most part. We had voices in the many conversations that transpired and in the final vote.

DATELINE: 2019

Over a quarter century later, I was asked to serve on an almost identical committee for my university's next (and current) provost, but this time as a department chair and representative for the humanities. Several crucial differences should be noted:

I now teach at a private university a little over half the size of my graduate alma mater.

Members of the board of trustees sat on the search committee.

Our search was organized and administered largely through a prominent executive search firm and its representatives, who wielded a de facto significant amount of influence by vetting and advocating for certain candidates.

The student senate president represented all students.

Once the search opened, it followed an aggressive schedule, with the finalist named within two months.

Most importantly, every single observation from 1992 proved to be true in 2019.

Universities and colleges, as well as the schools, departments, and programs within them, seek stability and access to resources as much as or more than they did a quarter century ago. It is now an axiom that members of upper administration are unlikely to stay in their positions for very long; to be a dean or provost for more than a decade is almost unthinkable. One is expected either to move up the administrative chain or on to a new post before then. And of course, many administrators don't stay more than a single contracted term (usually three to five years, depending on the institution). Without being too hyperbolic, faculty can often feel abandoned, or at least tossed hither and yon when a new administrator with new initiatives comes along. Adjusting and surviving requires additional energy—and *time*.

In addition, I noted how at private institutions, trustees wield influence to an extent not always seen at large, public universities. This is not to say, of course, that trustees do not play the same role at UCSB and other public institutions. But as faculty at public colleges and universities know, the state governing boards and legislatures hold more distant yet significant sway over institutions' directions.

LESSONS

Between these two searches, of course, I've had countless other experiences as a faculty member teaching, conducting research, and engaging in service to the university and profession. But the lessons from that first search have taught me how we can develop effective academic leadership.

First, leadership begins in academic programs, or even in graduate student governance. In my graduate program, our director of graduate studies and other faculty directly involved in the program regularly held seminars on professional matters. One of our core courses, which combined critical theory with research methods, had units devoted to these issues. Nearly every proseminar or seminar in the program took time, often a week or so, to discuss at least one of several professional subjects: how ideas in the course have influenced literary study; how to write abstracts to answer calls for papers; how to write publishable papers, where to send submissions, and why one should publish in the first place; the state of the academic job market, both in general and in specific fields; and how to write funding proposals.

Equally important, students within my graduate program frequently asked faculty to address questions about the program's structure (especially its examinations), about recruitment of women and people of color, about pedagogy, and about possible trajectories of academic careers. Admittedly, while most in the program were at least as concerned about the dearth of tenure-track jobs available in the 1990s, the movement to think of so-called alt-ac careers had not yet gained momentum.[7] That culture of open inquiry arguably resulted in a majority of my cohort's members becoming accustomed to both working within and questioning academic norms.

Questioning institutional structures in itself may not be unusual. When PhDs are comfortable with working for change within those structures, the net result is that assuming, even pursuing, positions of academic leadership becomes the new norm. Two-thirds of the eighteen people who began our graduate program completed the PhD; of those, 80 percent have served or are serving as program directors, department chairs, assistant or associate deans, deans, assistant or associate provosts, and provosts. At least one is a college president.

Let me pause. I recognize that this narrative may sound a bit triumphalist. While I unequivocally admire the faculty and students from my graduate program, they neither explicitly nor implicitly encouraged their students to become academic leaders, nor did they mention such positions as points along a career arc. Coincidence, needless to say, does not equal causality. But the program's assumptions—that all who matriculated had the potential to become faculty, to become part of academia, and should be equipped to work within it—served to remove some mystery from academic life.

About ten years ago at my current institution, our provost recognized that far too few members of the faculty had moved beyond the mystery. The university's history and operations remained opaque. In far too many departments, only a few people displayed both interest *and* aptitude for becoming program directors, department chairs, associate deans, or deans. The university had a leadership pipeline problem. In conjunction with the president's office, the provost asked deans and chairs to begin identifying potential leaders, those disposed to take on greater responsibilities, if only they knew how. The result was the Emerging Leaders Seminar, a semester-long series of weekly meetings at which potential leaders met with the president, the provost, several vice presidents, one or two deans or associate deans, and other officials who could explain everything from different offices' responsibilities and organizational charts to university finances, to admissions, to facilities, to the daily work of running departments, and so on. Identified as an "emerging leader," I found that my comprehension of—if not appreciation for—university bureaucracy grew exponentially.

Several colleagues who also participated in the seminar had different views. They strongly criticized the potential for such training seminars to reproduce or at least leave unquestioned hierarchies within the university. I cannot dispute that possibility; certainly, I doubt that upper administration wished to sow the seeds of its own destruction via a faculty revolt. But I looked around the room and saw the seminar as a potential tool for greater equity. Most of the participants were women. People of color were overrepresented in comparison to their numbers in the faculty's population. These two facts bring with them some caution, to the extent that women and faculty of color have historically been asked to take on a greater amount of service. The obvious difference, of course, is that upper administration was attempting to ensure that the university's future leaders would not be all White males. But true equity, then and now, would require that these future leaders be duly *compensated* for helping the institution to function effectively at all levels. More on this in the following section.

GETTING AWAY FROM GETTING AWAY FROM IT ALL

Perhaps the most valuable component of successful PhD programs is that they prepare students for academic realities, including the absurdities built into bureaucratic systems. No line from my graduate studies resonates more than "expect the unexpected," shared by two advanced students who'd made their first attempts at the academic job market. They described many of the horror stories that academic job seekers have shared: interviewing cheek by jowl with other job applicants at the Modern Language Association's Job Center; interviewees sitting on hotel beds while interviewers relaxed in solid chairs; interviewees being asked to care for interviewers' small children; uncomfortable, if not downright illegal questions; bizarre conversations; strange hotels; anxiety and despair.

More importantly, these graduate colleagues revealed how search committees, and therefore many faculty, think. Along with our professors, they stressed that search committees have to do their best because they have to answer to deans and provosts at their home institutions. If they bring to campus and hire candidates unlikely to gain tenure, then they risk not receiving future tenure-track positions for their departments. They have to think about the long-term consequences of their decisions. More to the point, these strange beings called "deans" and "provosts" wield power and influence meant to maintain and improve the institution's standards and culture. While I have little idea what my own professors thought of their deans and vice presidents for academic affairs, it's quite safe to say that they hoped and expected them to be competent. And if we were to become part of the professoriate, the hope was that we would be competent at our jobs.

Overwhelmingly, we are highly competent and capable. But out of several different motives, such as antipathy toward administrative work in particular or—to be honest—heavier work in general—we do find that a few faculty members attempt to ensure that they will not be asked to shoulder additional burdens, leaving it to others to learn how to do the jobs they can't or won't.

Learned or feigned incompetence is the quality of being decidedly bad at certain aspects of the job to avoid being asked to do them. Those aspects are almost invariably any administrative tasks. Faculty have devised or fallen into several habits to stay as far away from administration as possible; anyone reading this text can probably identify them. Most prominent is simply remaining purposefully ignorant of how one's institution works, in both the short and long terms. Thus one could be a member of one university's faculty for years, even decades, and not know how specific offices on campus work—or that they simply exist. This ignorance could even extend to one's own department, regardless of its size, however unlikely that might appear. Sometimes feigned incompetence means refusing to follow good email protocol or failing to communicate effectively.

To be fair, this apparent lack of competence may be the result of the impostor syndrome that afflicts nearly all of us from the moment we enter graduate study. It can be paralyzing and debilitating. Chairs and deans may attempt to help colleagues who struggle with a sense of their own inadequacy. But faculty doubts about authenticity and competence are frequently artificial, almost delusional, products of too many people being shielded from the university's inner workings during graduate study or in their early careers. Few graduate programs systematically offer graduate students opportunities to see how program directors, department chairs, or deans conduct their daily business similar to the one I described earlier. It is more common for students preparing to enter the academic job market to receive some advice about on-campus interviews when candidates are apt to meet associate deans, deans, and occasionally members of the provost's office. Until such training, though, most graduate students have little incentive to understand administrators' jobs, while assistant professors on the tenure track may be more focused on earning tenure than on studying a university organizational chart. Nevertheless, it requires either intense focus or severe avoidance not to learn, for example, that deans and provosts do have responsibilities, some degree of authority, and budgets (however limited), and why they are important.

I would characterize the second barrier to effective faculty governance or potential readiness for those leadership roles as a desire to reinvent the wheel, which frequently takes the form of re-legislating matters that members of the faculty had already legislated but a few years, months, weeks, or days earlier. Readers may nominate their own examples, but the most common would be matters of policy—anything from promotion and tenure guidelines, to undergraduate or graduate academic standards, or funding rules—that units had developed and settled upon after extensive and often vigorous discussion and debate. This often bespeaks not only a lack of trust between individuals and their units but also an assumption that *one* person's voice should overrule the work of many, no matter how idiosyncratic that voice might be. Faculty governance cannot take place without a healthy sense of collegiality and faith in others' abilities to decide on crucial matters. That begins at the program or department level. Faculty who slow a unit's progress by questioning every proposal decision without considering fairly the advantages, disadvantages, and outcomes can become toxic, and therefore undesirable, as potential leaders. While upper administration needs to earn faculty confidence as well by listening and valuing those who could lead their units, departments need to create processes for full vetting of proposals to obviate frequent revisiting of sound decisions.

I take to heart Jonathan R. Cole's admonition that an "essential feature of the American research university" and its notion of academic freedom is that

> no one speaks "for" the university—not even its official leaders. Although the president, the provost, and the board of trustees have the responsibility and the authority to formulate and carry out university policies, the essence of a university lies in its multiplicity of voices: those of its faculty, its students, its researchers, and its staff.[8]

For Cole, "there is no 'university position'" on "the writings, or remarks, or actions of Professor X" who may speak out of turn and threaten a university's image or standing; the university "does not decide which ideas are good and bad, which are right and wrong," as that is "up for constant debate, deliberation, and discourse among the faculty and students."[9] When faculty are not equipped or willing to engage in these debates, whether through learned incompetence or antipathy toward leadership roles or administrative work, then it becomes easier for the administrators, whom faculty and students rightfully fear to have free rein, to arrogate to themselves the responsibility to speak for the faculty.

The only way to avoid this outcome is for faculty to be fully engaged in their institutions' operations, to join the "war of position" and infiltrate the structures that need to be exposed and possibly rebuilt. This cannot happen when faculty attempt to escape their units, to give responsibility to an ever smaller group of faculty willing to serve. These forms of escape frequently consist of faculty building—and sometimes inventing—structural obstacles that prevent them from being fully engaged. At the basest and most egregious level, some members of the faculty might build artificial reasons why they could not possibly come to campus to participate in meetings, such as designated research days during the week that must always remain inviolate. More commonly, though, our colleagues may become so deeply ensconced in professional matters beyond the department and university that no one ever sees them. And so the burden falls to the same faculty again and again, with a shrinking number of voices carrying sway.

CONCLUSION: LOOKING FOR A LOT OF GOOD PEOPLE

What does it take to enter these positions? It certainly is not, as faculty repeat ad infinitum, a certain kind of character, as if good, highly competent administrators were born, not made. This is the most damaging narrative of all, that colleagues who become academic leaders are part of a de facto servant caste, one beneath those whose lives and research are more important than the odiousness of administrative or service work. Such narratives frequently reproduce hierarchical divisions of class, gender, and race in which women and people of color, ever inferior to the White male majority, must always pay a limitless set of "dues," while the faculty deserving of the full "life of the mind" are free to do their work without the burden of heavy service. Even when such narratives do not reify these structures, they relieve individual faculty members of the responsibility of working to improve their institutions. The avoidant define administrative offices and institutional policies as inscrutable at best, suited only for those whose teaching and research are deemed less valuable. And once again, our students lose; knowledge loses.

In the personal anecdotes I conveyed in this chapter, I concluded that the lessons learned from my early and recent experiences justified greater attention to professionalization and mentoring. I am an African American male, the first of my paternal and maternal families to earn a BA, MA, and PhD, one of the barely 5 percent of all Black faculty in the United States, 3.6 percent of all full professors, and—again, as an African American male full professor—one of one-half of 1 percent of all faculty.[10] The chances that anyone would receive the mentoring and professionalization needed to survive in the academy are already slim under the best of circumstances; for those in my subject position—for *all* faculty of color and the majority of women—they are infinitesimally small. As Chyna N. Crawford highlights elsewhere in this volume, mentoring and professionalization opportunities are not only unusual in academia, but also routinely closed off to women and to faculty of color, especially African American women. Crawford writes that her "peers were very quick to point out to me that they had years of training and practice, into an area where, I had little to no prior experience and expertise."[11] Her experience is all too common. Crawford also advocates good mentors because the mentor may help the "emerging leader to increase their self-efficacy by demonstrating that if their mentor can succeed, so can they."[12] Equally important, when women and people of color are asked to do more work with less support and mentoring while watching their White colleagues advance with less effort and more recognition, it is not only demoralizing but can militate against retention. Units that fail to provide such mentoring and support risk undoing any and all efforts to diversify their faculty, staff, and students. It's a butterfly effect that can have devastating consequences.

Yet the solutions here are almost maddeningly simple. They require integrating mentoring and professionalization into *all* graduate programs, rather than making these components the province of a few, elite institutions. They require creating and maintaining programs that identify and train faculty to become crucial players in their institutions' futures. They require active listening and discourse from the beginning of graduate study, through appointment in full-time positions, through promotion and tenure, and beyond. They require identifying and recruiting undergraduates, graduate students, and faculty invested in the academy's success. What they don't require is a deal with Lucifer.

NOTES

1. Jonathan Swift, "Travels into Several Remote Nations of the World. In Four Parts. By Lemuel Gulliver, First a Surgeon, and then a Captain of Several Ships," in *The Writings of Jonathan Swift*, eds. Robert A. Greenberg and William B. Piper (New York: W. W. Norton, 1973), 216.

2. "Change in Percentages of Full-Time Faculty Members Who Were Non-Tenure-Track, by Institutional Classification, 2008–9 and 2018–19," *The Chronicle of Higher Education*, August 18, 2019, https://www.chronicle.com/article/change-in-percentages-of-full-time-faculty-members-who-were-non-tenure-track-by-institutional-classification-2008-9-and-2018-19/.

3. Benjamin Ginsberg, "Administrators Ate My Tuition," *Washington Monthly*, September/October 2011, https://washingtonmonthly.com/magazine/septoct-2011/administrators-ate-my-tuition/.

4. Ivy Kaplan, "Breaking Down 'Administrative Bloat,'" The College Post, April 24, 2019, https://thecollegepost.com/breaking-down-administrative-bloat/.

5. Elissa Nadworny, "More than 1 Million Fewer Students Are in College. Here's How That Affects the Economy," NPR.com, January 13, 2022, https://www.npr.org/2022/01/13/1072529477/more-than-1-million-fewer-students-are-in-college-the-lowest-enrollment-numbers-. See also Larenda Mielke, "As Pandemic Pushes Higher Ed Closer to Demographic Cliff, Institutions Must Consider Strategic Options," October 29, 2021, https://www.kaufmanhall.com/insights/blog/pandemic-pushes-higher-ed-closer-demographic-cliff-institutions-must-consider.

6. Antonio Gramsci, *Prison Notebooks*, vol. 3, ed. Joseph Buttigieg (New York: Columbia University Press, 2007), 168–69. Gramsci writes that where "civil society was primordial and gelatinous," a war of maneuver that could upend a government would be more likely to succeed; where a "proper relation between state and civil society" existed, a tottering state revealed "a sturdy structure" that could not be moved. Save, perhaps, for those institutions (e.g., Sweet Briar College, which nearly closed in 2015) that have repeatedly or systematically threatened their own financial and administrative structures or otherwise been unable to sustain them, most universities have arguably maintained these structures within, even as the university has been under assault and defunding from without.

7. Short for "alternative academic," "alt-ac" has become a catchall term for careers that PhDs might pursue outside of the traditional professoriate. Like any general term, it subsumes many different, diverse paths and contains a number of problematic assumptions. Foremost among these is that the traditional path is the center; all other careers are marginal. In view of the horrendous academic job market, doctoral programs, especially those in the humanities, have been forced to alter this thinking; as Melissa Dalgleish writes, "Being an academic is just a job," one not inherently better than any other. To write these words would have been sacrilegious 25 years ago; to say so now is nearly routine. Melissa Dalgleish, *Hook & Eye*, March 17, 2016, https://hookandeye .ca/2016/03/17/questioning-that-altac-label-a-quit-letter-update/.

8. Jonathan Cole, *The Great American University: Its Rise to Preeminence, Its Indispensable National Role, Why It Must Be Protected* (New York: Public Affairs, 2009), 384–85.

9. Cole, *Great American University*, 384–85.

10. US Department of Education, National Center for Education Statistics, Integrated Postsecondary Education Data System (IPEDS), Table 315.20, "Full-Time Faculty in Degree-Granting Postsecondary Institutions, by Race/ Ethnicity, Sex, and Academic Rank: Fall 2015, Fall 2017, and Fall 2018," Spring 2016 through Spring 2019 Human Resources Component, Fall Staff Section.

11. Chyna N. Crawford, "Leading While Young, Black, and on the Tenure Track," in *Transforming Leadership Pathways for Humanities Professionals in Higher Education*, edited by Roze Hentschell and Catherine E. Thomas (West Lafayette, IN: Purdue University Press, 2023), 164.

12. Crawford, "Leading While Young," 165.

BIBLIOGRAPHY

"Change in Percentages of Full-Time Faculty Members Who Were Non-Tenure-Track, by Institutional Classification, 2008–9 and 2018–19." *The Chronicle of Higher Education*, August 18, 2019. https://www.chronicle.com/article/change -in-percentages-of-full-time-faculty-members-who-were-non-tenure-track -by-institutional-classification-2008-9-and-2018-19/.

Cole, Jonathan. *The Great American University: Its Rise to Preeminence, Its Indispensable*

National Role, Why It Must Be Protected. New York: Public Affairs, 2009.

Crawford, Chyna, N. "Leading While Young, Black, and on the Tenure Track." In *Transforming Leadership Pathways for Humanities Professionals in Higher Education*, edited by Roze Hentschell and Catherine E. Thomas, 157–73. West Lafayette, IN: Purdue University Press, 2023.

Dalgleish, Melissa. "Questioning That #Alt-Ac Label: A Quit Letter Update," *Hook & Eye*, March 17, 2016. https://hookandeye.ca/2016/03/17/questioning-that-altac-label-a-quit-letter-update/.

Ginsberg, Benjamin. "Administrators Ate My Tuition." *Washington Monthly*, September/October 2011. https://washingtonmonthly.com/magazine/septoct-2011/administrators-ate-my-tuition/.

Gramsci, Antonio. *Prison Notebooks*. Vol. 3. Edited by Joseph Buttigieg. New York: Columbia University Press, 2007.

Kaplan, Ivy. "Breaking Down 'Administrative Bloat.'" *The College Post*, April 24, 2019. https://thecollegepost.com/breaking-down-administrative-bloat/.

Mielke, Larenda. "As Pandemic Pushes Higher Ed Closer to Demographic Cliff, Institutions Must Consider Strategic Options." *Sustaining Higher Education* (blog), Kaufman Hall, October 29, 2021. https://www.kaufmanhall.com/insights/blog/pandemic-pushes-higher-ed-closer-demographic-cliff-institutions-must-consider.

Nadworny, Elissa. "More than 1 Million Fewer Students Are in College. Here's How That Affects the Economy." *NPR.com*, January 13, 2022. https://www.npr.org/2022/01/13/1072529477/more-than-1-million-fewer-students-are-in-college-the-lowest-enrollment-numbers-.

Swift, Jonathan. *Travels into Several Remote Nations of the World. In Four Parts. By Lemuel Gulliver, First a Surgeon, and then a Captain of Several Ships*. In *The Writings of Jonathan Swift*, edited by Robert A. Greenberg and William B. Piper, 1–260. New York: W. W. Norton, 1973.

US Department of Education, National Center for Education Statistics, Integrated Postsecondary Education Data System (IPEDS), Table 315.20. "Full-Time Faculty in Degree-Granting Postsecondary Institutions, by Race/Ethnicity, Sex, and Academic Rank: Fall 2015, Fall 2017, and Fall 2018." Spring 2016 through Spring 2019. Human Resources Component, Fall Staff Section.

2

THE POLITICS, PRACTICE, AND POETICS OF TEACHING LEADERSHIP

PHILIP ROBINSON-SELF

This chapter discusses the evolving role in higher education of teaching leadership. Leadership is a complex and contested practice in higher education and can sit particularly uncomfortably alongside the traditionally democratic and collegiate forms of discourse common to arts and humanities subjects. However, the humanities also offer us paths forward in terms of teaching us how to deconstruct and interrogate processes of leadership, how to lead in moral, value-driven ways, and hence present alternative paradigms for what leadership might mean, and how it can mean. The articulation of the critically complex, the problematic, and the subjective is one of the signature intellectual joys of the humanities, and it is precisely suited to understanding ways forward in the leadership of teaching.

TEACHING LEADERSHIP POLITICS AND CONTEXTS

The exercise of leadership has a long history in universities. In the early thirteenth century, the chancellor of the University of Paris registered a familiar dichotomy between the needs of teaching and of institutional governance, complaining that "things are hurried and little is learned, the time taken for lectures being spent in meetings and discussions."[1] Despite the long tail on the argument, however, it is fair to say that the last few decades have put issues of leadership in higher education under the spotlight in ways not seen previously, as both a subject for intense scrutiny and debate, and as an area ripe with opportunity. As I will briefly set out in the opening portion of this chapter, the higher education sector has, globally, increased and diversified in scope, size, and mission; at the same time, the links between universities, governments, publics, and private enterprises have shifted. These changes have brought tensions, pressures, and anxieties, but also greater opportunities to influence. Leadership within universities increasingly can mean leadership beyond. As I detail from a more personal viewpoint in the second section of this chapter, the ways in which we practice leadership offer the means to make genuine impacts beyond our own subject areas while carrying something distinctive about those subject areas with us.

The present chapter takes as its focus the developing role in higher education of teaching leadership, a role with a range of responsibilities conducted at varying degrees of seniority, and which comes with an equally varied nomenclature (associate dean, director of teaching, chair of studies, and so forth). There are, however, common threads and areas of interest running across such roles. Although the balance of responsibilities may vary, generally the activity of teaching leadership might be expected to involve something akin to the following: oversight of student learning and experiences, organization of teaching (if not always direct management of those colleagues doing the teaching), oversight of the development of new curricula and of the management of existing curricula, and the development, coordination, implementation, and communication of overall strategies regarding education. The level at which these responsibilities are conducted may again vary, as of course will individual agency in how such roles can be carried out.

Further complicating this picture of teaching leadership are the myriad ways in which the sector globally has changed, enlarged, and diversified over the past few decades. An increasingly diverse range of institutions with degree-awarding powers has led to a similarly diverse range of goals for learning and, consequently, a variety of notions of what constitutes, or what ought to constitute, good teaching practice.[2] Some institutions place greater strategic emphasis than others on research capacity, on the skills and employability of graduates, on links with industry, on attracting international students or offering placements abroad, or on particular cultural or pedagogical values; the balance of these kinds of priorities will affect how curricula can be shaped within each institution. The organization of teaching and of education strategy will likely look different in larger institutions with broader subject coverage than in smaller and more specialist providers, different again in institutions rooted in regional communities to those spread widely across multiple campuses, and different again in those with greater investment in online provision, and so on.

Thus, which goals are to be pursued, which innovations implemented, which stakeholders consulted, which staff involved and at what level of seniority are all variable by, and often also within, the institution.[3] Equally, particular goals may jar or find resonance with those of individual senior managers, academic staff, students, and other constituents within academia.[4] The role of meeting and matching such issues and competing demands with appropriate teaching is no simple business. Marshaling such complexity as a leader of other teachers is, if anything, yet more complex.

Beyond this essential complexity, though, there are other reasons why teaching leadership is fundamentally difficult. Most obviously, the concept of leadership generally in higher education has not been readily or easily accepted. Writing at the end of the '90s, Paul Ramsden noted that "ambitions for leadership, success in management and administration, a commitment to more efficient business operations [...] tend still to be looked on with disfavor by many academics."[5] Two decades later, management remains something of a dirty word in higher education, and leadership has not fared a great deal better. As Prichard puts it, "Management, managers and management activity are controversial and problematic in HE."[6]

Indeed, there is no single, clear, or broadly accepted definition of leadership in academia; a contentious area of scholarship, the literature features often competing and contradictory references to multiple leadership types, theories, styles, and models. In some ways this is, perhaps, unavoidable: leadership incorporates a considerable range of individuals, groups, actions, and activities, occurring in an equally considerable range of contexts, underpinned by distinct values and beliefs variable from person to person. Despite this essential variability, however, institutions have increasingly moved to structures that ask for, or require, forms of leadership tending toward the hierarchical, managerial, and positional. This focus on leadership as located in individuals can be seen as part of a structural and cultural shift in the organization and running of universities beginning in the 1980s, a shift that has involved movement from integrated academic cultures of administration to "executive management," from relatively flat organizational structures to increasingly hierarchical ones.[7]

There are well-rehearsed reasons behind these changes. External drivers commonly pointed to include the massification of the sector, internationalization, knowledge commodification, public scrutiny, and the onset of austerity. Increased regulation, oversight, competition, rising student fees and living costs (in some regions), questions of consumer satisfaction, data protection, and even something as prosaic as the sheer size of institutions have all encouraged movements toward more hierarchical forms of institutional organization. From this viewpoint, students, academic staff, and other constituents of the university are increasingly seen in terms of human capital: the stock of habits, knowledge, social, and creative attributes embodied in the ability to perform labor in the service of economic value. A range of matching cultural and organizational changes can be marked within institutions, including increased control (managerialism), increased competition between institutions (marketization), increased stress on transparency and measurement (bureaucratization), and the remodeling of structures and operations (corporatization). In much of the literature on leadership, this is regarded as invariably detrimental to higher education and to individuals working within it. There is some truth to all this, and we may particularly feel it in times of crisis. However, it is also worth acknowledging that a common, and useful, critique of this type of narrative is that it assumes an idyllic past to higher education borne more out of nostalgia than reality. After all, the history of universities, at least within the Western tradition of higher education, has been frequently elitist, imperialist, and marginalizing in nature.

The ensuing consequences of changes in the sector have been widely reported and debated, as have the effects on the organization of curricula.[8] Similar developments have been encouraged, and critiqued, globally; these can be seen as part of broader neoliberal movements in which higher education policy is increasingly based on "assumptions of global-ization, competition and meritocracy."[9] In this model, education is clearly "tailored to the needs of corporate interests" with increasingly less impetus to face "pressing social and ethical issues."[10] Similarly, Bulaitis describes the "adoption of economic value as the driving rationality of governance" for universities, with "the rhetoric of economic justification [...] a formal requirement for government subsidy of creative and cultural ventures."[11] How the university is conceived of (and particularly what purposes it is assumed to fulfill) affects what types of knowledge are valued, incentiv-ized, and rewarded; what shape our programs of study take; and the inter-actions and expectations of our students.

There are, then, a number of external issues facing those of us who move into teaching leadership. There are also extrinsic and intrinsic questions of recognition and value in the role itself. Though, by comparison, the con-cept of research leaders has grown in acceptance, aided by the language of promotion structures, grant accumulation, and various assurance exercises, teaching leadership can remain something of a contradiction in terms. The ethos of academic work, and particularly the work of teaching, tends to privilege individual academic judgment in its execution and collegiate action in its organization. While leadership *in* teaching has received in-creasing acknowledgment as both a legitimate career activity and a valid intellectual pursuit (the Scholarship of Teaching and Learning being one academic avenue that has burgeoned in recent years), leadership *of* teach-ing continues to imply an unwelcome and unmerited managerial inter-ference in day-to-day academic life.

These issues are all felt particularly acutely in the humanities, where the notion of individual and hierarchical leadership can sit uncomfort-ably with the signature pedagogies of our subject areas, and with the tra-ditionally democratic and collegiate forms of discourse common to arts and humanities subjects. On top of that, the neoliberal language of labor, skills, employability, public good, and so forth has put the humanities, par-ticularly, under significant economic pressure. Despite being in some re-spects the most economically viable courses, humanities and creative arts tend to be squeezed financially, and are often at pains to justify their ex-istence. The humanities have long been felt to be under attack or at least in need of defense. J. H. Plumb made the case for a "crisis in the human-ities" over half a century ago, and since then, the argument has reared its head in various ways.[12] The reorientation of universities in terms of mar-ket logic clearly privileges (even if it also constrains) scientific subjects that can show more immediate benefits of research investment to econo-mies.[13] Meanwhile, the humanities are seen to lag behind in terms of "in-creasing pressures on institutions to orient ... towards immediate socie-tal needs, most commonly the economic ones, manifesting themselves at the micro-level in the employability of graduates and at the macro-level in links to the knowledge economy."[14]

However, the humanities also offer us paths forward in terms both of deconstructing leadership as an idea and, perhaps more importantly, re-considering and enriching the ways in which we practice leadership along-side others. The articulation of the critically complex; the exploration of the subjective; and the imaginative, creative, and democratic deployment of discussion, interaction, reflection, and co-construction: these are some of the signature intellectual joys of the humanities, and they are, as I set out in the next section, particularly suited to understanding ways forward in the leadership of teaching.

LEADERSHIP POETICS AND PRAXIS

As I have sketched out in the foregoing, teaching leadership takes place against the context of several challenges at sector, institutional, and depart-mental levels. In offering my perspective on these issues, I draw directly from twin experiences as both a (past) teaching leader in humanities and a (present) teacher of leadership to others. Along the way, I want to point to the usefulness of critical and particularly aesthetic pedagogies in the exploration and practice of leadership in the humanities and more gener-ally. My own story may well be relatively familiar: partly by design, partly by chance, I moved several years ago from a path based primarily around teaching and research into one which also encompassed academic lead-ership across a number of subjects. From there (and mainly, at the time, with an eye on finding better work/life balance), I took something of a leap into leadership development. What began as a testing of the waters outside a home discipline has become, by various turns, a career. There are many positive aspects to such work. The range of ideas and perspectives brought up from the areas in which I engage has been both intellectually rich and professionally stimulating. The teaching aspects of my career have been enlivened by this work across disciplines: engagement with other academic areas has led me to learn about and in some cases to teach and research a variety of subjects that I might not have otherwise and to bring in some of their pedagogies into my own practice.

This engagement also has made me think differently about the nature of leadership, as I set out in the remainder of this chapter. It is not my intention here to propose new models of leadership per se. As has been noted, the field is already full of metaphors and models, and adding another risks confusion—and does not necessarily tell us anything new about the actions or outcomes of leadership.[15] What I do want to do, however, is to make a claim for the use of the humanities in understanding a practice and a particular approach to the ethos of leadership. As a whole, and with varying emphases, humanities disciplines work to reveal and to understand cultures, emotions, ethics, values, behaviors, and relationships; a critical understanding of these aspects of humanity has been seen as fundamental to competent, ethical leadership.[16] It is thus worth reminding ourselves of how the ways in which we teach can be productively reflected in the ways in which we lead.

Conducting effective teaching in humanities subjects often depends on the deployment and encouragement of rich, probing, and democratic discussion. Such discussion helps students to see events, objects, people, or ideas through a range of critical and theoretical lenses while developing their own lines of inquiry and insight. This teaching philosophy, that "discussion remains an indispensable part of democratic education," along with the skills that make it work as a practice, positively influences my own approach to leadership.[17] Of course, discussion and debate suit the humanities; they bring out and exercise key skills in specific disciplines while attuning students to subtleties in that skill set around active listening, creative response, and critical discourse. Such debate can also help to keep leadership a pleasurable, intellectually productive, and critically incisive activity.

To work in humanities is to "study the meaning-making practices of [. . .] culture, focusing on interpretation and evaluation with an indispensable element of subjectivity."[18] These methodological tools have been related powerfully to acts of pedagogy and emancipation by Maxine Greene, who saw the educational need to attune to "multiple patterns of being and knowing, to a regard for cultural differences, to an attentiveness when it comes to voices never listened to before."[19] Greene argued for the political and social power of the creative imagination: "Of all our cognitive capacities, imagination is the one that permits us to give credence to alternative realities [. . .] allows us to break with the taken for granted, to set aside familiar distinctions and definitions."[20] For Greene, human experience was a sedimentation of layers; as Kohli comments, successfully attending to such layers requires an "expanded notion of critical reflection—one that incorporates rational, emotional, ethical, and aesthetic sensibilities—in order to come to more complete understanding."[21] In a number of ways, then, the creative and reflective lenses which we use every day within our subject areas can be powerfully deployed in our approach to leadership.

Teaching leaders within the humanities have an opportunity to act as what Giroux has termed "transformative intellectuals," in as much as we take a critical stance toward our own practice and the practice of others that is inherently open, creative, and transformative. In shaping the curriculum, shaping policy, defining educational philosophies, and working with communities in diverse capacities, Giroux argues, transformative intellectuals are critically aware of their own theoretical convictions and become skilled in strategies for translating conviction into practice.[22] This is, essentially, the Gramscian/Freirean concept of praxis, or theoretically informed action. In both formulations, praxis involves the active combination of reflection and action in the service of social change, engaging teachers and students together in a critical examination of how power relations operate in education and how these relations sustain and propagate existing hegemonic social structures, particularly connected to the construction of knowledge (a process Freire famously referred to as conscientização, or conscientization; the gaining of critical consciousness). Equipping teachers and students with the language of critique and the rhetoric of empowerment enables "transformative agents who recognize, challenge, and transform injustice and inequitable social structures."[23] Praxis represents a vital approach in teaching and in leadership, offering empowered discourse in the service of transformative ends. We have an opportunity too, here, to be as open about our practices of leading as we are about those ends. The democracy of the humanities classroom ought also to be the democracy of leadership.

But in seeking transformation we must be careful not to become complicit in the flaws of transformational leadership practices. As Tourish has commented, "In stressing the need for leaders to 'transform' others—a project which increasingly seeks to reshape their most private values, attitudes and aspirations—transformational leadership has been complicit in attempts to extend the power of formal organizational leaders in ever more intrusive directions."[24] Genuine transformation is transformational for all, emerges from all, and does not operate at the cost of overriding identities or by forcing others to engage in a pretense of institutional values. This is the moral and democratic tension of leadership, leadership as responsibility to others, as obligation, "a reciprocal process of opening oneself up and learning from others in order to carve out new spaces of freedom."[25] It is not an easy process, and there are plenty of pitfalls along the way, but here again, I would argue that the humanities are well placed to cope with such tensions: "The humanities, centrally concerned as they are with the cultural practices of reflection, argument, criticism, and speculative testing of ideas, have a substantial contribution to make to the good working of democracy."[26] Democratic conversation, speculative and cooperative construction of knowledge, critical consciousness, attentiveness to argument, and care for both critique and kindness, these are the structural, intellectual and aesthetic building blocks of our subject areas in the humanities and are at the heart of the praxis of leadership.

Leadership should not then be enacted in terms of individual, personal, or positional attributes but rather seen in terms of a socially occurring nexus of ideas, events, and actors. According to Collinson and Tourish, leadership is "socially constructed and interpreted and [...] could mean very different things to different actors in different situations."[27] Thinking of leadership as a social process of mutual and reciprocal influence in the service of identifying and accomplishing collective goals is a rewarding if also clearly a complex proposition.[28] It necessarily involves identity work: who we choose to be, what identities we choose to enact, when we choose to perform them, how, with whom, and in what contexts are all central to the dynamics of leadership. Again, the critical reflection common to humanities disciplines is central here to the successful action of leadership because it provides space for considering the ways in which our own identity (subjectivity, biases, race, gender, class, culture) interrupts or, potentially, enhances, an ability to see other perspectives and hence provide effective arenas for the operation of leadership.[29]

A view of leadership as acquired and sustained (or lost) through constant social interactions necessarily shifts power away from any one leader and transfers it to the relationships within and around a community, "the social interactions in which people claim and grant leader identities."[30] This is not, it should be said, the same as distributed leadership, where responsibilities are determined from above by the nature of a task or situation. Distributed leadership tends to be a popular theory in higher education, in as much as the collegiality of the model fits an ideal of the university. In practice, however, this ideal can exclude, denigrate, or otherwise silence voices based on (for example) class, race, and gender. Distributed leadership, and to a certain extent ideas of collegiality as a whole, can mask contestation, discrimination, and conflict; it can also act as a method of pushing work onto junior colleagues.[31]

Equally, it is worth remembering that "sometimes making visible and opening the space for speech can contribute to rather than prevent harm."[32] There is a difference between appearing caring and engaged and creating spaces for actual dialogue or change. There is a sense in which creating spaces for speech and community risks also being coercive, in as much as what seems to us like a permission to engage may to others be a demand. Creating a genuinely engaged and democratic community among fellow academic staff can be—despite (or even because of) our experience in teaching—a more difficult proposition than with most students. Most obviously, differences in real or perceived seniority can create problems in discussion: "rational communication" may end up "distorted by the effects of unequal distribution of power."[33] Openness, a commitment to questions, and clarity in creating a learning space (again, all signature pedagogies in the humanities) can help in recognizing and carefully teasing out the problems. In believing in evolving forums for discussion based on genuine exchange and involvement, I take my cue from a point made some years ago in Edwards, McGoldrick, and Oliver (2006) concerning the quality of effective learning: "You've got to improvise—it's like a performance in a way. One in which the audience can heckle and change the ending [...] you just have to prepare as best you can and then cope."[34] Heckling and changing the ending is a wonderful description of what I would look for in genuinely engaged learning and just so in genuinely engaged leadership work. Everyone involved must have the capacity to change the ending, or there is not much point in being involved in the story.

Leadership, for better and worse, is about making meaning, and so in the same way that we teach creativity with the making of meaning in our own subject areas, we need leadership to make room for meaning-making on the part of everyone involved. For all the foregoing reasons touched on in this chapter, it seems ever more important to spend time with our communities, with colleagues, with students, with ourselves, thinking about what sort of leaders we want and what sort of leaders we want to be. Leadership should not be assumed but rather examined: the activities and practices of leadership ought not to begin and end with those in leadership roles but should instead work to bring in other voices, other members. This type of leadership, a leadership that I would argue is distinctive of the humanities, offers a way forward in catering to the many individual and group needs within and around our curricula—even as it also requires serious investment in terms of time and resources. In the final account, though, such a method of leadership offers intellectual and emotional sustenance to ourselves as well as to others.

NOTES

1. Graeme Moodle and Rowland Eustace, *Power and Authority in British Universities* (London: Routledge, 2012), 11.
2. Tony Harland and Neil Pickering, *Values in Higher Education Teaching* (Abingdon: Routledge, 2010), 65; Trevor Hussey and Patrick Smith, *The Trouble*

with Higher Education: A Critical Examination of our Universities (Abingdon: Routledge, 2010), 101.

3. Kerri-Lee Krause, "Interpreting Changing Academic Roles and Identities in Higher Education," in *The Routledge International Handbook of Higher Education*, ed. Malcolm Tight, Ka Ho Mok, Jeroen Huisman, and Christopher C. Morphew (London: Routledge, 2009), 413–25; Paul Blackmore and Camille Kandiko, "Change: Processes and Resources," in *Strategic Curriculum Change*, ed. Paul Blackmore and Camille Kandiko (Abingdon: Routledge, 2012), 111–27.

4. Craig Prichard, *Making Managers in Universities and Colleges* (Buckingham: SRHE/Open University Press, 2000), 124; Ronald Barnett and Roberto Di Napoli, ed., *Changing Identities in Higher Education: Voicing Perspectives* (Abingdon: Routledge, 2009), 23; Lee Bolman and Joan Gallos, *Reframing Academic Leadership* (San Francisco: Jossey-Bass, 2011), 4.

5. Paul Ramsden, *Learning to Lead in Higher Education* (London: Routledge, 1998), 58.

6. Prichard, *Making Managers*, 124. See also Doug Parkin, *Leading Learning and Teaching in Higher Education: The Key Guide to Designing and Delivering Courses* (London: Routledge, 2017), 15–16.

7. Robin Middlehurst, "Changing Internal Governance: A Discussion of Leadership Roles and Management Structures in UK Universities," *Higher Education Quarterly* 58, no. 4 (2004): 258–79.

8. Jeffrey L. Buller, *Change Leadership in Higher Education: A Practical Guide to Academic Transformation* (San Francisco: Jossey-Bass, 2014), 217–18; Bolman and Gallos, *Reframing Academic Leadership*, 4; Barnett and Di Napoli ed., *Changing Identities in Higher Education*, 20–21.

9. John Kenny, "Re-empowering Academics in a Corporate Culture: An Exploration of Workload and Performativity in a University," *Higher Education* 75 (2018): 32.

10. Henry Giroux, "The Corporate War Against Higher Education," *Workplace* 9 (2002): 106–7.

11. Zoe Hope Bulaitis, *Value and the Humanities: The Neoliberal University and Our Victorian Inheritance* (Palgrave Macmillan, 2020), 202–3.

12. Michael Bérubé, "The Utility of the Arts and Humanities," *Arts and Humanities in Higher Education* 2, no. 1 (2003): 23–40; Jerome Kagan, *The Three Cul-*

tures: Natural Sciences, Social Sciences, and the Humanities in the Twenty-First Century (Cambridge: Cambridge University Press, 2009), x–xi; Stefan Collini, *What Are Universities For?* (London: Penguin, 2012), 33; Eleonora Belfiore and Anna Upchurch, ed. *Humanities in the Twenty-First Century: Beyond Utility and Markets* (Basingstoke: Palgrave, 2013), 1.

13. Elizabeth Popp Berman, *Creating the Market University: How Academic Science Became an Economic Engine* (Princeton, NJ: Princeton University Press, 2012), 3.

14. Tristan McCowan, "Five Perils of the Impact Agenda in Higher Education," *London Review of Education* 16, no. 2 (2018): 279.

15. David V. Day, "The Future of Leadership: Challenges and Prospects," in *The Oxford Handbook of Leadership and Organizations*, ed. David V. Day (Oxford: Oxford University Press, 2014), 859–68.

16. Joanne B. Ciulla, "The Two Cultures: The Place of Humanities Research in Leadership Studies," *Leadership* 15, no. 4 (2019): 433–44.

17. Stephen Brookfield and Stephen Preskill, *Discussion as a Way of Teaching: Tools and Techniques for Democratic Classrooms* (San Francisco: Jossey-Bass, 2005), 16.

18. Helen Small, *The Value of the Humanities* (Oxford: Oxford University Press, 2013), 4.

19. Maxine Greene, "Teaching as Possibility: A Light in Dark Times," in *Critical Pedagogy in Uncertain Times: Hope and Possibilities*, ed. Sheila L. Macrine (New York: Palgrave Macmillan, 2009), 138.

20. Maxine Greene, *Releasing the Imagination: Essays on Education, the Arts and Social Change* (San Francisco: Jossey-Bass, 2000), 3.

21. Wendy Kohli, "The Dialectical Imagination of Maxine Greene: Social Imagination as Critical Pedagogy," *Education and Culture* 32, no. 1 (2016): 17.

22. Henry Giroux, "The Corporate War against Higher Education," *Workplace* 9 (2002): 103–17.

23. Michalinos Zembylas, "Critical Pedagogy and Emotion: Working through 'Troubled Knowledge' in Posttraumatic Contexts," *Critical Studies in Education* 54, no. 2 (2013): 177–78.

24. Dennis Tourish, *The Dark Side of Transformational Leadership: A Critical Perspective* (London: Routledge, 2013), 20.

25. Sabrina Ross, "The Dialectic of Racial Justice: Maxine Greene's Contributions to Morally Engaged and Racially Just Education Spaces," *Review of Education, Pedagogy, and Cultural Studies* 39, no. 1 (2017): 93.

26. Small, *Value of the Humanities*, 6.
27. David Collinson and Dennis Tourish, "Teaching Leadership Critically: New Directions for Leadership Pedagogy," *Academy of Management Learning and Education* 14, no. 4 (2015): 578.
28. Scott D. DeRue, "Adaptive Leadership Theory: Leading and Following as a Complex Adaptive Process," *Research in Organizational Behavior* 31 (2011): 125–50.
29. Lorri J. Santamaría and Andrés P. Santamaría, *Applied Critical Leadership in Education: Choosing Change* (New York: Routledge, 2012), 6–7.
30. Herminia Ibarra, Sarah Wittman, Gianpiero Petriglieri, and David V. Day, "Leadership and Identity: An Examination of Three Theories and New Research Directions," in *The Oxford Handbook of Leadership and Organizations*, ed. David V. Day (Oxford: Oxford University Press, 2014), 14.
31. Jacky Lumby, "Distributed Leadership: The Uses and Abuses of Power," *Educational Management, Administration and Leadership* 41, no. 5 (2013): 581–97.
32. Carolyne Ali-Khan, "Dirty Secrets and Silent Conversations: Exploring Radical Listening through Embodied Autoethnographic Teaching," *International Journal of Critical Pedagogy* 7, no. 3 (2016): 17.
33. Stephen Rowland, *The Enquiring University Teacher* (Buckingham: SRHE/Open University Press, 2000), 73.
34. Margaret Edwards, Chris McGoldrick, and Martin Oliver, "Creativity and Curricula in Higher Education: Academics' Perspectives," in *Developing Creativity in Higher Education: An Imaginative Curriculum*, ed. Norman Jackson, Martin Oliver, Malcolm Shaw, and James Wisdom (Abingdon: Routledge, 2006), 60.

BIBLIOGRAPHY

Ali-Khan, Carolyne. "Dirty Secrets and Silent Conversations: Exploring Radical Listening through Embodied Autoethnographic Teaching." *International Journal of Critical Pedagogy* 7, no. 3 (2016): 13–32.
Barnett, Ronald, and Roberto Di Napoli, eds. *Changing Identities in Higher Education: Voicing Perspectives*. Abingdon: Routledge, 2009.
Belfiore, Eleonora, and Anna Upchurch, eds. *Humanities in the Twenty-First Century: Beyond Utility and Markets*. Basingstoke: Palgrave, 2013.

Bérubé, Michael. "The Utility of the Arts and Humanities." *Arts and Humanities in Higher Education* 2, no. 1 (2003): 23–40.

Blackmore, Paul, and Camille Kandiko. "Change: Processes and Resources." In *Strategic Curriculum Change*, edited by Paul Blackmore and Camille Kandiko, 111–27. Abingdon: Routledge, 2012.

Bolman, Lee, and Joan Gallos. *Reframing Academic Leadership*. San Francisco: Jossey-Bass, 2011.

Brookfield, Stephen, and Stephen Preskill. *Discussion as a Way of Teaching: Tools and Techniques for Democratic Classrooms*. 2nd ed. San Francisco: Jossey-Bass, 2005.

Bulaitis, Zoe Hope. *Value and the Humanities: The Neoliberal University and Our Victorian Inheritance*. Basingstoke: Palgrave Macmillan, 2020.

Buller, Jeffrey L. *Change Leadership in Higher Education: A Practical Guide to Academic Transformation*. San Francisco: Jossey-Bass, 2014.

Ciulla, Joanne B. "The Two Cultures: The Place of Humanities Research in Leadership Studies." *Leadership* 15, no. 4 (2019): 433–44.

Collini, Stefan. *What Are Universities For?* London: Penguin, 2012.

Collinson, David, and Dennis Tourish. "Teaching Leadership Critically: New Directions for Leadership Pedagogy." *Academy of Management Learning and Education* 14, no. 4 (2015): 576–94.

Day, David V. "The Future of Leadership: Challenges and Prospects." In *The Oxford Handbook of Leadership and Organizations*, edited by David V. Day, 859–68. Oxford: Oxford University Press, 2014.

DeRue, D. Scott. "Adaptive Leadership Theory: Leading and Following as a Complex Adaptive Process." *Research in Organizational Behavior* 31 (2011): 125–50.

Edwards, Margaret, Chris McGoldrick, and Martin Oliver. "Creativity and Curricula in Higher Education: Academics' Perspectives." In *Developing Creativity in Higher Education: An Imaginative Curriculum*, edited by Norman Jackson, Martin Oliver, Malcolm Shaw, and James Wisdom, 59–73. Abingdon: Routledge, 2006.

Giroux, Henry. "The Corporate War against Higher Education." *Workplace* 9 (2002): 103–17.

Greene, Maxine. *Releasing the Imagination: Essays on Education, the Arts and Social Change*. San Francisco, CA: Jossey-Bass, 2000.

Greene, Maxine. "Teaching as Possibility: A Light in Dark Times." In *Critical*

Pedagogy in Uncertain Times: Hope and Possibilities, edited by Sheila L. Macrine, 137–49. New York: Palgrave Macmillan, 2009.

Harland, Tony, and Neil Pickering. *Values in Higher Education Teaching*. Abingdon: Routledge, 2010.

Hussey, Trevor, and Patrick Smith. *The Trouble with Higher Education: A Critical Examination of our Universities*. Abingdon: Routledge, 2010.

Ibarra, Herminia, Sarah Wittman, Gianpiero Petriglieri, and David V. Day. "Leadership and Identity: An Examination of Three Theories and New Research Directions." In *The Oxford Handbook of Leadership and Organizations*, edited by David V. Day, 285–302. Oxford: Oxford University Press, 2014.

Kagan, Jerome. *The Three Cultures: Natural Sciences, Social Sciences, and the Humanities in the Twenty-First Century*. Cambridge: Cambridge University Press, 2009.

Kenny, John. "Re-empowering Academics in a Corporate Culture: An Exploration of Workload and Performativity in a University." *Higher Education* 75 (2018): 365–80.

Kohli, Wendy. "The Dialectical Imagination of Maxine Greene: Social Imagination as Critical Pedagogy." *Education and Culture* 32, no. 1 (2016): 15–24.

Krause, Kerri-Lee. "Interpreting Changing Academic Roles and Identities in Higher Education." In *The Routledge International Handbook of Higher Education*, edited by Malcolm Tight, Ka Ho Mok, Jeroen Huisman, and Christopher C. Morphew, 413–25. London: Routledge, 2009.

Lumby, Jacky. "Distributed Leadership: The Uses and Abuses of Power." *Educational Management, Administration and Leadership* 41, no. 5 (2013): 581–97.

McCowan, Tristan. "Five Perils of the Impact Agenda in Higher Education." *London Review of Education* 16, no. 2 (2018): 279–95.

Middlehurst, Robin. "Changing Internal Governance: A Discussion of Leadership Roles and Management Structures in UK Universities." *Higher Education Quarterly* 58, no. 4 (2004): 258–79.

Moodle, Graeme, and Rowland Eustace. *Power and Authority in British Universities*. London: Routledge, 2012.

Parkin, Doug. *Leading Learning and Teaching in Higher Education: The Key Guide to Designing and Delivering Courses*. London: Routledge, 2017.

Plumb, John H. *Crisis in the Humanities*. Harmondsworth: Penguin, 1964.

Popp Berman, Elizabeth. *Creating the Market University: How Academic Science Became an Economic Engine*. Princeton, NJ: Princeton University Press, 2012.

Prichard, Craig. *Making Managers in Universities and Colleges*. Buckingham: SRHE/Open University Press, 2000.

Ramsden, Paul. *Learning to Lead in Higher Education*. London: Routledge, 1998.

Ross, Sabrina. "The Dialectic of Racial Justice: Maxine Greene's Contributions to Morally Engaged and Racially Just Education Spaces." *Review of Education, Pedagogy, and Cultural Studies* 39, no. 1 (2017): 90–105.

Rowland, Stephen. *The Enquiring University Teacher*. Buckingham: SRHE/Open University Press, 2000.

Santamaría, Lorri J., and Andrés P. Santamaría. *Applied Critical Leadership in Education: Choosing Change*. New York: Routledge, 2012.

Small, Helen. *The Value of the Humanities*. Oxford: Oxford University Press, 2013.

Tourish, Dennis. *The Dark Side of Transformational Leadership: A Critical Perspective*. London: Routledge, 2013.

Zembylas, Michalinos. "Critical Pedagogy and Emotion: Working through 'Troubled Knowledge' in Posttraumatic Contexts." *Critical Studies in Education* 54, no. 2 (2013): 176–89.

3

ACADEMIC DUCK-RABBIT

Faculty Leadership at the Smaller College or University

EMILY RUTH ISAACSON

I mean *Negative Capability*, that is, when a man is capable of being in uncertainties, mysteries, doubts, without any irritable reaching after fact and reason.

JOHN KEATS, "LETTER TO GEORGE AND
TOM KEATS, DECEMBER 1817"

AS HUMANISTS, WE OFTEN THINK OF OURSELVES IN VERY SPECIFIC TERMS, PERHAPS UNDER-valuing our skills and talents that can be useful outside of research and teaching. Somewhat relatedly, many of us find ourselves in leadership positions, sometimes deliberately pursuing such work, sometimes winding up in those positions in what amounts to a giant game of "not it." Being a humanist in a leadership position means leveraging our skills in a new way. As humanists, we are often quite good at storytelling about others, but we are not always as comfortable with telling our own stories or drawing the conclusion that, indeed, our training as humanists is precisely what got us to this point. We look to other places for advice (as you are doing with this book), and many of us continue to seek ideas about how to manage the things that we cannot solve. But sometimes, we don't quite find what we are looking for. When I was first appointed to a quasi-administrative role, I did what any good English professor would do: I bought some books. While the books I have read through the years include useful information,

I recognize that the intended audience worked at a larger university and in a larger department than I work in. For example, George Justice's excellent *How to Be a Dean* discusses managing an administrative staff and mentions budgets ranging from $500,000 to $50,000,000.[1] I have neither of those things. I know that whatever useful advice I can glean from these books has to be adapted to my own experiences at a very different sort of institution. Quite simply, the work I see in those books doesn't match my day-to-day experience of faculty leadership and administrative work.

Thus, what I want to do is speak more directly about the work done at the smaller institutions of higher learning. By this, I mean the liberal arts schools of fewer than 2,000 students, the small seminaries, and conservatories.[2] These are institutions that fall into a wide range of financial situations, with some having sizable endowments and others being entirely tuition-dependent. Geographically and in mission, they are diverse, but in terms of expectations for faculty participation in campus leadership, I suspect that they are similar. Whether the faculty number 50 or 150, service by all faculty is necessary to ensure that the institution functions. Those academic administration and leadership books include useful advice, but they rarely acknowledge the many different roles a single professor at small institutions will play. For many at larger institutions, the shift to a purely administrative role moves them into a different circle of influence; however, at a small institution, the faculty administrator remains squarely a member of the faculty and remains in the classroom. This may mean taking on leadership roles within the faculty through elected positions, even when serving in a role viewed as administrative by colleagues; this likely also means taking on many roles in a single academic year.

To make it clearer: at one point, I was director of the Honors Program, chair of the English Department, chair of the faculty (the equivalent of faculty senate president), and a faculty representative to the board of trustees in a single year. I continue in several of those roles, though my elected faculty positions change every couple of years. Moreover, I remain on an entirely faculty letter of appointment, even though a portion of my job is twelve months, and a portion is nine months. My experience is not universal, though it is one that can be instructive for anyone who is working at a small institution. While my work may sometimes move between the administrative and the faculty, it's all work I'm doing at essentially the same time; hence, my suggestion of feeling like a duck-rabbit.

The experiences that I have accrued in leadership, both as a faculty member and as a sometime administrator have been varied and have been far from my own training as an early modernist. I use the term "sometime administrator" here rather purposefully: much of what I've taken on blends from one area to the next. This ambiguity of the role is something that I've come to be comfortable with, and it's something that I think I was built for. While much of my current work feels far from my training in early modern literature, my experiences as a humanist research and humanist teacher have helped me develop a set of tools essential in my growth as a faculty leader. Other chapters in this book will delve into the specifics of those skills, so what I want to do here is discuss the way that that relationship with ambiguity—that negativity capability described by Keats—can inform any humanist interested in administrative work or faculty leadership work. This is true of those at any institution, but most especially true for those of us at the 1,000-plus small institutions of higher education across the United States. Comfort in ambiguity means openness, and it is this openness that leads to our ability to do the things that can help us find our footing as leaders.

Working at a small college is a different experience from working at a large university, and it is one that most of us did not prepare for in graduate school at Carnegie R1 or R2 institutions, as those PhD programs tend to be part of large institutions. President emeritus of Dickinson College A. Lee Fritschler explains that "the small college is different from larger academic institutions, as well as other institutions in society, in that the faculty are central in managing the institution. The liberal arts college has two dominant constituencies: faculty and mostly undergraduate students. The large university has several faculties, and they vary greatly in terms of academic specialties, outside interests, experience, and aspirations."[3] That is to suggest that the interests of the faculty of the small college are more closely tied to the institution as a whole. This closeness to the campus plays out in any number of ways, but most especially in our involvement outside of the classroom: we are leaders of campus committees, we take on administrative work, we sponsor various student organizations, and we attend all manner of campus activities (and for many of us, the expectations that we do these things are spelled out in contracts, letters of appointment, or faculty manuals). While each campus will be idiosyncratic and each faculty member's experience will be their own, faculty can learn from one another and take stories from each other's experiences and think about how to apply those lessons elsewhere.

But what's most important from my story, and what I think others can take away from what I'm explaining is this: I have found that my training in the humanities allows me to operate in both realms and to move between the various roles I have played on campus and will continue to play. The humanist's pleasure in ambiguity, I believe, serves me better than any other central skill that I continue to hone in my development as a higher education professional. We have a set of core skills and values that can help us move forward in leadership roles, developed in our training, and not simply things that we learn through the literature of organizational leadership. We simply need to be better at naming this skill and telling our story about it.

To think about the idea of comfort in ambiguity, we need only think of our experiences with students. Students often group themselves into "science students" and "humanities/arts students." This shows most clearly in their anxieties about their general education coursework: humanities students sometimes express fear of taking science or math courses because of the expectation of "the right answer," whereas many "science" students have expressed their concerns to me about taking courses where they interpret poetry because there's simply not a single "right" answer. This is, of course, something of a sweeping generalization, but it does point to a fundamental expectation that we have about the interpretation of texts because it assumes some skill in Keats' negative capability. Those of us who train in the interpretation of texts are immersed in a way of thinking that embraces the complexity and instability of meaning as central to our intellectual pursuits.

This sort of comfort with ambiguity, then, connects to the other skill sets of the humanist that bear on our ability to move into positions of leadership. That negative capability of Keats's experience is linked deeply with openness and curiosity about the world: while Keats argues that we should not reach "after fact and reason" when confronted with uncertainties, he is not arguing for irrationality. Rather, he is arguing against using rationality as a way to refuse to acknowledge the inevitable uncertainties of life. What our work in the humanities requires of us, especially in the context of faculty leadership, is a flexibility that benefits from this view of ambiguity. I want to suggest that for the faculty leader/faculty administrator at the smaller institution, this acknowledgment of the tensions is essential for success, even more so than at larger institutions where lines are clearly drawn.

In *The Essential Department Chair*, Jeffrey L. Buller outlines several practical strategies for chairs of small departments, but even here, he does not address the fluid nature of faculty leadership at the very small institution.[4] He asserts, "Chairs of small departments tend not to have the buffers available to their colleagues in larger programs," and by this he's talking about the buffers of support staff who initially field calls. He further explains that "chairs in smaller departments tend to find that, in most cases, their departments are less hierarchical and more collegially organized than are large departments. The chair of a small department is less frequently the 'boss' in a top-down manner than a colleague who is willing to provide some organizational support to the unit for a fixed period."[5] The suggestion that the chair isn't a boss but someone doing logistics for the department doesn't quite jibe with my experience though, because the need for someone to help steer the future of the department, program, or committee still exists; however, the point that is particularly relevant is the idea that the hierarchy is relatively flat. You remain a colleague; you generally try to remain friends.

The ability to navigate the politics of this situation is exactly why comfort with ambiguity is important. Part of daily life on the small college campus is to be able to accept the tension of being both "colleague" and "boss" at the same time. This tension can crop up in unfortunate settings, certainly: if I'm having a disagreement with a faculty member about how to handle a situation with a student, am I acting in my administrative role or as a fellow classroom instructor? In my own mind, I'm thinking of myself as an experienced classroom instructor. But a colleague who I interact with only infrequently likely sees me as an administrator rather than a fellow traveler. This can also be a failure to read the room appropriately. I made a mistake early in my tenure in the Honors Program because I saw myself only as a faculty member and not as a member of the academic leadership team. I was on the Faculty Development Committee, and we were hosting a speaker on campus. Because she had a handout that I wanted to make available to all faculty who were absent from the event, I wanted to figure out who was missing so that I could later hand deliver the materials. Other people in the room saw the situation differently: I later got feedback that the administration was taking attendance at an optional event. Since that event, I have been more conscientious about how I might be viewed in those sorts of situations, and I have learned to live with that.

As should be clear from my example, it's important to learn how to read a situation, and the politics of the smaller institution are as idiosyncratic as each institution is. This is complicated by the fact that you will routinely work not only with fellow faculty members and students but often closely alongside various staff members. When working with our colleagues (and to be clear, staff members are our colleagues in the endeavor), we must work with a commitment to the entire institution and not just our departments. Our ability as humanists to recognize patterns and to view texts within a social context helps us do this. This works in a different direction from our analysis of the text: this is the synthesis of ideas and the interdisciplinary nature of our work. This is the inherent curiosity required for humanistic work and for our leadership.

Working across campus with others means that essential in your work as a leader is your ability to bring people together, building relationships across the campus; much of that work is linked to the idea of storytelling but also links to the idea of an openness to other ways of knowing. This will certainly work in different ways for different people, but at the heart of it is the humanist aspiration of centering the human experience, centering human expertise and experience across the disciplines. As an example, I want to point to my work as the director of the Honors Program, which involves recruiting faculty to teach in the program, as well as to mentor senior projects. Because of my position as both a faculty member and an administrator, I have a rapport with my colleagues that I might lack at a larger institution with clearer lines of separation. When I first began this work, I set up individual meetings with any faculty member who was interested in working with honors students. We simply discuss what the faculty member is interested in. I ask questions. I point to the connections I see. We brainstorm. My own basic knowledge about a wide range of things helps me know what to ask, but even more, my general excitement for people's work helps build rapport. It takes time but building these relationships to recruit faculty to teach in my program also allows me to better know my colleagues and their skills. And this type of understanding of my colleagues' work helped me build a reciprocal trust that I relied upon as faculty chair and as a faculty representative to the board. My work in faculty leadership builds on my work in my administrative capacity.

Because of this position as both a faculty member and an administrator, I have the political capital to build relationships with not only my faculty colleagues but also the administrators and board members I report to. We spend so much time talking about relationships between characters when we're studying literature that the reading of the human condition carries over into our daily work at the university. Freeman A. Hrabowski III, president of University of Maryland Baltimore County, explains his success as being based on those kinds of relationships: "This is one of the great challenges facing higher education institutions today. We must start by building strong relationships on campus that allow faculty, staff, students, and administrators to ask tough questions of themselves and one another, to have difficult conversations, and to embrace change. We may not always move quickly, but together, we can go far."[6] I think that this is all the more important at the small institution, where relationships are exactly what we market when we try to recruit students. This is further linked to the way that, in my experience, many small institutions' presidents tend to talk about the campus community as "a family."

The institutional relationship building and the bird's-eye view of the campus that we gain in leadership roles require a move away from our own egos, including sometimes a move away from a laser focus on our own disciplines. This is the challenge facing all of us as the humanities seem often to be the easy target of outside ire and the frequent victim of campus downsizing. But, as George Justice points out, "true leadership on campus involves making the case for *all* of the disciplines in the college and, in particular, for the contributions the college's faculty members and students make locally as well as nationally."[7] This is true not only for the administrative leader; this is also true for the faculty leader. As a faculty senate president, a committee chair, or a faculty representative to the board, we must think about the value of all the majors and programs on campus. We need to be able to articulate the value of our colleagues and their work; we need to be able to articulate the value of these intellectual pursuits for our students' development. When majors are euphemistically "sunsetted" whether by administrative or faculty decision, we can find ways to support our colleagues and find ways to demonstrate the value of those subjects on campus. Students opting not to major in a subject like Spanish or philosophy does not make the subject less valuable from an intellectual perspective: instead, we must help figure out how to make the case for our colleagues' fields, and we must help figure out how those subjects can appear in the campus curriculum in a way that both benefits our students and supports our colleagues. It may just look different than a major. What our work can be for the humanities is the work of preserving the humanities in some form because they help us all deal with ambiguity, they help us think about human interactions, and they help us tell the story of who we want to be. This applies to the students just as much as to the faculty.

What this can translate into—and *must* translate into—is a willingness to focus on the work and success of other people. It's essential that the success of the entire institution be part of the focus of the faculty leader and/ or administrator. As Simon Sinek argues, "What makes a good leader is that they eschew the spotlight in favor of spending time and energy to do what they need to do to support and protect their people."[8] That is, our work in these roles requires that we do the work for other people, not for ourselves and not just for our departments. We may think of our departments as distinctive and separate, but we also must remember that every department is part of the larger institution, and all departments must work in tandem to keep the campus moving forward. On the small campus, the difference between being a faculty leader and an administrator is nearly nonexistent when it comes to doing the work of improving the institution and strategizing for the future. At my current institution, for example, faculty members work alongside administrators, staff, and board members on committees that oversee strategic budgeting, assessment, faculty development, and the institutional strategic plan, among many other topics. Additionally, most administrators teach at least one course a year. Our roles blend together, and we are all trying to steer our boats in the same direction.

It is true that the aptitudes and skills I'm talking about here (and others speak of elsewhere in this book) are not exclusive to humanists, but what I want to emphasize about my experience is this: I learned these things through *being* a humanist. Telling our stories as leaders and future leaders is about recognizing what we have done, what we have learned, and how it applies to future situations. I think most important in this is an idea I began with: comfort in ambiguity. All of us recognize students who are not comfortable in that ambiguity; we probably recognize that in some of our colleagues as well. This is not a flaw in any individual, but rather it creates a different way of viewing the world. Keats's concept of negative capability, in action, is deeply uncomfortable. Between my study of literary texts and my study of literary theory, I have developed a comfort with troubling situations that require holding and considering multiple viewpoints simultaneously. My ability to reconcile these difficulties has been central to my ability to contribute to my institution beyond my classroom teaching. It's also what has allowed me to navigate between my faculty leadership roles and my administrative roles.

You are perhaps, at the least, looking for some practical solutions to this problem of feeling like a duck-rabbit. Let me offer you what may work because sometimes it's important to separate out which role you are playing, even though I've generally argued for the power of blending all the roles together. First and foremost, schedule time thoughtfully, whatever time management system you prefer. Blocking out time for administrative projects and projects linked to faculty leadership is important so that you aren't simply spending all your time putting out fires. If you can compartmentalize the work through different workspaces or work in different capacities on different days of the week, you will likely find yourself navigating your identities more readily (for example, I do English Department work on Mondays, Honors Program work on Tuesdays). Second, get to know staff members throughout campus and in every office. Third, understand the organizational hierarchy and all your locations within it. Fourth, remember that you are not doing this work alone. Find a mentor on campus or a mentor at another institution. It's helpful to have a mentor and confidant when you're trying to sort out the problems of your work. And fifth, lean into the weirdness of being a duck-rabbit. Some days you will be a duck. Some days you will be a rabbit. Some days you will be both at once. And most days it's a good thing.

NOTES

1. George Justice, *How to Be a Dean* (Baltimore, MD: Johns Hopkins University Press, 2019), 46.

2. The National Center for Education Statistics' Integrated Postsecondary Education Data System's (IPEDS) College Navigator lists at least 1,000 small private baccalaureate institutions numbering under 2,000 students.

3. A. Lee Fritschler, "Building Strong Ties with Faculty and Staff at Liberal Arts Colleges," in *Leading Colleges and Universities: Lessons from Higher Education Leaders*, eds. Stephen Joel Trachtenberg, Gerald B. Kauvar, and E. Gordon Gee (Baltimore: Johns Hopkins University Press, 2018), 56.

4. At the time he was writing the book, Buller was vice president for academic affairs and dean of the college at Mary Baldwin College, a small liberal arts institution.

5. Jeffrey L. Buller, *The Essential Department Chair: A Practical Guide to College Administration* (San Francisco: Jossey-Bass, 2006), 178.

6. Freeman A. Hrabowksi III, "Go Far Together: Creating a Healthy, Inclusive Culture for Faculty and Staff," in Leading Colleges and Universities: Lessons from Higher Education Leaders, eds. Joel Trachtenberg, Gerald B. Kauvar, and E. Gordon Gee (Baltimore: Johns Hopkins University Press, 2018), 54.

7. Justice, *How to Be a Dean*, 165.

8. Simon Sinek, *Leaders Eat Last: Why Some Teams Pull Together and Others Don't* (New York: Portfolio/Penguin, 2014), 83.

BIBLIOGRAPHY

Buller, Jeffrey L. *The Essential Department Chair*. San Francisco, CA: Jossey-Bass, 2006.

"College Navigator." National Center for Education Statistics. Accessed October 5, 2021. https://nces.ed.gov/collegenavigator/.

Fritschler, A. Lee. "Building Strong Ties with Faculty and Staff at Liberal Arts Colleges." In *Leading Colleges and Universities: Lessons from Higher Education Leaders*, edited by Stephen Joel Trachtenberg, Gerald B. Kauvar, E. Gordon Gee, 55–62. Baltimore: Johns Hopkins University Press, 2018.

Gunsalus, C. K. *The College Administrator's Survival Guide*. Cambridge, MA: Harvard University Press, 2006.

Hougaaard, Rasmus, and Jacqueline Carter. *The Mind of the Leader: How to Lead Yourself, Your People, and Your Organization for Extraordinary Results*. Boston: Harvard Business Review Press, 2018.

Hrabowski III, Freeman A. "Go Far Together: Creating a Healthy, Inclusive Culture for Faculty and Staff." In *Leading Colleges and Universities: Lessons from Higher Education Leaders*, edited by Stephen Joel Trachtenberg, Gerald B. Kauvar, E. Gordon Gee, 47–55. Baltimore: Johns Hopkins University Press, 2018.

National Center for Education Statistics. "Integrated Postsecondary Education Data System (IPEDS)." Accessed October 4, 2021. https://nces.ed.gov/ipeds/datacenter/DataFiles.aspx?goToReportId=7.

Justice, George. *How to Be a Dean*. Baltimore, MD: Johns Hopkins University Press, 2019.

Sinek, Simon. *Leaders Eat Last: Why Some Teams Pull Together and Others Don't*. New York: Portfolio/Penguin, 2014.

4

NAVIGATING NETWORKS AND SYSTEMS

Practicing Care, Clarifying Boundaries, and Reclaiming Self in Higher Education Administration

GENESEA M. CARTER, AURORA MATZKE, AND BONNIE VIDRINE-ISBELL

The transition from faculty to administration requires you to reframe your sense of professional accomplishment and understand that you are fueling student success from a different vantage point. Instead of flying the airplane, you are designing new airplanes, repairing broken airplanes, controlling air traffic, ensuring safety, building new airports and serving the general welfare of all.

BRADLEY FUSTER, "MOVING TO THE 'DARK SIDE' IN DARK TIMES"[1]

THE ADMINISTRATIVE ROLES HUMANITIES FACULTY TEND TO FILL ARE COMPLEX: MUCH LIKE running an airport, they must navigate a myriad of roles and responsibilities. And much like an airport exists within a super system of airports, higher education is a super system: it is a series of microsystems and networks influencing the macrosystem. While systems and networks are necessary to keep universities and colleges running smoothly, they can also act like agentive beings, shaping policies and processes, such as imposing deficit-based pedagogies and perpetuating problematic labor practices.[2] Systems and networks are vital to academia, and they are also all-consuming by nature because systems and networks' primary function is to ensure the success and survival of the institution. As a result, the institution may become more economically focused to (try to) ensure financial success and survival.[3] The neoliberalization of higher education, especially with the emphasis on institutional auditing and economics, is one example of how systems and networks create tensions for humanities faculty administrators. Many neoliberal systems and networks undermine the training many humanities scholars receive in communities of practice, mindfulness, contextual exigency, organizational psychology, social justice efforts, and academic labor issues, among others.[4]

In our chapter, we will first introduce systems theory as a lens through which humanities' faculty administrators may understand and reflect upon the work they accomplish in the systems and networks they are working within. Second, we will provide examples from our own faculty administrative roles and accompanying recommendations to help readers see how systems and networks shape the challenges of leadership roles. Finally, we conclude by returning attention to the self and the system as an organic pairing deserving of attention. Throughout our sections, we include reflection-in-process practices common in our field of rhetoric and composition to spark personal application and reflection. We believe offering readers an introduction to systems theory, sharing our own experiences, and engaging in reflection-in-process begins to provide readers with the knowledge, language, and metacognition tools needed for clarity, self-care, and boundaries. Our roles often call us to give so much of ourselves, and we need clarity, self-care, and boundaries to honor our own needs, effectively determine where change and potential are possible, and understand the needs of our colleagues and students.

REFLECTION IN PROGRESS

But first: grab a journal or tablet and your favorite beverage. Then, choose one of the following reflection questions and spend five minutes freewriting your answers:

- Try and identify one primary academic system or network impacting, positively or negatively, the work you do and/or want to do.

- Who might help you better understand the systems and networks shaping your program, department, college, and/or university?
- How do systems and networks affect your personal life?

We find focusing problem-solving on the systems and networks—rather than focusing on individuals—more effectively works toward positive, inclusive change. In addition, "writing to learn" is an effective strategy often used by humanities scholars to unpack complex topics and theories. We'll come back to your reflection. Because communication is, as collection contributor Michael Austin writes, "the coin of [the] realm" in many of the positions we have held, we draw from our collective experience communicating through writing and reflection as tools for readers to further develop or share with colleagues.[5]

Our Positionalities: Providing Context for Our Experiences and Perspectives

We are cisgender, white, and female professors. Two of us are first-generation college students. Two of us hail from California; one of us comes from Louisiana. We have taught at institutions ranging from 5,000 students to 40,000 students and have held adjunct, non-tenure-track, and tenure-track positions. We have held various administrative roles, including writing program administrator, director of English language programming, director of general education, and senior associate provost of operations and strategic planning. Advocacy for and attention to under-represented student populations have been hallmarks of our careers. As we write here and have written elsewhere, we are committed to approaching administrative work as human work. Our view is that we cannot be effective administrators without considering our humanity in that work.

Of course, a large part of our combined approach (in our larger work but also evidenced in this chapter) is heavily influenced by our backgrounds as humanities scholars. With backgrounds in literature, teaching English as a second or foreign language, composition, and rhetorical studies, we have spent most of our careers studying language and language systems. Language and the control, access, and understanding of its systems and uses, often represent a dual seat of power and access. It is in this vein we pursue systems studies. Our hope is this chapter might be useful to anyone, at any level of administration, and may be especially thought-provoking for faculty from academic humanities disciplines, ranks, and positions who are either administrators or admin-curious.

Systems Theory

Systems theory is the study of interrelated and ecosocial systems and networks, human-made and natural. Fields such as social work, sociology, psychology, biology, and cybernetics use systems theory to understand how systems and networks shape human, biological, social, and technological behavior and action.[6] They affect higher education leadership by defining and shaping the structure of the university. Ferd J. Van der Krogt explains, "In order to survive, any organization must meet a number of functional requirements, such as the realization of set objectives.... Structures are designed to realize these functions: the production structure, the policy structure, and the human resource management structure."[7] Systems and networks ensure an organization's structural functionalism works from the top to the bottom. For example, in 2018 when the California legislature shifted the requirements of remedial classes, institutions scrambled to adjust everything from individual coursework to transfer and general education credits. Many of the adjustments involved records—the keeping, transferal, and adjustments of records necessary to allow students to enroll in, in some cases, entirely different course sequences. The Cal State System depended on the networks and systems to verify and guarantee the human components—administrators, faculty, staff, and students—were working toward the functional requirements set by the system.

Networks and systems are vital to ensuring university goals are achieved. However, when the university's structural functionalism takes precedence over the local, organic needs of administrators, faculty, staff, and students, there are consequences: disciplinary best practices are ignored, the emotional and physical well-being of faculty and staff are stifled, and problematic labor practices may continue.[8] For example, when administrators try to change student pronouns in the learning management system, and the information technology (IT) office reroutes the query to the enrollment management office, who then reroutes them to another department, administrators go around in circles trying to update students' pronouns.

While there are several layers of interaction among individuals, the system is so complex that making changes to students' pronouns is complicated and requires multiple departments to problem-solve. There is a human(e) cost to navigating systems and networks out of sync with the humans working within them, which often results in faculty, staff, and student disenfranchisement, disillusionment, and resentment.[9]

REFLECTION-IN-PROCESS

Applying Stephen Covey's circle of concern (e.g., issues of which I am aware but cannot control) and circle of influence (e.g., issues of which I am aware and over which I do have partial or full control), we want you to evaluate where your energies might be the most useful.[10] Choose one of the reflection questions you answered already and complete the following:

- Underline, circle, or highlight the people, locations, offices, artifacts present in your system or network.
- Create a concern/influence x- y-axis.
- Of the system elements you identified in the first "Reflection-in-Process" section, place them on the axis.
- Evaluate your axis (see figure 4.1). How many of the elements are high concern/low influence? And the reverse—high influence/low concern? What about the other quadrants: high concern/high influence and low concern/low influence?

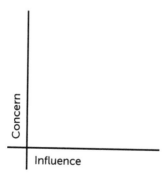

FIGURE 4.1 Concern/influence axis.

This exercise offers an evaluation of the human and nonhuman players in a system, as well as your level of concern and your level of influence. The axis can help you identify who is influencing whom, where the real authority connected to the processes might rest, and how to deploy change agents (including yourself) effectively. In addition, it may highlight for readers the different approaches needed for the differing systems in which we find ourselves.

Practicing Care, Clarifying Boundaries, and Reclaiming Self

In this section, we dovetail our faculty administrative stories with practical strategies that have worked for us—and we hope will work for you too. We recognize faculty administrative experiences are contextual and institution-specific and share these stories and strategies with the hope they are widely applicable or at least recognizable. Each section is written by a different author and in a different university context to demonstrate the depth and breadth of our collective experiences. To honor anonymity, the following narratives will not use universities' or persons' names.

STRATEGIES FOR CHANGE: WRITING TO CREATE CHANGE

One of the systems encountered within the university is the system for evaluation of English language proficiency. Inherent in this process is the deficiency model, which often indicates what is lacking in a human. Within the context of international students' language proficiencies and entrance exams, this deficiency model is found in the physical objects embedded within the US university system: Visa/I-20 application documents, textbooks for immigration officers, proficiency tests, immigration officers' exams, and nonobjects such as websites or virtual training seminars. These existing objects and nonobjects hold within their very semiotics a philosophy of lack and an implicit message of superiority. Suhanthie Motha and Angel Lin discuss this ideology of lack in their theory of desire for the English language. Using Jacques Lacan's psychoanalytic notion of the *object petit a*—the object cause of desire, these two authors connect the desire for the English language to the experience of lack. When one recognizes (or believes) something is missing, its absence makes the subject believe herself to be incomplete. For example, they write, "Establishing the absence of English as a lack changes the positionality not only of those who do not speak English but also of those who are able to claim ownership over English by reaffirming their primacy."[11] The philosophy of language deficiency often fixates on international or domestic multilingual students' lack of language rather than on their diverse linguistic resources, their cultural intelligence, or their ability to act as translingual liaisons.

I have encountered this deficiency model at both universities I have worked at, and gratefully, my first university explicitly named and worked to unravel the deficiency model. Teams of instructors both within the English Writing Program and in the English Language Program met and studied ways of change. Some of the activities for change included writing new outcomes that addressed the interconnection of discrimination and English language, creating training manuals and mandatory training seminars for new instructors, and developing a textbook for First-Year Composition that explicitly addressed the concept of deficiency through readings, such as "Mother Tongue" by Amy Tan or excerpts from *Borderlands/La Frontera: The New Mestiza* by Gloria Anzaldúa. Being part of this process and involved in this training prepared me to enact similar changes when I began at my second university as a new college-level director.

At this university and in a new position as leader rather than participant, I noticed elements of the deficiency model that users of the system were unaware of. Often, the humans I interacted with had power to only *use* the problematic physical objects/nonobjects (e.g., textbooks for immigration officers), not rewrite them. As human agents within this system, they were part of the construction and socializing of this lack, but they did not create it nor did they actively have power to change it. As the director, I did have the power to create and recreate these objects. I had both high concern and influence. To process moments of frustration or resistance, journaling, prayer, and exercise were tools I relied on to move my brain activation from limbic flooding to prefrontal cortex thinking. Here, I could productively analyze the diction and semiotics associated with the situation specific to my university context. I realized I needed to focus my high concern and influence on the physical objects themselves; therefore, those of us within the program began work to change the language within the documents. I asked to see the letters from admissions; we rewrote them. I asked to see the textbooks; we changed them. I asked to rewrite the catalog; we completed three revisions. We drafted and redrafted a program manual and training materials. These were the first steps.

Once completed, the next step was to find the person on campus who "pushes the button" and ask them to push it on behalf of our program. We needed to change some of the methods and workflow used by intercampus constituents, and this would require a different level of rhetorical analysis than needed previously— one of relational networks within the university.

With human agents, change often happens relationally, as our brains are social in nature, working systematically and often unconsciously to regulate emotion and navigate social groups. [12] Thus, our sphere of influence remains tied to the human bodies connected to the work. Coupled with the unique paradigms, hierarchies, and historical context of my university, it became clear that, for my requests to be granted, someone else needed to convey my message. The best chance would be a live conversation in a private setting between two relationally close individuals who could convince others to do what I needed for things to change. It also required me to humble myself and realize I was asking to change course from a long history of using a familiar workflow system that functioned well enough for the users. It was a big ask for a newcomer, and my attitude of superiority and systemic frustration only mirrored the larger concern I was facing.

After a two-year process, these changes have been realized, and our university is more aware of the deficiency model and more active in naming the resources of cultural knowledge and linguistic diversity that students bring to our classrooms. Though hopeful, this story ended where my sphere of influence ended. I had little influence to change our immigration system's philosophy. I tried. When I received paperwork laden with deficiency-laden language inherited from larger networks, I wrote back. However, my emails landed in the wrong laps. In one answer, the writer replied, "While I do understand your concern, the terms are not determined by the State Approving Agency for Education, rather they're derived from the Code of Federal Regulations published in the Federal Register by the executive departments and agencies of the federal government of the United States."[13] Email exchanges showed I had to (re)consider my span of influence. I did not have the power to rewrite those documents. What could I do to unravel a philosophical system built upon this *lack*? How could I teach the English language to students who are told they are insufficient because they do not own it?

Begin with objects in the system. Begin with documents. Find a program textbook that teaches from a philosophy of linguistic resources so that everyone who comes through your program reads and wrestles with the construct of deficiency. Rewrite your outcomes. Rewrite your syllabus. Rewrite your catalog. Write. And write more. Produce meaning with your language. As humanities scholars, we are comfortable with using writing to produce the meaning we want and need to see. I encourage you to use writing—and the careful attention to words—to create the change needed in the systems and networks that affect your programs, your department, your college, and your institution.

REFLECTION-IN-PROCESS

Return to your reflection notes. Review your concern/influence axis and take five minutes to answer at least one of the following questions:

- What artifacts/objects (emails, policies, websites, institutional research, syllabi) are connected to one or two of your high influence moments?
- What is the process of revision for these artifacts?
- Are there any other offices, procedures, or individuals connected to the artifacts that should be consulted to articulate a clear pathway prior to beginning the revision process?

We believe we can practice personal and professional care by locating and revising documentation. Documentation—from office to office, meeting to meeting, and person to person—holds the key to systemic change, one word at a time. Yet, of course, there are situations where no amount of writing will shift the realities of a system in crisis.

CLARIFYING BOUNDARIES: FINDING NUANCE AND SETTING LIMITS

January 2020, the World Health Organization declared COVID-19 a global health emergency.[14] In March and April of 2020, COVID-19 had spread to the point that much of higher education shut down in-person education opportunities in response to the COVID-19 global pandemic, *Inside Higher Ed* began tracking institutional case rates, policies changes, and vaccine requirements, and many administrators across the landscape of higher education began watching the changes on an hourly basis.[15] Over the past two years, the pandemic has brought with it the need to mask up, distance, and isolate, as well as death tolls in the millions.[16] While the individual and communal experience of the pandemic has been and continues to be traumatizing on multiple levels, higher education institutions are experiencing the effects of large budget deficits at the hands of declining enrollments, slipping persistence rates, and the loss of income from auxiliary services.[17]

My institution, to remain fiscally balanced and retain as many employees as possible in the fall of 2020, moved to mandatory furloughs (instead of mass layoffs) offset by banked vacation. In the spring of 2021, as a mid-level administrator, I found myself the recipient of a university mandate: the organization would no longer allow employees to bank vacation hours; we were moving to flexible time off (FTO); there would be additional furloughs.

The cessation of vacation accrual in alignment with the request for continued furloughs was clearly a fiscal strategy designed to pull down the amount of money the institution had tied into banked vacation. The difficulty here was threefold:

1. The administration was looking for ways to preserve faculty and staff lines as much as possible through the shrinking of banked vacations.

2. In order to positively impact the current fiscal year, the decision needed to be made swiftly.

3. FTO is a policy change that during regular operations is often hailed as a top employee desire.[18]

But, when you stir these decisions into the same pot and oversalt with a scarcity economy, you end up with an unpalatable soup. I found myself leading teams of individuals with their safety nets removed. Employees were confused, frustrated, and scared. While some might have been excited about the prospect of "no limits" vacation, any positive press was marred by concerns about continued furloughs. Banked vacation hours, under the pressure of furlough, would dwindle. Leave connected to baby bonding, often augmented by banked hours, seemed to be in flux. Additional time to heal after planned surgeries, was that also gone? The questions came fast and furious. What could be done?

The answer was not to rage against the amorphous "powers that be." The decision was the decision. We were in a pandemic. First, I read every piece of information I could get my hands on in connection with the new policies. I also encouraged several of the seasoned leaders I worked with to do the same. Collectively, we came up with listings of scenarios and potentialities that would need to be addressed in the new materials (i.e., new mothers in financial hardship, medical leave options, bereavement alternatives). Academic affairs leadership then held emergency meetings of our chairs and directors, highlighted the salient points of the policies, and allowed them to share their concerns directly. We then sent out an anonymous survey based on their concerns to all affected employees under our span and collected additional concerns and examples. Next, we created two pathways: (1) make the benefits of FTO immediately and explicitly clear to employees by encouraging prompt use, and (2) meet with human resources (HR) to start an action plan for addressing gaps and fissures in the policies that negatively impacted subsets of employees (with direct examples and problem-solving action plans brought to the meetings). As each gap was resolved, we brought that resolution to the larger group, so they understood their needs were being clearly addressed. In addition, some of the concerns were already addressed in the materials initially released by HR, but the materials were missing the mark. Audience evaluation and messaging were lacking in the initial release—something humanities scholars are skilled at spotting and addressing. We also continued to meet with HR regarding their messaging and have since coordinated additional university-wide materials. As Austin asserts in his chapter in this volume, "People who are trying to negotiate a crisis do not need, and cannot process, multiple messages from different departments of the university."[19] To this end, we had to simplify and streamline, and these concerns continue to be a point of negotiation, even as we continue to experience pandemic realities.

This was not a policy, procedure, or decision I could rewrite or revise on a mass scale. However, every systemic decision has boundaries and gaps, and my work was setting limits and exploring the nuance to clearly mitigate anxiety and give opportunity where it was possible. Focusing on the structure and purpose of the decision, finding and naming the confines, and articulating clear resolution pathways for participants with difficulties helps recenter the institutional conversation appropriately at the level at which you find yourself and those in your span of care. If the decision is unjust, the gathering of evidence and examples will be the first step toward bringing a case forward to the decision-makers. In the end, it is important for us to identify our circles of influence, to clarify boundaries between people and policy, and to get to work where we can get to work. Otherwise, the issues exacerbating employee tensions and challenges will remain unclear and unresolved.

REFLECTION-IN-PROCESS

Return to your reflection notes and take five minutes to write responses to the following questions:

- What or who is missing from your notes and/or concern/influence axis?
- Where are the gaps in communication and/or considerations of difference (from people group to people group, department to department, area to area, etc.) articulated?
- What might be one or two solutions you can facilitate to close the gaps?

Continue to use your freewriting to focus your efforts and energies—or to help you know when to pull back and take a break.

RECLAIMING SELF: LEARNING TO SEE IT IS NOT MY FAULT

After completing my doctorate in 2013, I applied to over seventy rhetoric and composition jobs across the United States. I had fifteen interviews, two campus visits, and two offers. I took an assistant professor job at a midwestern university with a teaching load of four sections of composition and rhetoric courses a semester in addition to research and service requirements. As a doctoral student, I had trained to be a writing program administrator and, in 2015, I became the director of First-Year Composition at the university overseeing a two-course general education sequence. While I had taken a graduate course in writing program administration and had several years' experience in program administration as a doctoral student, I had no training in navigating the human consequences of working within a monolithic system designed around neoliberal principles. I certainly had no graduate training in setting boundaries or saying no—quite the opposite. Workaholism was rewarded and expected. Naively bright-eyed and hopeful that my passion and workaholism could create systematic change, the human consequences in such a system were palpable:

- Admissions-rejected students were later accepted to boost enrollment numbers, yet very little infrastructure academically supported these students.
- The university wanted to cancel the noncredit developmental composition course, despite increasing enrollment numbers due to the university accepting international and US students with need.
- Full-time, tenure-track faculty (TTF) taught four sections a semester; full-time, non-tenure-track faculty (NTTF) taught five sections a semester. Faculty were so worn out from teaching writing-intensive courses and constant budget cuts and furloughs; they were disillusioned and disheartened.
- TTF and NTTF salaries were significantly lower than peer institutions, which meant faculty often taught overloads during the summer

and/or during winter break. The high teaching load plus extra courses meant faculty, although passionate about their teaching, were simply trying to keep their heads above water and didn't have additional energy for program initiatives.

As a new assistant professor, I thought if I worked harder, I could create meaningful and ethical change within the system. I thought my enthusiasm and commitment to students and the program would be infectious and could mitigate the exhaustion and resentment colleagues felt about the university system. But what I did not understand was I could not counteract a system set up to burn us out. (In new faculty orientation, the provost said faculty turnover was 47 percent with no mention of what the university was doing to retain faculty.)

During my four years at that institution, I thought that, if I agreed to all service opportunities, I might find mentors and allies who would help me create change. I thought if I worked toward aligning our composition and rhetoric courses with the discipline's best practices (e.g., starting program assessment and aligning curriculum with course outcomes), colleagues would be passionate about that work. But, unfortunately, many of my colleagues were burned out, suspicious, resentful, tired, and apathetic—and in many instances, rightfully so. At the same time, colleagues' negative emotions festered, went unaddressed by the larger system, and sometimes resulted in toxicity. It was not unusual that well-meaning colleagues would tell me about anonymous complaints regarding how I worded an email or objected to a program initiative. (At one point I was told by a colleague that "someone and I won't say who" thought I was "a dictator" for implementing program assessment.) While I had a handful of allies, I never felt emotionally or professionally safe because of the lack of transparency and because the system had set us up to fail. As a result, my work motivation eroded and health problems followed: I developed adrenal fatigue, woke up every day for a year with a panic attack, and second-guessed my career choice, among other work-related physical and emotional issues. Ultimately, working in the system was unsustainable because it refused to be self-reflective and/or support change, and I went back on the job market.

In my own effort to heal from adrenal fatigue and to process my emotions relating to my time at that institution, I've realized a few home truths

I want to share with readers who may have had or currently have similar experiences:

- We cannot single-handedly change the university system—even if we desperately want to. That I couldn't change the system is not *my* fault. That you cannot change the system is not *your* fault. We need to be realistic about what we can achieve and know when to let go.
- If we want to try to change the system, we need a team of allies to share the work and any accompanying mental and emotional stress. But, also, we should not allow our emotional and mental health to suffer as we attempt to find allies. There is often the desire to "just keep looking" with the hopes we'll find our dream allies in a meeting or workshop. But we should not keep looking for allies to the detriment of our health and well-being.
- We should not let our professional passions become consumed by the system. Does your role allow space for your passions? Are there colleagues who will support your professional passions? If not, I encourage you to look elsewhere—perhaps stepping out of your role to nurture those passions.
- We must get honest with ourselves about our workloads. Are we workaholics, overworkers, or a little of both? Workaholics work excessively because they believe their and the organization's rewards are worth the excessive work. Overworkers work excessively but do not believe they are fairly rewarded for their excessive work.[20] In both cases, the system benefits more than the individual. When we set precedents as workaholics or overworkers, the system will continue to expect excessive work from us.

In learning to honor and respect my own boundaries, my own professional needs, and my personality traits, I realized I couldn't be the complete version of myself I wanted to be in this position; I also realized the longer I stayed in a job with a high teaching load, low salary, and low administrative compensation, the more I was enabling the system to perpetuate untenable working practices. I felt like a cog in a machine that was duct-taped together, and I no longer wanted to be that cog. Through my time at this university, I learned that as much as I may crave changing the system, it may not be possible. The way forward for me—and working through the disappointment and frustration—was implementing one self-care activity or setting one new boundary every term and learning that moving on is not a personal failure. I did not fail the system; the system failed me, my colleagues, and the students. I encourage you to listen to and honor your personal and professional needs, so you can unlock new (and healthier and happier) ways of seeing, thinking, and being.

REFLECTION-IN-PROCESS

In this final reflection, take five minutes and pick one or more freewriting questions to answer:

- Are you an overworker, a workaholic, a little bit of both, neither?
- Do you feel like you can say "no" and set boundaries for your personal and professional well-being?
- Where might you have to let change go, despite what you understand as the benefit to the system, in order to maintain your momentum for the greater good?

Because we cannot single-handedly create change within systems and networks, sometimes for our greatest good—our mental, emotional, physical, and/or cognitive health—we need to reevaluate the ways we have dedicated ourselves to our administrative work. Sometimes we need to get really honest with ourselves before we can move forward in sustainable and meaningful ways.

CONCLUSION

Humanities faculty administrators can use systems theory and reflection practices, as we have done here, to critically look at the micro- and macrosystems and networks that affect faculty administrators' lives and work. While we would not argue that we are at the mercy of higher education systems, we are also not autonomous—and neither are the individuals with whom we work. Careful consideration of self, communities of practice, and larger state and national networks can lead to more fruitful, sustainable workplace practices over time. And while our chapter does not explicitly address COVID-19 as more than a foil for administrative change, let us take a moment to acknowledge the space in which many of us now find ourselves.

With the onset of the pandemic, many of us watched as our systems and networks rapidly adapted or calcified and crumbled under socioeconomic and psychosocial stressors. The long-term benefits or drawbacks of these changes remain to be seen. This places humanities scholars with administrative roles at an interesting fulcral point. Humanities scholars study power—the uses, distribution, and (in)access points—and now, perhaps more obviously than ever before, these abilities have been strained, as we rest in the spaces between best practice and reality.

In closing, we urge you to consider the concentric circles in which you find yourself operating.[21] Ultimately, we hope to draw readers' attention to how systems and networks function in higher education and affect humanities faculty administrators. We believe awareness of how systems and networks shape and influence our roles, departments, colleges, and universities provides an exigence for meaningful conversations, problem-solving tools, and meditative moments. Furthermore, a deeper examination of where we fit into the systems and networks around us can foster a praxis for individual self-care that lays the systems and networks, and our own culpabilities and opportunities within them, bare.

NOTES

1. Bradley Fuster, "Moving to the 'Dark Side' in Dark Times," *Inside Higher Ed*, August 20, 2020, https://www.insidehighered.com/advice/2020/08/20/faculty -member-describes-lessons-hes-learned-moving-administrative-position.

2. Adrianna Kezar, Tom DePaola, and Daniel T. Scott, *The Gig Academy: Mapping Labor in the Neoliberal University* (Baltimore: Johns Hopkins University Press, 2019); Alpesh Maisuria and Svenja Helmes, *Life for the Academic in the Neoliberal University* (Oxon: Routledge, 2020); Jason Brennan and Phillip Magness, *Cracks in the Ivory Tower: The Moral Mess of Higher Education* (Oxford: Oxford University Press, 2019); D. Bruce Johnstone and Jason E. Lane, eds., *Higher Education Systems 3.0: Harnessing Systemness, Delivering Performance* (Albany: State University of New York Press, 2013).

3. Cris Shore and Susan Wright, "Audit Culture Revisited: Rankings, Ratings, and the Reassembling of Society," *Current Anthropology* 56, no. 3 (2015): 421–44, https://www.jstor.org/stable/10.1086/681534.

4. Jeffrey R. Di Leo, *Corporate Humanities in Higher Education: Moving Beyond the Neoliberal Academy* (New York, NY: Palgrave Macmillan, 2013).

5. Michael Austin, "Communication and Crisis Management: A Case Study and a Cautionary Tale," in *Transforming Leadership Pathways for Humanities Professionals in Higher Education*, eds. Roze Hentschell and Catherine E. Thomas, (West Lafayette, IN: Purdue University Press, 2023), 230.

6. To read more about systems theory, we recommend: Ludwig von Bertalanffy, *General Systems Theory: Foundations, Development, Applications* (New York: George Branziller, 1969); Werner Schirmer and Dimitris Michailakis, *Systems Theory for Social Work and the Helping Professions* (Oxon and New York: Routledge, 2019); Shelly Smith-Acuña, *Systems Theory in Action: Applications to Individual, Couples, and Family Therapy* (Hoboken: John Wiley & Sons, 2011); Paul Thibault, *Brain, Mind and the Signifying Body: An Ecosocial Semiotic* (London and New York: Continuum, 2004); Jay Lemke, "Across the Scales of Time: Artifacts, Activities, and Meanings in Ecosocial Systems," *Mind, Culture, and Activity* 7, no. 4 (2000): 273–90, https://doi.org/10.1207/S15327884MCA0704_03.

7. Ferd J. Van der Krogt, "Learning Network Theory: The Tension between Learning Systems and Work Systems in Organizations," *Human Resource Development Quarterly* 9, no. 2 (2006): 159, accessed May 17, 2021, https://doi.org/10.1002/hrdq.3920090207.

8. Alison L. Black and Susanne Garvis, eds., *Lived Experiences of Women in Academia: Metaphors, Manifestos and Memoir* (Oxon and New York: Routledge, 2018); Patricia A. Matthew, ed., *Written/Unwritten: Diversity and the Hidden Truths of Tenure* (Chapel Hill: The University of North Carolina Press, 2016); Sheyin Chen, ed., *Academic Administration: A Quest for Better Management and Leadership in Higher Education* (New York: Nova Science Publishers, 2009).

9. Kezar, DePaola, and Scott, *The Gig Academy*.

10. Stephen R. Covey. *The 7 Habits of Highly Effective People: Powerful Lessons in Personal Change* (New York: Free Press, 1989).

11. Suhanthie Motha and Angel Lin, "'Non-coercive Rearrangements': Theorizing Desire in TESOL," *TESOL Quarterly* 48, no. 2 (2014): 334, https://doi.org/10.1002/tesq.126.

12. Louis Cozolino, *The Neuroscience of Human Relationships: Attachment and the*

Developing Social Brain (New York: W. W. Norton & Company, 2014), 367–68.

13. Anonymous, email message to author, August 6, 2020.

14. "Statement on the First Meeting of the International Health Regulations (2005) Emergency Committee Regarding the Outbreak of Novel Coronavirus (2019-nCov)," *World Health Organization*, January 23, 2020, https://www.who .int/news/item/23-01-2020-statement-on-the-meeting-of-the-international -health-regulations-(2005)-emergency-committee-regarding-the-outbreak -of-novel-coronavirus-(2019-ncov).

15. "Live Updates: Latest News on Coronavirus and Higher Education," *Inside Higher Ed*, May 18, 2021, https://www.insidehighered.com/news/2021/05/14 /live-updates-latest-news-coronavirus-and-higher-education.

16. "Coronavirus Death Toll," *Worldometer*, May 19, 2021, https://www.worldo meters.info/coronavirus/coronavirus-death-toll/.

17. Rowena M. Tomaneng, "Ito Ang Kwento Ko: Pinayist Pedagogy/Praxis and Community College Leadership," in *Transforming Leadership Pathways for Humanities Professionals in Higher Education*, eds. Roze Hentschell and Catherine E. Thomas, 195–208; Victoria Jackson and Matt Saenz, "States Can Choose Better Path for Higher Education Funding in COVID-19 Recession," *Center on Budget and Policy Priorities*, February 17, 2021, https://www.cbpp.org /research/state-budget-and-tax/states-can-choose-better-path-for-higher -education-funding-in-covid; Bob Blankenberger and Adam Williams, "COVID and the Impact on Higher Education: The Essential Role of Integrity Accountability," *Administrative Theory & Praxis* 42, no. 1 (2020): 1–20, https:// doi/10.1080/10841806.2020.1771907.

18. "Thriving in the New Work-Life World: MetLife's 17th Annual U.S. Em-ployee Benefit Trends Study 2019," *MetLife* (2019): 39, https://www.metlife .com/content/dam/metlifecom/us/ebts/pdf/MetLife-Employee-Benefit-Trends -Study-2019.pdf.

19. Austin, "Communication and Crisis Management," 236.

20. Maury Peiperl and Brittany Jones, "Workaholics and Overworkers: Produc-tivity or Pathology?," *Group & Organizational Management* 26, no. 3 (2001): 374, https://doi.org/10.1177/1059601101263007.

21. "Differentiation of Self," The Bowen Center for the Study of the Family, 2021, https://www.thebowencenter.org/differentiation-of-self; John Hassard, Ruth Holliday, and Hugh Willmott, eds., *Body and Organization* (London: SAGE Publications, 2000).

BIBLIOGRAPHY

Austin, Michael. "Communication and Crisis Management: A Case Study and a Cautionary Tale." In *Transforming Leadership Pathways for Humanities Professionals in Higher Education*, edited by Roze Hentschell and Catherine E. Thomas, 229–40. West Lafayette, IN: Purdue University Press, 2023.

Bakhtin, Mikhail. *Speech Genres and Other Late Essays*. Translated by Vern W. McGee. Austin: University of Texas Press, 1986.

Black, Alison L., and Susanne Garvis, eds. *Lived Experiences of Women in Academia: Metaphors, Manifestos and Memoir*. Oxon and New York: Routledge, 2018.

Blankenberger, Bob, and Adam Williams. "COVID and the Impact on Higher Education: The Essential Role of Integrity Accountability." *Administrative Theory & Praxis* 42, no. 1 (2020): 1–20. https://doi.org/10.1080/10841806.2020.1771907.

Bottrell, Dorothy, and Catherine Manathunga. *Resisting Neoliberalism in Higher Education, Volume I: Seeing Through the Cracks*. Cham: Springer International Publishing, 2019.

The Bowen Center for the Study of the Family. "Differentiation of Self." 2021. https://www.thebowencenter.org/differentiation-of-self.

Bowen, Murray. *Family Therapy in Clinical Practice*. Northvale: Jason Aronson Inc, 1978.

Brennan, Jason, and Phillip Magness. *Cracks in the Ivory Tower: The Moral Mess of Higher Education*. Oxford: Oxford University Press, 2019.

Burgin, A. J., Stephanie Hankinson, and Candice Rai, eds. *Writer/Thinker/Maker*. Plymouth: Macmillan Learning Curriculum Solutions, n.d.

Chen, Sheyin, ed. *Academic Administration: A Quest for Better Management and Leadership in Higher Education*. New York: Nova Science Publishers, 2009.

Covey, Stephen. *The 7 Habits of Highly Effective People: Powerful Lessons in Personal Change*. New York: Free Press, 1989.

Cozolino, Louis. *The Neuroscience of Human Relationships: Attachment and the Developing Social Brain*. New York: W. W. Norton & Company, 2014.

Di Leo, Jeffrey R. *Corporate Humanities in Higher Education: Moving Beyond the Neoliberal Academy*. New York: Palgrave Macmillan, 2013.

Fuster, Bradley. "Moving to the 'Dark Side' in Dark Times." *Inside Higher Ed*. August 20, 2020. https://www.insidehighered.com/advice/2020/08/20/faculty-member-describes-lessons-hes-learned-moving-administrative-position.

Hassard, John, Ruth Holliday, and Hugh Willmott, eds. *Body and Organization*. London: SAGE Publications, 2000.

Jackson, Victoria, and Matt Saenz. "States Can Choose Better Path for Higher Education Funding in COVID-19 Recession." *Center on Budget and Policy Priorities*. February 17, 2021. https://www.cbpp.org/research/state-budget-and-tax/states-can-choose-better-path-for-higher-education-funding-in-covid.

Johnstone, D. Bruce, and Jason E. Lane, eds. *Higher Education Systems 3.0: Harnessing Systemness, Delivering Performance*. Albany: State University of New York Press, 2013.

Kerr, Michael, and Murray Bowen. *Family Evaluation*. New York: Norton and Company, 1988.

Kezar, Adrianna, Tom DePaola, and Daniel T. Scott. *The Gig Academy: Mapping Labor in the Neoliberal University*. Baltimore: Johns Hopkins University Press, 2019.

Latour, Bruno. "On Actor-Network Theory: A Few Clarifications." *Soziale Welt* 47, no. 4 (1996): 369–81. https://www.jstor.org/stable/40878163.

Lemke, Jay. "Across the Scales of Time: Artifacts, Activities, and Meanings in Ecosocial Systems." *Mind, Culture, and Activity* 7, no. 4 (2000): 273–90. https://doi.org/10.1207/S15327884MCA0704_03.

"Live Updates: Latest News on Coronavirus and Higher Education." *Inside Higher Ed*. May 18, 2021. https://www.insidehighered.com/news/2021/05/14/live-updates-latest-news-coronavirus-and-higher-education.

Maisuria, Alpesh, and Svenja Helmes. *Life for the Academic in the Neoliberal University*. Oxon: Routledge, 2020.

Matthew, Patricia A., ed. *Written/Unwritten: Diversity and the Hidden Truths of Tenure*. Chapel Hill: The University of North Carolina Press, 2016.

MetLife. "Thriving in the New Work-Life World: MetLife's 17th Annual U.S. Employee Benefit Trends Study 2019." 2019, 1–56. https://www.metlife.com/content/dam/metlifecom/us/ebts/pdf/MetLife-Employee-Benefit-Trends-Study-2019.pdf.

Motha, Suhanthie, and Angel Lin. "'Non-coercive Rearrangements': Theorizing Desire in TESOL." *TESOL Quarterly* 48, no. 2 (2014): 331–59. https://doi.org/10.1002/tesq.126.

Peiperl, Maury, and Brittany Jones. "Workaholics and Overworkers: Productivity or Pathology?" *Group & Organizational Management* 26, no. 3 (2001): 369–93. https://doi.org/10.1177/1059601101263007.

Schirmer, Werner, and Dimitris Michailakis. *Systems Theory for Social Work and the Helping Professions.* Oxon and New York: Routledge, 2019.

Shore, Cris, and Susan Wright. "Audit Culture Revisited: Rankings, Ratings, and the Reassembling of Society." *Current Anthropology* 56, no. 3 (2015): 421–44. https://www.jstor.org/stable/10.1086/681534.

Shore, Cris, Susan Wright, and Davide Però, eds. *Policy Words: Anthropology and the Analysis of Contemporary Power.* New York and Oxford: Berghahn Books, 2011.

Smith-Acuña, Shelly. *Systems Theory in Action: Applications to Individual, Couples, and Family Therapy.* Hoboken: John Wiley & Sons, 2011.

Sue, Derald Wing, and David Sue. *Counseling the Culturally Diverse: Theory and Practice.* New York: John Wiley & Sons, 2003.

Thibault, Paul. *Brain, Mind and the Signifying Body: An Ecosocial Semiotic.* London and New York: Continuum, 2004.

Tomaneng, Rowena M. "Ito Ang Kwento Ko: Pinayist Pedagogy/Praxis and Community College Leadership." In *Transforming Leadership Pathways for Humanities Professionals in Higher Education,* 195–208, edited by Roze Hentschell and Catherine E. Thomas. West Lafayette, IN: Purdue University Press, 2023.

Van der Krogt, Ferd J. "Learning Network Theory: The Tension Between Learning Systems and Work Systems in Organizations." *Human Resource Development Quarterly* 9, no. 2 (2006): 157–77. https://doi.org/10.1002/hrdq.3920090207.

von Bertalanffy, Ludwig. *General Systems Theory: Foundations, Development, Applications.* New York: George Branziller, 1969.

World Health Organization. "Statement on the First Meeting of the International Health Regulations (2005) Emergency Committee Regarding the Outbreak of Novel Coronavirus (2019-nCov)." January 23, 2020. https://www.who .int/news/item/23-01-2020-statement-on-the-meeting-of-the-international -health-regulations-(2005)-emergency-committee-regarding-the-outbreak-of -novel-coronavirus-(2019-ncov).

Worldometer. "Coronavirus Death Toll." Accessed May 19, 2021. https://www .worldometers.info/coronavirus/coronavirus-death-toll/.

PART 2

Interdisciplinarity and Innovation in Higher Education Administration

5

ADMINISTERING ANTIDISCIPLINARITY

Navigating a Diverse Career Path from Theory to Institutional Practice

RYAN CLAYCOMB

I n a recent conversation with colleagues on the subject of my next career steps, one said, "Ryan's interested in pretty much everything." And while that's not quite true, like many in the humanities, I find that my curiosity is wide-ranging. This has been the case across my academic life: even though all of my degrees are in the literature field, I took significant coursework in cultural studies and performance studies and trained as a teacher in rhetoric and composition. Even that modest interdisciplinary travel was frustrating enough—like finding ways to make courses in a theater department meaningfully count toward the English PhD—but became more so when I hit a tightening job market. Too theatrical for English, too literary for theater. I cannot complain; my early career administrative experiences as a graduate writing program coordinator during my PhD, and a great first job teaching in the newly constituted University Writing Program at George Washington University (GWU) afforded me just enough insight into how and why one might develop new forms of composition pedagogy in an interdisciplinary context.

That writing program was predicated on a four-credit model new to GWU, wherein faculty teaching composition skills were nonetheless encouraged to spend roughly a quarter of our time on thematic subjects, developing deeper academic content with which to teach those writing skills. The idea was that faculty would bring expertise from many disciplines to the program, creating spaces in our classrooms for richer conversations among students, and making room for discussions among colleagues that would sparkle with ideas coming newly into contact. So, in addition to subfields common to English studies (rhetoric, literary criticism creative writing, critical theory), we also rubbed elbows with working scholars from game studies, women's studies, history, psychology, philosophy, religious studies, and, over time, disciplines even further afield. The director and associate director of that program built an extraordinarily collaborative environment, such that much of the visioning work of the new program grew directly from faculty conversations, both in formal sessions and at lunch or in hallway conversations. We set up peer-mentoring structures, devised shared learning goals, formulated approaches to assessment, invented a first-year student symposium, and workshopped ideas for program research. I was especially happy to extol (in perhaps predictably callow new-faculty ways) the virtues of teaching interdisciplinarity as an overt learning goal: its pleasures afforded by creating new contact zones between lines of thought, the challenges of integrating knowledge from many fields to tackle the hard problems of our world, the rigor of learning the standards of knowledge production from multiple disciplines, honed over time.[1] I'm sure I was rhapsodic. *Interdisciplinarity!*

"Or even antidisciplinarity," interjected my new colleague, Rachel Riedner, at lunch one day. I stopped in my tracks. I might have even blinked a little extra hard, processing the concept. *Antidisciplinarity?*

This chapter begins from that paradigm-shifting conversation and follows a path that mirrors my own career: from exploring antidisciplinarity (and other "open" disciplinarities) as a scholarly and theoretical concept, traveling through a range of higher ed locations, and cultivating a mindset for navigating that career. While many of the scholars who have advocated antidisciplinary stances in particular have made anti-administrative (or even anti-administrator) arguments, I believe that those stances offer imperatives for scholars to take on administrative positions in order to effect the changes that they want to see in the university, as, for example,

Anne-Marie Walkowicz describes later in this volume. Further, an antidisciplinary disposition goes hand-in-hand with certain habits of mind—an emphasis not just on making knowledge but also on *how* knowledge is made and an appreciation for the gray areas and ambiguities that necessarily arise. It offers tools to thrive in different spaces. Indeed, the interaction of scholarly humanities research with open disciplinarities has only become sharper as I have engaged those spaces in applied practice, with immediate stakes for scholarship, teaching, and learning. In what follows, I revisit some of those arguments through the lens of practical experience and then trace out the ways that leading with a mindset of opening up disciplinary enclosures can offer exciting and flexible career experiences with similarly exciting implications for our academic communities. Ultimately, I point to the value of addressing academic problems from a vantage point that views disciplinary knowledge both appreciatively and critically, but with an understanding of the limitations of any single approach to knowledge-making and problem-solving.

In those first years at GWU, Riedner, our colleague Randi Grey Kristensen, and I began a dialogue, eventually producing our 2009 collection, *Writing Against the Disciplines: Antidisciplinarity in the Writing and Cultural Studies Classroom.* There, we made arguments (following Michel Foucault in *The Order of Things*) for how the structures and practices of conventional academic disciplines can limit certain kinds of academic knowledge-making. Moreover, we argued, these limits are imposed with implicit, and sometimes explicit, aims of restricting the flows of power through scholarship that challenged ideological norms.[2] In the face of this observation, we located the counter-disciplinary potential available in rhetoric, composition, and cultural studies classrooms as a mechanism to labor against that disciplining of knowledge. Both critical theory and our contributors' classroom experiences informed our volume, which advocated for humanities practices of cultural studies analysis, self-reflexivity, and process-oriented teaching, through which we might push back on the kinds of academic disciplinary policing that can encourage conformity and muffle politicized ideas.

The terms that mark off our knowledge-making endeavors can be dizzying: pre-, multi-, inter-, trans-, post- and antidisciplinarities abound in our self-searching lexicons. And readers of this volume will surely have some familiarity with—and likely some strong opinions about how we might make distinctions among—these categories. I won't belabor them here except to make a few points. First, these ideas each respond specifically to forms of knowledge-making that are themselves structures for sorting epistemological, rhetorical, and political approaches to how we know and interact with the world. Each term comes with its own limits and limitations, situating knowledge in time (affected both by historical context and the processes of academia), in culture, and in systems of power. For instance, knowledge-making can take place prior to students' sorting into disciplinary majors; there are operations that we might undergo to place fields alongside one another and make them interact; there are rules for how we might make exceptions to those operations and social and economic consequences for breaking them. In the academy, the sorting of disciplines and fields has over time sedimented into a regimented set of rules and norms that appears from the outside to be a closed system. Each of these approaches imagines different ways of prying that system open, and so I tend to use the term "*open* disciplinarities" as an umbrella to encompass several ways we might critique knowledge-ordering systems and redress that critique.

Second, critiques of disciplinarity that arose in the '80s and '90s tended to focus (in the Foucauldian cultural studies mode that initiated them) on disciplinarity as a tool for exercising political control over knowledge. As the culture wars set up political stakes for making cultural knowledge, challenging disciplinarity on political lines was perhaps as common in the humanities as practices that replicated disciplinary modes. Louis Menand, interpreting the disciplinarity debates in "The Marketplace of Ideas" notes that "outside the discipline became the good place to be, and there was a period in the 1980s and 1990s when many disciplines were almost defined by the internal criticisms they generated."[3] The fact that we antidisciplinary scholars flourished in the millennial academy to a certain extent undermines our argument that politically resistant paradigms were hemmed in by disciplinary processes of hiring and tenure. Indeed, writing twenty years ago, Menand could already say that a postdisciplinary moment, defined by "a determined eclecticism about methods and subject matter" had arrived, and the field of English, in the moment I earned my degree, had "become almost completely postdisciplinary."[4] But disciplinarity is not dead, and departments certainly aren't. So what remains in the place of epistemological-methodological rigor is not knowledge production that flies in the face of explicitly political controls. Rather, knowledge production operates within the confines of political-economic controls, as Menand's "marketplace of ideas" has assuredly fallen into the grasp of supply-and-demand approaches to curriculum design and scholarly training: surely an effect of cultural neoliberalism. While scholars spill plenty of ink critiquing neoliberalism in the academy, that logic still rules the day, as virtually every contributor to this volume who deals with strategic enrollments, course caps, and contingent faculty salary rates can ruefully attest. Third, even this supposedly postdisciplinary moment hasn't abandoned boundaries and structures, and scholars doing "unruly" work will still often critique deans and provosts and presidents for hemming in knowledge that just wants to be free (I have done so myself). But even when the trumpets of open disciplinarities finally do blow the walls of departmental structures down, what we end up rebuilding is no promised land of free knowledge production. What we get instead are schools and centers justified with a blending of the cultural studies rationales of community and political resistance, together with buzzwords from the twenty-first-century economic landscape: "nimble," "responsive," and "scalable." I'm not against this, per se—I want to preserve this work within the climate we inhabit. So, I also note at this later stage of my career the challenges of supporting wide-ranging work, while also preserving enough of the systems to keep wide-ranging knowledge workers employed, an administrative task often regarded with derision and suspicion by some faculty members.

Consider the stance of historian of science D. Graham Burnett, writing with Matthew Rickard and Jessica Terekhov, graduate students in Burnett's 2017 course for Princeton's interdisciplinary doctoral program in the humanities, "Interdisciplinarity and Antidisciplinarity." As a final project for the course, faculty and staff alike produced a brief book, *KEYWORDS; for Further Consideration and Particularly Relevant to Academic Life, Especially as It Concerns Disciplines, Inter-Disciplinary Endeavor, and Modes of Resistance to the Same*, a text inspired in equal parts by

Raymond Williams's landmark cultural studies text, and Ambrose Bierce's satirical *The Devil's Dictionary*.[5] It's a wry and witty look at the way that we talk about what we do, but the collaboratively produced text (attributed formally to "A Community of Inquiry") also puts itself at a remove from actual administration. In an *Inside Higher Ed* interview on their book, they collectively write,

> It's common to hear university administrators encourage graduate students to perform interdisciplinary work in order to make them competitive applicants in an increasingly exigent job market, the idea being that students who can teach (or better yet, publish) in multiple fields are likelier to appeal to colleges and universities trying desperately to cover the same amount of labor with fewer full-time employees.... By treating interdisciplinarity as another accolade in the endless pursuit of incremental advantage, we risk subjecting academic experimentation to the same protocols as disciplinary inquiry, albeit with less judiciousness. That's why the entry on "irony" says that interdisciplinarity is not "more knowing" but "less": while we admire (and practice!) the intellectual activity that flourishes within disciplinary constraints, we also want to shelter interdisciplinarity—or perhaps it is *anti*disciplinarity that we mean – from the dynamics that would assimilate it to business as usual within university life.[6]

The winking flourishes here that decry exploitative administrators who tout "interdisciplinarity" while quashing actual antidisciplinarity misses a point that I want to underscore in the remainder of this chapter: that yes, theory, critical analysis, and scholarly playfulness can reveal ways that our institutional structures constrain us, and that humanities scholars can meaningfully attune ourselves to those political, economic, and cultural constraints.[7] But it is not enough to take potshots in articles and at conferences at tenured administrators who have "gone over to the dark side." Instead, there is intellectually honest work to be done in academic leadership to build better infrastructures to support free inquiry, but doing so involves operating within precisely the politically and economically contested confines of university administration. To put it another way, if we want a scholarly utopia, some people are going to have to do the nuts-and-bolts work of making that change. That work is slow, frustrating, messy, contested, and complicated. Yet the intellectual frameworks of open disciplinarities are rich assets for doing this work, even as we might think seriously about how to orient them affirmatively toward new models of producing ideas.

———————

I first joined those conversations on antidisciplinarity years ago. Since then, I have experienced the slow, frustrating, messy, and complicated nature of this work first-hand, across a range of academic spaces as a humanities scholar and administrator at several research-intensive universities. I have been a contingent faculty member in a predisciplinary writing program, a tenure-track faculty member in a conventional English department, an associate dean in a multidisciplinary honors college, a director of an interdisciplinary humanities center, and now an associate dean (this last position after two years as a kind of a project-based utility infielder in the dean's office). Moving through these varied academic spaces and occupying differently empowered positions at solidly funded institutions has afforded me avenues for thinking through modes of disciplinarity in both theoretical and pragmatic ways. In part, these have presented occasions to see that yes, sometimes infrastructural disciplinarity delimits resistant forms of knowledge, often those that grow out of identities and experiences that challenge the centrality of White, middle-class patriarchy. But these ethical and political values frequently are navigated in bureaucratic ways—through budgets, structures, and policies—such that occupying administrative positions offers affirmative and practical tools to effect changes in academia that (as several contributors to this volume attest) are informed by theory, close reading, and an attention to affects alongside rationales.

While it would be imprecise to claim an administrative career dedicated to the goal of opening up disciplinarity, I have gravitated to spaces where that work was possible. More specifically, that path depends on notions that institutions consist of people, and people do their work by prioritizing certain values. One way to shape institutions—even large, complex bureaucracies—with values hospitable to people of diverse identities, knowledges, and perspectives, is to enter its administration in good faith and with an eye toward embedding those values within its structures, policies, and practices. We don't have to take on leadership roles just to maintain the status quo; we can use the insights earned from deep study to identify the social, cultural, and philosophical underpinnings of our own spaces, and then work to make them better.

Even in conventional departments in the humanities, open disciplinarity can and does flourish, in part in the ways that Menand describes. So, after spending two formative years in GWU's University Writing Program, I secured a tenure-track English job at West Virginia University (WVU), teaching in a curriculum with little room for the disciplinary play that I often valorized. The undergraduate major and graduate degrees in English literature attracted few students interested in performance studies, and the School of Theater was situated in another college altogether. My teaching in those first years was almost completely conventionally disciplinary. Yet, Kristensen and I published our collection on antidisciplinarity in those same years, a publication that contributed to my tenure dossier. A combination of institutional and identity-based privilege (as a cis-gendered, heterosexual, White man at a research institution) functioned alongside a conventionally administered department structure, which provided me a measure of security, even as I struggled to find new spaces to engage cross-disciplinary ideas with students and like-minded colleagues. At that moment, my intellectual interests, scholarship, and politics all tended toward antidisciplinarity, and I worried that conventional career pathways would necessarily follow disciplinary lines in a department with little room to make an interdisciplinary impact.

What I've since learned is that humanities skills are helpful across the academy, and an approach to open up disciplinary thinking can point to new ways to navigate our institutions. Locating differently disciplinary spaces and embracing a flexible approach to career building can create ways to thrive while actively advocating for more flexible structures in the academy. Specifically: to make institutional space for open-disciplinary thinking, it helps to get into new administrative spaces to establish those structures and policies and practices. A mindset built upon humanities habits of cultural analysis, context-sensitive communication, rigorous self-reflexivity, and process orientation can encourage ongoing learning from different ways of knowing, and therefore offers ways to find and further open those spaces. For my part, I've taken several tacks. First, I joined, supported, and enriched an existing structure that fostered open disciplinarity in the Honors College at WVU; I built a new structure to enable the kind of open disciplinarity I wanted to see at my institution in the form of the new Humanities Center that I founded at WVU soon after; and then I returned to lead the Honors College for a time. In each of those roles, I was able to employ humanities mindsets and skills to foster and sometimes even create structures informed by open disciplinarity. And currently, I am learning to make the most of a new institutional environment to foster these conversations in potentially unlikely places in an administrative role in the College of Liberal Arts at Colorado State University (CSU). The combination of humanities training and an orientation toward opening up disciplinarities has become useful across these institutional locations—both in handling the day-to-day tasks of academic leadership and in charting a meaningful career path in academic administration in fraught times.

One thing that this combination has shown me is a central tension between disciplinarity and antidisciplinarity: what I learned within the frame of a humanities discipline, and how humanities thinking has itself sometimes pointed away from, and even against that very same disciplinary training. Further, it would be disingenuous to underplay how those habits of mind have come into play in a wide variety of spaces. For example, a humanities-focused (and critical theory–informed) understanding that disciplines don't just have different problems or methodologies but different ways of knowing informed by historical and political contexts was crucial to working with faculty from every discipline across campus in the Honors College. And the skills developed in crafting arguments for various audiences, skills I learned and taught in years of writing instruction, were more than handy in navigating spaces across the disciplines: campus committees, outward-facing activities like admissions and recruitment and new student orientation, and internal projects like working as a trained facilitator to foster equitable dialogues within department cultures.

Across those spaces, habits that humanities disciplines intentionally cultivate can be central and crucial to making change at our universities: sometimes transformational changes we might adopt around disciplinarity itself and sometimes small changes for which we might advocate that align with humanities principles of thoughtful and equitable discourse.

For example, in 2014, the WVU Honors College went through a visioning process that involved devising a new curricular structure. I had the opportunity over the next two years to design, refine, and implement a new two-year program—the Honors Foundations Program—to enrich students' general education by providing both in-discipline and interdisciplinary options for fulfilling components of their general education curriculum. That process was the first time that I understood the idea of open disciplinarity both as a goal for institutional structures and as a design for my own continued learning. At the same time, the process of developing the Honors Foundations program depended on those critical humanities skills. The habits of cultural analysis, forged in a climate of Marxist cultural theory, gender studies, and Black studies, pointed out ways that our existing admissions process excluded certain kinds of access for students who otherwise might be well equipped to thrive in our program. An attention to cultural knowledges required to navigate our admissions processes—specifically, the kinds of middle-class and often White cultural experiences that foreground higher education and are invisible—helped me to revise our intake practices to reach out proactively to more (and more diverse) students. Contextual writing skills honed over years of teaching writing and rhetoric helped me craft less exclusionary communications with incoming students and more encouraging ones for continuing students. And those epistemic approaches led to results, with larger and more diverse entering classes whose first cohorts finished at a much higher rate than the previous program's curriculum enabled.

The challenge of opening up disciplinarity is no less rewarding to pursue on the research side of the academy's mission, and the tension between disciplinary ways of thinking and open disciplinarities can find new expressions in the context of interdisciplinary research centers. For example, as director of the new WVU Humanities Center, I found a structure designed specifically to nurture and sustain intellectual pursuits that didn't fit neatly into departments. This approach to humanities scholarship was simultaneously antidisciplinary and disciplinary, held in productive tension. Antidisciplinarity inhered in the endeavor's focus on traversing boundaries across departments, across colleges, across individual scholarly agendas, and even across the town-gown divide. Our new advisory board, composed of faculty from across the university, focused on supporting and incentivizing public scholarly production, nonconventional publishing formats, and cross-disciplinary and collaborative projects that weren't well accounted for in fields that prioritized solo work. Whereas honors administration *crossed* many departments, this research center was able to support work that might have fallen in between those departmental structures. One upside of navigating this new challenge was the chance to develop a new set of tools to shape the intellectual climate we were making: applying for programmatic grants, administering small internal research grants, planning and co-sponsoring public programming, and having new kinds of conversations with other administrators.

Even as we sought to support these in-between spaces, I was reminded—as our advisory board undertook deliberate self-reflexive practices around our vision and practices—that the broad category of humanities scholarship is itself anchored by some common disciplinary premises: the focus on qualitative interpretation, the emphasis on theoretical frameworks (as opposed to what my colleagues in the sciences understand as capital-T Theories), the celebration of inductive reasoning, the comfort (even exultation) in gray areas, and the warm embrace of the messier ethical and affective components of human experience. This reminder, that despite my commitment to opening up the disciplines, I was still deeply steeped in these methodologies, revealed to me some of the limits of antidisciplinarity, for I was unable and ultimately unwilling to shed these common humanities premises. Plus, this kind of leadership role specifically requires the durable skills that humanities scholars as a group are well equipped to deploy.

Effective communication here matters, especially with the new partners I encountered across and beyond the degree-granting enterprise: brilliant campus colleagues in the university libraries, our Center for Digital Publishing, the art museum, and a small but vibrant university press, as well as off-campus partners like the state Humanities Council, the National Endowment for the Humanities (NEH), our local public libraries, even legislators who might advocate for humanities funding for our region. Indeed, the opportunity to lobby West Virginia's congressional delegation for NEH funding was a surprising new arena that I might never have expected to encounter had I limited my scholarly career to writing and teaching in the discipline and is a site where humanities scholars broadly might find new focus to advocate for our fields.

Finally, I am learning that experience administering programs in open-disciplinary environments has had real application value in more conventional disciplinary spaces. After a surprising turn in my career path—when my spouse's career took us halfway across the country to CSU—I found that I had developed a varied skill set that soon helped me, as the popular saying goes, bloom where I was planted. Even though I arrived in a privileged faculty role to return to my own scholarship, I encountered a restlessness about engaging this new institution, restlessness I correlate also with my humanities training. That restlessness (and an attendant curiosity about how this new institution worked) pointed me back to administrative work. Certainly, restlessness and curiosity are not unique to liberal arts disciplines. I have learned much from having worked across university contexts and having seen how large swaths of our institutions operate from a range of disciplinary thought patterns: business world approaches to strategy, engineering approaches to solving academic problems, social sciences approaches to seeing students navigate a large bureaucracy, just to name a few. All of this has shown me new tools, but also helped me value my own, specifically in the form of an openness to seeing the challenges of our moment as interconnected across ways of knowing, an openness that we humanities scholars learn in the study of cultures and their artifacts. The connections between my scholarly research into how theatrical performance advances feminist or progressive politics ends up shedding light on how, for example, the stories we tell about academic cultures structurally undermine minoritized students, exploit contingent labor, or reinforce disciplinary norms as givens. And in academic leadership, we can find plenty of sites to turn these cultural and critical impulses toward addressing real issues.

Admittedly, I arrived at the university with some navigational capital, and so making my capacities known was easier for me than it might have been for others. In the years I've been here, then, I have worked on some familiar pursuits across the disciplines—strategic planning for honors education, common reading programming, and proposing a Center for Engaged Humanities. But these cross-disciplinary experiences also can help inform the kinds of tasks that occupy traditional department and college structures. For example, in 2020, I worked on a project with the college's diversity coordinator to prepare resources around academic freedom and inclusive pedagogy in tense times—a set of resources built specifically for liberal arts classrooms. I have gotten to work on faculty issues for our non-tenure-track faculty, a concern with quite specific applications in English in particular. I have worked on some student success initiatives and some strategic planning work for the college, both of which have provided a chance to apply lessons learned in multidisciplinary spaces directly to liberal arts disciplines. These examples show how humanities scholars can not only *employ* administrative skills developed in these multiple locations but—alongside our disciplinary inclination toward close reading, theoretical framework, and nuanced interpretation—can also *apply* them as tools to learn about our new institutional homes.

What can the combination of humanities training and an instinct to work across disciplinary lines add up to for others considering administration? Yes, being "interested in pretty much everything" is both a disciplinary feature and a useful administrative disposition. That is to say, our fields in the humanities give us tools to identify challenges to address everywhere and frameworks to see cultural operations in every mechanism. They also show us that our fields are not in and of themselves sufficient, especially if we acknowledge that knowledges and contexts are historical, contingent, and structured by the operations of power. And at the same time, our disciplinary training helps us practice the tools needed to address these contexts—deep reading, persuasive writing, careful research, self-reflexivity about our own roles, and an emphasis on becoming interested and cultivating learning around those interests.

As of this writing, I find myself looking forward to a permanent associate dean role in a traditional disciplinary college, still compelled (and a bit driven to distraction) by my many interests. But I have come to understand that like the different academic contexts in which we might work, our administrative skills are forged within disciplinary mindsets but also are enriched immeasurably by a humanities-inflected openness to hearing *and learning* other ways of understanding the world and approaching problems. Learning those administrative tools will always be a transdisciplinary pursuit. This is evidenced by the ways that academic leadership across the academy is populated by thinkers from every field, almost none of whom are administering directly from their field of expertise but are also nearly always inflected by their ways of knowing, gathering evidence, and solving problems. Humanities scholars can and should still approach academic problem-solving as a task that benefits from applying theoretical frameworks, reading situations closely and interpretively, and insisting upon the ethical and affective dimensions of administrative challenges. At the same time, we might admire the data-sensitivity of quantitative social scientists, the budgetary deftness of colleagues in business, the elegantly pragmatic problem-solving of our engineer friends, the listening-first approach of social work scholars, the creative experimentation of arts faculty in leadership roles, and the awareness of ecosystem complexity of peers working in natural resources and other life sciences. There is real joy to be had in working with folks who cherish these ways of knowing. As members of a community of scholars who are together laboring to help our colleges and universities survive and thrive as places to make, protect, and share knowledge, let's be glad that we are all working together.

NOTES

1. Allen F. Repko, *Interdisciplinary Research: Process and Theory* (Los Angeles: SAGE Publications, 2008), 3–6.
2. Michel Foucault, *The Order of Things: An Archaeology of Human Sciences* (New York: Vintage Books, 1994).
3. Louis Menand. "The Marketplace of Ideas," *ACLS Occasional Papers* 49 (2001), http://archives.acls.org/op/49_Marketplace_of_Ideas.htm.
4. Menand, "Marketplace."
5. A Community of Inquiry, *KEYWORDS; for Further Consideration and Par-*

ticularly Relevant to Academic Life, Especially as It Concerns Disciplines, Inter-Disciplinary Endeavor, and Modes of Resistance to the Same, eds. D. Graham Burnett, Matthew Rickard, and Jessica Terekhov (Princeton, NJ: Princeton University Press, 2018).

6. D. Graham Burnett, Matthew Rickard, and Jessica Terekhov, "'Keywords' for Understanding Academe: Co-editors Discuss Their No-Holds-Barred Dictionary for Academic Life," Interview by Scott Jaschik, *Inside Higher Ed*, January 11, 2018, https://www.insidehighered.com/news/2018/01/11/co-editors-discuss-their-new-work-keywords-understanding-academe.

7. Laurie Ellinghausen's exploration of "academic innovation" in the next chapter does precisely this sort of work.

BIBLIOGRAPHY

Burnett, D. Graham, Matthew Rickard, and Jessica Terekhov. "'Keywords' for Understanding Academe: Co-editors Discuss Their No-Holds-Barred Dictionary for Academic Life." Interview by Scott Jaschik. *Inside Higher Ed*. January 11, 2018. https://www.insidehighered.com/news/2018/01/11/co-editors-discuss-their-new-work-keywords-understanding-academe.

A Community of Inquiry. *KEYWORDS; for Further Consideration and Particularly Relevant to Academic Life, Especially as It Concerns Disciplines, Inter-Disciplinary Endeavor, and Modes of Resistance to the Same*. Edited by D. Graham Burnett, Matthew Rickard and Jessica Terekhov. Princeton, NJ: Princeton University Press, 2018.

Foucault, Michel. *The Order of Things: An Archaeology of Human Sciences*. New York: Vintage Books, 1994.

Menand, Louis. "The Marketplace of Ideas," *ACLS Occasional Papers* 49 (2001). Accessed November 8, 2021. http://archives.acls.org/op/49_Marketplace_of_Ideas.htm.

Repko, Allen F. *Interdisciplinary Research: Process and Theory*. Los Angeles: SAGE Publications, 2008.

6

"WE KNOW WHAT WE ARE, BUT KNOW NOT WHAT WE MAY BE"[1]

Academic Innovation and the Reinvention of Professional Identities

LAURIE ELLINGHAUSEN

As teachers, we take it as a given that our students must be challenged to stretch their comfort zones to grow intellectually. I would add that we as higher education professionals also stand to grow personally and contribute more to our institutions when we are compelled to absorb new and different kinds of knowledge, learn new tasks, work with colleagues in different roles, and accommodate our thinking to unfamiliar landscapes. For humanities faculty in particular—often unfairly stereotyped as lacking "real-world" skills—taking on administrative roles can facilitate personal expansion into an identity far more empowering than the customary ribbing about "going over to the dark side" would suggest. Academic innovation and professional reinvention, I will propose in this chapter, can be marshaled into a productive dialogue by which humanities faculty not only bring our unique skills and backgrounds to the leadership table but also grow individually along with our institutions. The embrace of self-innovation while pursuing academic leadership charts possible ways to synthesize knowledge, experience, and interests into new and creative approaches to professional and institutional development.

MY START IN ACADEMIC INNOVATION

When the description for a new "associate vice provost for academic innovation" first landed in my email, I didn't pay much attention. Having recently received promotion to full professor, I knew I wanted to consider administration to give back to my institution and explore a broader range of potential for myself. However, I assumed that a provost-level position would require having served as a department chair or a dean, whereas my roles to that point had included program directorships (interdisciplinary PhD coordinator, director of graduate studies, and director of undergraduate studies in my home department of English) and shared governance positions (faculty senator, vice chair/secretary and then chair of the College of Arts and Sciences). My current roster of skills included curriculum design, assessment, a significant amount of online teaching, and faculty leadership. Still, a role in the provost's office seemed too big a step for someone who had never worked in a dean's office or as a department chair.

Yet later that day, a colleague forwarded the job announcement with a note: "Sounds like an interesting position—you should check it out." I examined the announcement more closely this time and found that many of the duties did indeed speak to my experience: "providing collaborative institutional leadership," "overseeing program implementation while ensuring quality programs and teaching standards across a variety of delivery formats," and "coordinating the work" of various teams—academic and administrative—to achieve critical goals. Moreover, nowhere did the description list chair- or dean-level experience as a requirement. "Why not? Let's see what happens," I told myself, setting an intention to think about my cover letter on the drive home.

Two months later, I found myself sitting in an "academic innovation retreat" with other provost's office staff, introducing myself with a brand-new title. I had landed there after a round of interviews and presentations in which I shared my ideas about curricular innovation. In one presentation, I described a course I had recently co-taught on Shakespeare's First Folio. Innovation, I argued, is about seizing and optimizing opportune moments. My two collaborators and I had done just this in formulating our course, which we designed to coordinate with the Folger Shakespeare Library's fifty-state national "tour" of First Folios in 2016. Missouri's copy, as it happened, would be displayed at the downtown branch of the Kansas City Public Library (KCPL), less than five miles from our campus. This windfall presented a unique opportunity for our students, many of whom had interests in print culture and museum studies, as well as literature and drama. Accordingly, we designed a hybrid course (blended online and in-person delivery) that included reading and discussion of four recent books on Shakespeare and the First Folio, an introduction to the KCPL staff and facilities, and training to become docents for the exhibit, with two additional opportunities for a formal internship. This course, I argued, represented an approach to academic innovation that connected traditional humanities study with the acquisition of "real-world" skills and experience, an approach that much of the current literature on academic innovation advocates.

Yet my new job, I learned at the retreat, would require me to stretch considerably beyond course-level innovation. As I listened to the provost describe our charge, self-doubt began to creep in. "Who am I to be here? Aren't I just an English professor?" I wondered. Looking back on that moment, I realize now that this very sentiment signals a personalization of the innovation process, whereby we are called upon to learn new things quickly and work through the discomfort of not knowing everything right away. Despite my apprehension that day, I since have done the following things:

- learned to run data reports from the Integrated Postsecondary Education System, the Bureau of Labor Statistics, Academic Analytics, and Burning Glass and interpret that data in terms of workforce and student demand;
- become a voracious daily reader of higher education news, paying special attention to innovation efforts throughout the postsecondary education market;
- expanded my professional network to include academic and administrative colleagues from all over my campus and the University of Missouri system;
- attended a Higher Learning Commission national conference at

which I learned about the business of accreditation and its many requirements;

- learned about the rigors of academic program approval from our campus, to our four-campus system, to the Missouri Board of Curators, to our accrediting body, and finally to the US Department of Education;
- worked with schools of business, education, law, computing and engineering, pharmacy, biological sciences, medicine, nursing, and arts and sciences on creating new undergraduate and graduate programs;
- wrote policies identifying new program approval procedures for our campus;
- chaired campus-wide task forces and served on campus committees in need of an "academic innovation" perspective; and
- reviewed programs nominated to scale in our new Missouri Online initiative, for which I also provided initial input during the initiative's inception.

My dissertation on early modern laboring writers prepared me for virtually none of these things; my years of research and teaching as a faculty member helped only in a limited way. Yet, just as when I transitioned from graduate school to faculty life, I learned and adjusted, and I now feel strongly that I am better for the expansion itself.

INNOVATION, PAST AND PRESENT

The personal story outlined in the previous section illustrates two features inherent in innovation itself: risk and discomfort. These features—which lend an element of awkwardness, if not outright peril, to a brand-new endeavor—characterize not only my own professional journey but also the challenge of innovation itself. After all, for much of human history, "innovation" has been considered a dangerous thing. In early modern England, the term conveyed suspicion toward dubious novelties, as when Shakespeare's *Hamlet* notes "the late innovation" of introducing children's companies to the stage.[2] In more threatening registers, "innovation" suggested the disturbance of entrenched social norms and their supporting forms of authority, disturbances that included heretical religious practices, rebellion, sedition, and the creation of new honors rendering older forms of social distinction meaningless.[3] As such, "innovation" also conveys the heady excitement of revolutionary change. The political economist Joseph A. Schumpeter captured both senses of the term in the influential theory of "creative destruction" he advanced in his 1943 book.[4] Schumpeter's argument was later developed by theorists such as the business consultant and professor Clayton Christensen, who conceived of innovation as thriving on "disruption."[5] These commentators emphasized the productive and creative potential of "destruction," positing innovation as a process that cleared out the old in favor of the new and subjected all assumptions undergirding the status quo to a finite life cycle.

It is important to know this history because, most recently, innovation seems to have lost its edge from sheer overuse of the term. In the realm of higher education, "innovation" now is a mainstay of mission statements and strategic plans. In 2014, 10 percent of American Council of Education member institutions reported dedicated institutional efforts toward academic innovation; from 2010 to 2015, higher education job descriptions using the word "innovation" rose 211 percent.[6] This rapid growth has given rise to a proliferation of literature, if not yet a defined set of best practices, on how best to innovate within the postsecondary education space. Some writers look toward the American institutions most widely celebrated for innovation—Stanford, Harvard, and MIT—to extract several suggestions for the rest of us: that institutions invest serious money in research and development ("R&D"), build physical infrastructure supporting innovation (i.e., dedicated "innovation centers"), and create long-term industry partnerships (along the lines of those clustered in Silicon Valley and Boston).[7] Other writers specify such recommendations by looking directly to technology and entrepreneurship as society's most promising pathways to innovative growth, citing genomics, energy storage, automation, mobile internet, the Internet of Things, cloud computing, advanced robotics, energy storage, 3D printing, advanced materials, and renewable energy as areas inviting optimization. A widely disseminated 2020 workforce trends report concurs with the general direction of this notably tech-heavy list.[8] These areas of emerging demand frequently are suggested as the basis for fostering entrepreneurship as part of the academic experience and seeking private-sector collaboration to fund R&D and create opportunities for students.

Even as such suggestions prompt great excitement, humanities faculty seeking to participate in or even lead campus innovation initiatives would be justified in balking at this picture. Such resistance encompasses genuine concerns well beyond the previously described discomfort that frequently comes with large-scale change. For one thing, commentators who express skepticism toward academic innovation describe these efforts as merely the latest iterations of an unimaginative "dark side," one associated with resource-intensive (i.e., those expensive "innovation centers"), but ultimately useless, public posturing and bureaucratic pencil-pushing. One observer, for example, detects in academic innovation the "ability to encompass so much, while specifying so little," while attributing this perceived stagnation to "administrators, [who] like most people, aren't particularly innovative."[9] Likewise, at least one major study has found scant evidence that investment in academic innovation yields much in the way of either job growth or institutional revenue.[10] These accounts evoke the worst "dark-side" stereotypes, conceptions that hold little attraction for faculty considering academic leadership. No one wants to be thought of as "[not] particularly innovative," much less be responsible for administrative bloat at a time when humanities-oriented academic missions go perpetually underfunded.

Moreover, the academic innovation movement's particular focus on entrepreneurship and technology replicates cultural trends that leave faculty from the humanities disciplines out in the cold. At first glance, this exclusion would not seem to be the case, as most of us are familiar with "STEAM" mandates that add "A" ("arts") to science, technology, engineering, and mathematics, thus including humanistic inquiry in the interdisciplinary mix. Rationales for including "arts," a term that captures a broad range of humanistic disciplines, are several. Since "disruptive" forms of innovation tend to exacerbate inequality in society, the humanistic focus helps keep innovators attuned to the need to promote diversity and inclusion. A focus on the "human" also keeps ethics at the front of disciplines such as data science, a field beset by ethical problems, such as algorithmic bias, digital redlining, and facial recognition technology, not to mention more general concerns about data security and privacy.[11] The inclusion of "A," in other words, represents an acknowledgment of—even an apology for—STEM's potential to do more harm than good. Humanities scholars will recall how such cautions abound within the Western literary canon—from the unfortunate Prometheus of Greek myth, to Shakespeare's imperious magus Prospero, to Mary Shelley's beleaguered Victor Frankenstein.

Yet given the way most grant and development money flows—overwhelmingly to schools of business, engineering, and health care—humanists might be forgiven for sensing that the "A" in "STEAM" remains largely on the margins of institutional strategy. Certainly, we humanists are free to "innovate" on the level of our courses, as my colleagues and I did with our First Folio course in 2016. We can also innovate in the realm of new approaches to research and apply for funding from the perennially tapped-out National Endowments for the Arts and Humanities, as well as seek out smaller grants supporting humanities-based work. At the same time, those humanities projects that are awarded relatively high funding tend to be ones that apply computational methods to their data, thus lending technological legitimacy to the study of "A." To be clear, I do not dismiss the important insights of such research projects and neither do my humanist colleagues, if the packed ballroom I witnessed at a recent Shakespeare Association of America panel on computational linguistics is any indication. However, current allocations of research funding do suggest that the more "technical" a project is, the more it stands to attract real investment and thus become the basis for an institution's innovation efforts.

So how can a humanities scholar-teacher, such as I was when I took on my current role and still am, actively publishing and teaching, substantively participate in and even lead academic innovation projects? Are we merely here to service allegedly more urgent things? Should we console ourselves with supplying the so-called soft skills addendum, which seems like a consolation prize, even though these skills make a major difference in graduates' employability?[12] When considering such questions, the uncomfortable but ultimately healthy challenge of personal reinvention that

I describe at the start of this chapter is displaced by serious qualms about what exactly we stand to promote when taking on administrative roles. I do not have an answer (yet) as to how to give humanities faculty a bigger and more authentic seat at the innovation table, aside from continuing to argue for the "real-world" purchase of the skills in critical thinking, writing, and research that we teach. However, I do want to suggest a place to begin—and that is by utilizing the humanities as the basis for thinking about an *innovation culture* that not only improves our institutions but drives the expansion of ourselves as teachers, as professionals, and as colleagues—a personal expansion that has collective and institutional benefits as well.

HUMANITIES AND INNOVATION CULTURE

By "innovation culture," I mean an institutional habit of being that makes innovation something we do organically, not something intermittently embraced in moments of panic about revenue shortfalls. This habit, cultivated on a personal level and then extended outward, is fundamental to the creation of sustainable learning outcomes, completion rates, employment outcomes, and—yes—revenue streams as well. My vision of such a culture emerges in large part from my study and teaching of one of early modern England's great innovators: the poet and pamphleteer John Milton (1608–1674). Milton's life and career, as well as several of his works, offer a compelling case study in how we scholar-teachers can contribute to our professional culture through leadership roles that make the most of our humanistic training.

Since innovation today largely shares associations with entrepreneurial and STEM endeavors, Milton's name may not come to mind immediately. After all, his century witnessed the cutting-edge contributions of scientists such as Isaac Newton, Robert Boyle, Robert Hooke, and Christopher Wren. Milton, on the other hand, is a figure associated with literature and language—he was a multilingual scholar and writer whose poetic output included the greatest epic in the English language, *Paradise Lost* (first edition, 1667; second edition, 1674). But in addition to this record of artistic achievement, he also spent a turbulent decade on "the dark side" as an administrator (secretary for foreign tongues, where he put his prodigious talent for ancient and modern languages to use) in the republican Commonwealth government. Recall here the previously cited assertion that administrators "aren't particularly innovative." Perhaps it is true Milton did not have much room to "innovate" within the perimeters of his official government role. Yet in line with early modern senses of "innovation" as a disturbance of norms, Milton embraced the revolutionary politics of his day and wrote copious amounts of prose arguing for his positions while also serving the bureaucratic machinery of a government that, at least initially, espoused his most cherished ideals. These ideals, for many of his early modern contemporaries, encapsulated "innovation" in its most dangerous sense: as a threat to established social order.

Milton's career demonstrates several other meanings of "innovation," meanings more directly relevant to humanities faculty considering the call to academic leadership. In terms of his poetic output, Milton innovated in a way that literary artists often do, in dialogue with tradition, with the works of the past becoming the basis for generic innovations that yield new reflections on old ideas.[13] *Paradise Lost*, written during the aftermath of the Commonwealth's demise (a time in which Milton, as a former government official, narrowly escaped execution) demonstrates by its very existence that creation can occur under restraint. I strive to keep this fact in mind while negotiating higher education's regulatory landscape of government accountability mandates and accreditation requirements, features that certainly can limit the scope of innovation but, at the same time, give rise to creative thinking about how to negotiate such strictures. *Paradise Lost* itself, in fact, is a poem about limits. It charts, first, the fall of Satan from heavenly favor and then the fall of humankind from its perfect state due to disobedience of heavenly prescription. Yet at the same time, the epic form itself is commodious and expansive; it is, in the terms of Renaissance literary criticism, a compendium of all things.[14] Over the course of twelve books, Milton draws on a staggering variety of contemporary discourses: literary, political, theological, scientific (incorporating both old and new science), environmental, astrological, mythological, historical, botanical, and more. This proliferation of knowledge reflects the author's own ambition to write a definitive epic of the English language, one incorporating "things unattempted yet in prose or rhyme,"[15] all despite his lifelong anxiety that he might never bring such a thing to pass. The very creation of *Paradise Lost* thus illustrates how innovation demands a bold vision in the face of personal, professional, and institutional limitations that encourage otherwise.

An earlier work, Milton's prose essay *Of Education* (1644), also is instructive on the topic of academic innovation, this time insofar as it proposes a comprehensive humanities-based educational program for leadership. This tract, in which Milton articulates what he feels to be the ideal school curriculum, blends traditional scholastic endeavor with practical knowledge, all with an eye toward preparing boys for citizenship: "I call therefore a complete and generous education that which fits a man to perform justly, skillfully and magnanimously all the offices both private and public of peace and war." Such preparation aligns with the philosophy of early modern European humanists who regarded education as a means by which to cultivate civic virtue and right action among the ruling classes. For Milton, this cultivation would come about not through repetitive scholastic exercises—"the most intellective abstractions of logic and metaphysics"—but through a blend of artistic, scholarly, *and* practical endeavors. The students in Milton's school would learn languages, philosophy, and science with an eye toward fostering eloquence, a broad base of wisdom, and aptitude for such applied sciences as "fortification, architecture, enginry, or navigation." Milton's program, in essence, resembles a modern general education curriculum of the kind still required at most universities. Moreover, the present-day dictum to teach "transferable skills"[16] echoes Milton's own emphasis on practical applications of learning. Within this model for students, we might also detect a program for humanities faculty seeking leadership roles, whereby our training in the arts and humanities productively combines with the cultivation of "practical" skills such as team management, budgeting, and strategic planning.

To be sure, Milton's vision is not something we would wish to implement wholesale. His regicidal politics, his theocratic views, and the fact that *Of Education*'s curriculum applies only to upper-class boys clearly delimit twenty-first-century adaptation. What I wish to emphasize, however, is the distinct lack of boundaries in Milton's otherwise highly disciplined world, a world in which there are no "humanities people," "STEM types," or excuses made along the lines of "I'm just bad at math; I'm much better at English." Milton's epic poem made plenty of room for physics, astronomy, and botany among iambic pentameter lines replete with biblical and mythological lore. Likewise, the graduates of Milton's hypothetical school would know how to fish, till land, brandish a sword, manage a household, translate biblical languages into English, and deliver a convincing oration. They would know, in other words, how to perform a variety of endeavors, the "STEM" things as well as the "A" things, with grace, thoughtfulness, and skill.

This multidisciplinary model, which combines broad-based scholarly attainment with the practical skills of public service, charts a way in which we too, as humanities faculty considering the prospect of academic leadership, can combine our humanistic training with meaningful service to our institutions. Milton's own career demonstrates that such a thing can not only be imagined but implemented. Why, then, do we higher education professionals so sharply limit ourselves? I ask this question as a challenge to humanities faculty contemplating academic leadership within our rapidly changing educational landscape.

I distinctly recall the first moment in graduate school when I became aware of the supposed necessity of categories in crafting my own professional identity. During my first year, a mentor advised me: "When you go on the job market, you *become* your dissertation." This advice came just as I had completed a weeklong new student orientation in which I was constantly asked, "What's your *field*?" In all honesty, I did not mind being required to choose one, as it gave me a chance to delve deeply into the historical period I loved. The dissertation years, of course, required even greater specialization and, sure enough, once I entered the academic job market, I became identified as the candidate with the project on Tudor-Stuart writers of the laboring classes. After my job talks, my profile narrowed further to render me "the candidate who works on John Taylor 'The Water Poet.'"

Such discrete identifications no doubt make our broad and diverse field easier to navigate. Self-presentation and job searching become more focused and, on the other side of the job search, hiring becomes easier when departments can identify precisely how a candidate will contribute to the curriculum. Still, I have yet to encounter a colleague who feels that graduate training, focused as it is on research, writing, and sometimes teaching, adequately prepares us for the diverse commitments of faculty life. Suffice it to say that, when I started as an assistant professor in 2003, I was *not* my dissertation. Rather, I was

- a colleague in my department, my academic unit, my campus, and the University of Missouri System;
- a teacher of undergraduate and graduate students;
- a mentor for students doing projects in early modern English studies;
- the go-to Shakespeare scholar for students, colleagues, and members of the community, including staff at the local Shakespeare festival;
- the author of a research monograph and collection of articles that I strove to complete as the tenure clock ticked away;
- a member of several new committees, all of which were working on ongoing projects unfamiliar to me;
- a reviewer of books and manuscripts upon request; and
- the brand-new resident of a city and state that I had never visited prior to my campus interview.

The reader could no doubt add even more professional and personal demands to this list. For colleagues transitioning into non-tenure-track positions, the challenges number even higher. In all cases, the mental adjustment to such sudden expansion can take time as we work through a considerable degree of befuddlement and panic, and hopefully excitement as well.

That said, tenured faculty may have the most difficulty of all taking on the risk of discomfort inherent in personal and institutional innovation, that is, the scariness of not knowing things and of embracing roles for which we may believe ourselves to be unsuited due to the restrictive self-categorizations encouraged by the profession. Even as the business of higher education responds in unaccustomed ways to pandemics, racial reckoning, political dysfunction, and budget crises, our position remains relatively privileged and secure, barring the ever-looming threat of "financial exigency" that might alter that comfortable status. Innovation, whether personal or institutional, inspires a mixture of trepidation and excitement, thus posing a difficult landscape of reactions to navigate as change hurtles us forward into unknown terrain. But it is a prospect worth the risk, one that invites us to, to paraphrase Shakespeare, know not only what we *are*, but what we *may be*.

NOTES

1. William Shakespeare, *Hamlet*, in *The Complete Works of Shakespeare*, 5th ed., ed. David Bevington (New York: Longman, 2003), 4.5.43–4. All citations from Shakespeare are taken from Bevington's edition.

2. Shakespeare, *Hamlet*, 2.333.

3. *Oxford English Dictionary*, *s.v.* "innovation, n." (Oxford: Oxford UP, 2020), https://www.oed.com.proxy.library.umkc.edu/view/Entry/96311?redirected From=innovation#eid. The social meanings I list here are derived from the textual examples cited under each definition.

4. Joseph A. Schumpeter, *Socialism, Capitalism, and Democracy* (Abingdon, UK: Routledge Classics, 2010), 71–75.

5. Clayton Christensen, *The Innovator's Dilemma: When New Technologies Cause Great Firms to Fail* (Boston: Harvard Business Review Press, 1997), xi.

6. Christina M. Sax, "Five Steps to Building an Academic Innovation Engine," *The EvoLLLution: A Destiny Solutions Illumination*, August 1, 2016, https://evolllu tion.com/managing-institution/operations_efficiency/five-steps-to-building -an-academic-innovation-engine/.

7. Erika Gimbel, "Three Strategies of the Most Innovative Universities," *Ed Tech: Focus on Higher Education*, January 2, 2019. https://edtechmagazine.com /higher/article/2019/01/3-strategies-most-innovative-universities.

8. Farnham Jahanian, "4 Ways Universities are Driving Innovation," *World Economic Forum*, January 17, 2018, https://www.weforum.org/agenda/2018/01/4 -ways-universities-are-driving-innovation/ and *2020 Emerging Jobs Report*, LinkedIn Business Solutions, https://business.linkedin.com/content/dam /me/business/en-us/talent-solutions/emerging-jobs-report/Emerging_Jobs _Report_U.S._FINAL.pdf.

9. John Patrick Leary, "Enough with All the Innovation," *The Chronicle of Higher Education*, November 16, 2018, https://www.chronicle.com/article/enough -with-all-the-innovation/.

10. Mark V. Levine, "The False Promise of the Entrepreneurial University," *University of Wisconsin—Milwaukee Center for Economic Development*, September 1, 2009, https://dc.uwm.edu/cgi/viewcontent.cgi?article=1025&context=ced_pubs.

11. David Skorton, "Branches from the Same Tree: The Case for Integration in Higher Education," *PNAS* 116, no. 6 (February 2019): 1865–69.

12. "What Is Career Readiness?," NACE Center for Career Development and Talent Acquisition, National Association of Colleges and Employers, 2022, https://www.naceweb.org/career-readiness/competencies/career-readiness defined/; Ryan Jenkins, "This Is the Most In-Demand Skill of the Future." *Inc.*, July 19, 2019, https://www.inc.com/ryan-jenkins/this-is-most-in-demand-skill-of-future.html; "New Survey: Demand for 'Uniquely Human Skills' Increases Even as Technology and Automation Replace Some Jobs," *Cengage*, January 16, 2019, https://news.cengage.com/upskilling/new-survey-demand-for-uniquely-human-skills-increases-even-as-technology-and-automation-replace-some-jobs/; and "Robot Ready: Human + Skills for the Future of Work," Strada Institute for the Future of Work, *Strada Education Network*, 2019, https://stradaeducation.org/report/robot-ready/ (report is sent free in PDF when user submits contact information to web portal). See Anne-Marie E. Walkowicz's chapter in this volume for an example of how these skills can be built into an academic program.

13. T. S. Eliot, "Tradition and the Individual Talent," reprinted by *Poetry Foundation*, 2021, https://www.poetryfoundation.org/articles/69400/tradition-and-the-individual-talent.

14. Barbara Lewalski, "The Genres of *Paradise Lost*," in *The Cambridge Companion to Milton*, ed. Dennis Danielson (Cambridge: Cambridge UP, 1989), 81.

15. I.16. All quotes from Milton's works are from the digital editions in *The John Milton Reading Room*, ed. Thomas H. Luxon (Hanover, NH: Trustees of Dartmouth College, 1997–2001), https://milton.host.dartmouth.edu/reading_room/contents/text.shtml.

16. Adam Adamopolous, "Universities Should Be about Transferable Skills and Continuing Education," *Forbes*, January 3, 2019, https://www.forbes.com/sites/forbesbostoncouncil/2019/01/03/universities-should-be-about-transferable-skills-and-continuing-education/?sh=5cf58353432f.

BIBLIOGRAPHY

Adamopolous, Adam. "Universities Should Be About Transferable Skills and Continuing Education." *Forbes*, January 3, 2019. https://www.forbes.com/sites /forbesbostoncouncil/2019/01/03/universities-should-be-about-transferable -skills-and-continuing-education/?sh=5cf58353432f.

Cengage. "New Survey: Demand for 'Uniquely Human Skills' Increases Even as Technology and Automation Replace Some Jobs." January 16, 2019. https:// news.cengage.com/upskilling/new-survey-demand-for-uniquely-human -skills-increases-even-as-technology-and-automation-replace-some-jobs/.

Christensen, Clayton. *The Innovator's Dilemma: When New Technologies Cause Great Firms to Fail.* Boston: Harvard Business Review Press, 1997.

Eliot, T. S. "Tradition and the Individual Talent." Reprinted by *Poetry Foundation*, 2021. https://www.poetryfoundation.org/articles/69400/tradition-and-the -individual-talent.

Gimbel, Erika. "Three Strategies of the Most Innovative Universities." *Ed Tech: Focus on Higher Education*, January 2, 2019. https://edtechmagazine.com/higher /article/2019/01/3-strategies-most-innovative-universities.

Jahanian, Farnham. "4 Ways Universities Are Driving Innovation." *World Economic Forum*, January 17, 2018. https://www.weforum.org/agenda/2018/01/4-ways -universities-are-driving-innovation/.

Jenkins, Ryan. "This Is the Most In-Demand Skill of the Future." *Inc.*, July 19, 2019. https://www.inc.com/ryan-jenkins/this-is-most-in-demand-skill-of -future.html.

The John Milton Reading Room. Edited by Thomas H. Luxon. Hanover, NH: Trustees of Dartmouth College, 1997–2001. https://milton.host.dartmouth.edu /reading_room/contents/text.shtml.

Leary, John Patrick. "Enough with All the Innovation." *The Chronicle of Higher Education*, November 16, 2018. https://www.chronicle.com/article/enough-with -all-the-innovation/.

Levine, Marc V. "The False Promise of the Entrepreneurial University." *University of Wisconsin–Milwaukee Center for Economic Development.* University of Wisconsin–Milwaukee, September 1, 2009. https://dc.uwm.edu/cgi/view content.cgi?article=1025&context=ced_pubs.

Lewalski, Barbara. "The Genres of *Paradise Lost.*" In *The Cambridge Companion to Milton*, ed. Dennis Danielson, 79–95. Cambridge: Cambridge UP, 1989.

LinkedIn Business Solutions. *2020 Emerging Jobs Report*. https://business.linkedin .com/content/dam/me/business/en-us/talent-solutions/emerging-jobs-report /Emerging_Jobs_Report_U.S._FINAL.pdf.

National Association of Colleges and Employers. "What Is Career Readiness?" NACE Center for Career Development and Talent Acquisition, 2022. https:// www.naceweb.org/careerreadiness/competencies/career-readiness-defined/.

Oxford English Dictionary. "Innovation." Oxford: Oxford UP, 2020. https:// www-oed-com.proxy.library.umkc.edu/view/Entry/96311?redirectedFrom =innovation#eid.

Sax, Christina M. "Five Steps to Building an Academic Innovation Engine." *The EvoLLLution: A Destiny Solutions Illumination,* August 1, 2016. https://evolllu tion.com/managing-institution/operations_efficiency/five-steps-to-building -an-academic-innovation-engine/.

Schumpeter, Joseph A. *Capitalism, Socialism, and Democracy.* Abingdon, UK: Rout- ledge Classics, 2010.

Shakespeare, William. *The Complete Works of Shakespeare.* 5th ed. Edited by David Bevington. New York: Longman, 2003.

Skorton, David. "Branches from the Same Tree: The Case for Integration in Higher Education." *PNAS* 116, no. 6 (February 2019): 1865–69.

Strada Institute for the Future of Work. "Robot Ready: Human + Skills for the Future of Work." Strada Education Network, 2019. https://stradaeducation .org/report/robot-ready/.

7

ADMINISTERING INSTRUCTIONAL REFORM

Interdisciplinary Learning and the Humanities Profession

ANNE-MARIE E. WALKOWICZ

Interdisciplinary inquiry has become pervasive within the humanities in recent decades. One look at the work of historians, literary scholars, philosophers, and communication researchers in publications by major academic presses uncovers the frequent disciplinary-boundary crossing that occurs. Historians draw on a wide range of sources—written and visual—to examine historical events from multiple perspectives; literary scholars employ methods of cultural history to discuss literature; and studies in philosophy are informed by areas of sociology, anthropology, and religion. My own work focuses on early modern drama, cultural history, and political theory, analyzing the place of the early modern stage within the political debates on counsel in the public sphere. This emphasis on interdisciplinary methods seems a natural outpouring of the complexity of the areas of interest that humanities professionals study. Our research topics are multifaceted, and by employing methods from across disciplines, we synthesize a more comprehensive understanding of the topic and produce knowledge that encompasses sets of relationships.

Trained in fields that embrace interdisciplinary methodologies, humanities professionals often bring their research into the classroom and create courses that integrate knowledge from across disciplines. This chapter explores the role of humanities leaders in creating interdisciplinary undergraduate curricula that connect their research, teaching, and administrative endeavors. Based on my work as an administrator of the newly created bachelor of arts in humanities-interdisciplinary studies (IDS) at Central State University, I take up two questions not widely addressed in the scholarship on the humanities profession: why should humanities faculty incorporate interdisciplinary inquiry into undergraduate education, and how can humanities leaders cultivate a culture of change to develop and administer curricula?

The first part of the chapter discusses the construction of Central State University's interdisciplinary program and the faculty leadership opportunities that stemmed from the degree's creation. I then discuss my role as the program's administrator in implementing curriculum change. Whether revising a preexisting curriculum or creating a new one, implementing curriculum change demands a shared and cooperative responsibility among faculty and administrators. These administrative roles are rewarding because they provide opportunities for faculty leaders to take ownership of curricular decisions, envision connections between their scholarly work and innovative teaching, and see beyond their own courses to positively affecting the curriculum as a whole. Ultimately, purposeful curriculum development makes a difference in how faculty—as leaders and educators—can prepare students for their future careers.

CREATING AN INTERDISCIPLINARY UNDERGRADUATE EDUCATIONAL PROGRAM

Central State University is an 1890 land-grant institution, located in Wilberforce, Ohio. The university has an undergraduate enrollment of 2,000 traditional students and an increasing component of another 4,000 distance learners, who attend through a low-cost educational program as a member of a union affiliated with the American Federation of Labor and Congress of Industrial Organization (AFL-CIO). Central State has typically served first-generation students, and 85 percent of students are Federal Pell Grant eligible.[1] The recent addition of the distance learning program has attracted new nontraditional students to Central State. These students are working while attending college, transferring previously completed credits, and have families of their own. For both our traditional and distance learners, most of our students enter college for the purpose of earning the degree and credentials essential for their professional careers. Within this institutional context, the Humanities Department houses degree programs in communications, English, and history, and minors in international languages and philosophy.

In fall 2019, the Humanities Department was approached by the university administration to create an interdisciplinary bachelor of arts degree to meet the needs of distance learners transferring with a large number of previously earned college credits or an associate of arts degree. I was invited to lead the endeavor and used this as an opportunity to shape an undergraduate educational program that was based on intentional integration of content knowledge and empowering students to develop their own academic work aimed at career goals. Taking a leadership role in this project was a natural extension of my service work at Central State. Previously, I was a member of the leadership team that created our Writing Across the Curriculum Program and revised our general education curriculum. As an early career faculty member, I chose to be a part of these university initiatives because they were occasions where I could combine my formal training from my bachelor's degree in education with my professional interests in the role of the liberal arts in workforce preparation. Working on these two initiatives drew attention to my understanding of curriculum development in enhancing teaching and learning, and my ability to communicate this to others.

This work led to taking a part-time administrative position in fall 2015 as director of faculty development and the Center of Teaching and Learning, which I held for five years. Much of my work in faculty development supported the university's accreditation by the Higher Learning Commission (HLC) and the accreditation of the College of Education by the Council for the Accreditation of Educator Preparation (CAEP). I conducted professional development seminars on curriculum mapping and writing and assessing student learning outcomes (SLOs), and I served on the writing teams for the accreditation documents. Leadership development in assessment and accreditation is one of the rare cases in higher education administration where faculty can engage in professional training. Accreditation organizations sponsor conferences and seminars, higher education institutions can hire consultants, and assessment is a disciplinary field in the scholarship of teaching and learning. For me, participation in Central State University's accreditation initiatives included opportunities for professional development at seminars sponsored by the Teagle Foundation, HLC, and CAEP, where teams focused on curriculum planning, assessment, and program review procedures to prepare us for accreditation site visits. As a faculty leader in these endeavors, I realized assessment requires skills in reading, analysis, and communicating the effectiveness of academic programs to various audiences. I had honed these skills in my disciplinary practices in English literature and composition, and easily transferred them to evaluating academic programs, using evidence to make decisions on their effectiveness, and contextualizing data to define improvement efforts.

Stepping into administration is often accompanied by a growth in leadership skill sets. In my case, these university initiatives required cultivating faculty buy-in, and I viewed my role as a facilitator. I developed a leadership style that was dependent on listening to objections and considering them as part of the cocreation process. By inviting discussion and working to address concerns, I helped faculty feel invested in the process. In some ways, this was comparable to addressing counterarguments and taking into consideration differing perspectives, which is part of the study of the humanities. Through these experiences, I molded a talent for formulating a coherent vision, leveraging feedback, and creating a culture of working together to benefit the academic program. Assessment, accreditation, and program review are part of twenty-first-century higher education culture that require collaboration and shared responsibility among faculty. Leadership roles in accreditation activities and program evaluation can be empowering experiences that encourage innovation in teaching and learning and have wide-ranging impacts on the university's academic community.

When the opportunity presented itself to develop a new interdisciplinary degree, I saw it as an occasion to bring together my knowledge on curriculum design, high-impact practices, and assessment based on related and applied learning. What I had not expected was for this to be an administrative opportunity to be a visionary and to lean into my leadership skills in building a vision and mobilizing faculty to meet its goals. The vision of the course curriculum was developed with a deep understanding of integrative learning, and with the research and expertise of the committee members.[2] Several of the committee members actively engaged in interdisciplinary research, and three of the members had attended the 2018 Institute on Integrative Learning and Signature Work by the Association of American Universities and Colleges (AAC&U), for which I was the team lead. The committee members agreed that we did not want to create a general studies degree. A previous initiative had been voted down by faculty in the Humanities Department, because of concerns that such degrees lacked depth in the skills and knowledge that derived from well-grounded education in a field of study. Instead, the committee chose to concentrate the degree in the humanities. As a faculty leader, I formed a vision of this degree by defining why the degree should be created and implemented at Central State and then articulating its primary purpose and direction.

Communicating the primary purpose and direction of the degree was crucial to convincing faculty—both in the Humanities Department and across the university—that a humanities degree would prepare students with the career competencies and content knowledge necessary for workplace success. Humanities disciplines share the development of student skill sets in communication and critical thinking. Students hone and perfect these through study across the fields of English, history, communications, and philosophy. Nationally, the humanities appear widely in public debates on the necessity of higher education to produce graduates with specific communication and technical skills. A 2017 study by Google's People Analytics Team and the 2019 Job Outlook Survey by the National Association of Colleges and Employers (NACE) stress that competencies necessary for workplace success are not vocational skills, but those in coaching, communication, listening, critical thinking, and empathy toward others.[3]

These studies reinforce what many humanities leaders have already known: the conventional wisdom that college students need to study and master technical and vocational job skills is a gross simplification of what graduates need to know and be able to do for career success. However, while these studies advocate that liberal arts degrees meet the needs of rapidly changing employment fields, others support the trend for higher education to provide specific occupational training. Substantial declines in humanities undergraduate majors have occurred since the Recession, and the high cost of a college education has placed greater pressure on universities to meet a diversity of technical and vocational outcomes for career readiness.[4] A 2010 study by Hart Research Associates demonstrated that only 20 percent of employers believed "a broad range of skills and knowledge that apply to a range of fields or positions" prepared students for the workplace.[5] At Central State, we serve minoritized students and nontraditional working adults, so it was important to communicate to faculty and administrators how the IDS degree prepared students with practical skills in ways that could compete with vocational degrees in business and education, as well as integrate with STEM degrees to address ethical and philosophical needs related to human-centered design.[6]

In my role as a faculty leader, I wanted to move beyond making a theoretical case for the relevancy of a humanities degree and purposefully integrate employment skills within the degree design and course offerings. To be frank, I no longer wanted to pay lip service to the idea that the humanities prepared students for jobs. My leadership strategy was based on my training in best practices of accreditation and assessment, and I consistently focused the conversation on the sets of pedagogical strategies, assignments, and course content that worked to meet the goals of recursive practice and development of job-related skills. The resulting degree curriculum focuses on the broad essential employment skills of communication, critical thinking, and cultural fluency. These skills are a direct reflection of NACE's Career Competencies and skills that are developed through study in the humanities.[7]

The committee members based the curriculum on the principles and practices of integrative learning as promoted by AAC&U, which many of us had acquired in the 2018 Summer Institute, including a curricular design that connects learning experiences across stages of development, incorporates inquiry-based assignments, and applies integrative learning in a variety of contexts.[8] Program coursework includes four core courses that develop skills in written and oral communication, critical thinking, problem-solving, and intercultural fluency; two interdisciplinary seminars—an introductory course and a senior capstone; a concentration of courses within a single subject in the humanities; and electives across the humanities.[9] Within the introductory interdisciplinary seminar, students create a plan toward graduation and are asked to consider fulfilling these university electives with a minor or a selection of courses that prepare them for their career field. At the mastery level, the course curriculum culminates in a research-based senior capstone experience and project. Additionally, the faculty have closely aligned minors and lists of elective courses to high-demand fields, including data science, information security, national intelligence and law enforcement, and public health. Integrating career readiness within a curriculum is a crucial step to ensuring students are prepared for the transition to the workplace. In order to provide students with the skills they want and need as future professionals, course curricula require a high level of intentionality for students to develop skills through practice and application, synthesize their work across a variety of learning experiences, and integrate knowledge and insights from their chosen concentration with other disciplines.

At Central State, the strengths of a degree based on career competencies that are acquired through studies in the humanities, rather than a general studies degree, were perceived by the faculty from its early conceptions. As the committee chair, my role was to articulate its purpose and direction, and then mobilize faculty members to sustain a supportive instructional environment to meet the vision. This was accomplished through cultivating innovation, collaboration, and communication. By encouraging an open exchange of ideas, faculty were empowered to be innovative. Building a strong team required giving everyone a voice and collaborating to design a degree that met the various challenges of our vision. Collaboration and communication helped us push through failures by exchanging advice and developing solutions to problems. In some ways, I was creating a culture of change—a shift in values, norms, and habits—asking faculty to imagine a powerful degree and working toward creating and implementing it.[10] In other ways, the creative breakthroughs we achieved in revising course content and instructional methods to meet the design and

purpose of the degree occurred because the humanities faculty were utilizing the very essential skills we believed were the product of the bachelor of arts in humanities-IDS.

CULTIVATING COLLABORATIVE FACULTY ENGAGEMENT IN CURRICULUM DESIGN

In fall 2020, I took on the part-time role of the coordinator of IDS. The
position stemmed from my work as chair of the ad hoc committee and was
created by the university administration to manage the degree program.
The coordinatorship is a position within the Department of Humanities
and is one of several program coordinators who assist the chair with the administrative responsibilities of a specific degree program within the larger
department. Some of the administrative work includes the day-to-day
running of the program—making teaching schedules, addressing student
inquiries, managing program assessment, and hiring faculty. The managerial duties were not what interested me in the position. I was attracted
to leading the dynamic revision of courses that would support the design
and purpose of the degree program. The position transformed my role as a
faculty member and as an administrator because I was working collaboratively with other faculty to promote deep approaches to learning. Through
this position, I was able to implement a culture of change aimed at revising instructional methods and course content, lead the revision of courses
to integrate career competencies into coursework across various fields in
the humanities, and establish an ePortfolio initiative in the degree curriculum to make student learning visible.

My leadership style is aimed at cultivating an environment of teamwork based on inspiring faculty to be creative and to think innovatively as
part of the cocreation process. Through a culture of discussion and mutual
decision-making, faculty are genuinely part of the collaboration that envisioned and executed the degree program. Connecting faculty with the
vision meant that at times it took new shapes and directions. One of the
conditions that helped to make this initiative successful at Central State
was it aligned with the moment online learning was taking an unprecedented role in transforming our institution. This break from established

educational models of teaching was occurring internally as Central State was implementing new and rapidly growing online programs and externally because of the sudden forced closure of our institution due to the COVID-19 pandemic. The combined shift to online learning and the implementation of the new degree provided an acute awareness of why a change in learning was taking place. These changing instructional conditions helped to promote interest in adapting teaching and course content. Another condition that helped sustain the initiative was the opportunity for faculty who taught a large number of general education courses to engage in teaching that was aligned with their research interests in upper-division courses. Faculty reaped intellectual rewards as course revision and implementation of the new degree program brought opportunities to enrich their teaching experience.

Leading a transformation of culture within a higher education institution requires shared meaning and beliefs among the faculty. Faculty leaders and administrators are often placed into the role of a change agent, the person who initiates change within the institution and motivates others to accept the change.[11] The challenge for academic leaders is often defining how to employ a change. As the coordinator of IDS, I lead the curriculum development across the fields in the Humanities Department. In this role, I aim to promote the development of integrated learning, increase the transparency of student learning, and demonstrate the degree's effectiveness to students, faculty, and outside stakeholders.

Change in teaching and learning entails that faculty, who are in the classroom and directly working with students, position themselves for reinvention and growth. In the case of the curriculum development for the IDS degree, these changes included the creation of new courses and the revision of previously offered ones. To meet this goal, I created a faculty learning community (FLC), a small peer group of faculty focused on investigating and implementing the best practices in integrated learning.[12] The FLC emerged out of members from the IDS degree committee and faculty interested in revising face-to-face courses or creating new online courses that are taught in the program. Rather than formal workshops, faculty members maintain a meeting schedule of informal collaborative planning, sharing ideas for assignments, and exchanging feedback on assignment and course design. These informal sessions encourage continuous improvement and foster an environment for faculty to take risks, but they also are sustainable and accessible for faculty who feel pressure from other aspects of their work. I chose the FLC as the means to revise the curriculum because it provided a collaborative structure that invited faculty to take ownership of the change by seeking their insight. FLCs involve an element of cocreation. The structure promotes discussion and ideation, acknowledges varying viewpoints, and leverages those ideas back into the whole. Faculty become invested in the initiative because they feel their voices are being heard, see key takeaways, and formulate their role in the process of change.

Degree programming and curriculum development are natural places for implementing change. The current higher education culture of accreditation and assessment includes recursive examinations of student learning and adjustments in pedagogy to meet student needs. At Central State, the conversations in the FLC on course development and revision often focused on our shared scholarly interests as humanities professionals, and the career competencies students acquire through study in our courses. Humanities research develops understandings of human events and expressions, and explores how history, culture, and intellectual thought influence them. These discussions strongly influenced how we wanted to revise courses so that students acquire specific learning content in the course and then apply their holistic knowledge to a context, problem, or theme within the signature assignment. In developing these signature assignments, the members of the FLC shifted their focus from a set of knowledge and skills that are required for the course toward seeing undergraduate education as a means to teach students the discipline's integrative ways of thinking and career competencies. They pushed advanced levels of intellectual activity into classes and focused on student-centric learning experiences, where students are actively engaged in the type of intellectual work that we do as scholars.

Faculty leadership enables curriculum development so that educational goals may be achieved. These leadership opportunities couple faculty members' specialized content expertise to the larger context of the institution and provide occasions for faculty leaders to expand their own research, engage students, and advance the institution through strengthened educational programs. The curriculum development of Central State's IDS degree promoted in-course integration, where integrative learning is blended into already established courses.[13] This means faculty are not developing new interdisciplinary seminars but rather reenvisioning content within courses already offered through our Humanities Department. The revision of courses incorporates concepts, theories, and methods from at least two disciplines into course content and includes at least one student signature assignment that engages in integrative inquiry and develops career competencies. These genres include presentations, informational reports, evaluations, and peer reviews, which reflect the types of contexts they will experience professionally, such as participating in reviews, giving presentations, and writing for social media. The faculty often leaned on their own research interests to generate this course content and assignments. The ongoing process of curriculum development benefits faculty, students, and institutions. For faculty, when their research is directly applied to their teaching, research productivity enhances their interest in course subject material. The process provides an opportunity to sustain research while maintaining a high teaching load in a primarily undergraduate institution. For students, they engage in the kinds of inquiry that are common in humanities fields. Through their coursework, they pose questions to common assumptions, uncover new meanings and insights from integrative inquiry, and communicate their ideas and research to others through various genres and in multiple contexts. Faculty leaders support the purposeful design and implementation of degree programs, and strengthen the institution's goals of achieving high levels of student learning.

Promoting the kinds of instructional methods to achieve learning outcomes in career competencies requires creating a shared culture focused on learning experiences that connect content knowledge and career skills. Faculty leaders facilitate a culture focused on student achievement when they provide structures that support the ability of faculty to continuously discover how to produce more student learning. In order to document how students achieved subject content knowledge and career competencies in the IDS program, the FLC decided to implement an ePortfolio into the curriculum, a high-impact practice that provides an opportunity for students to archive their learning and reflect upon their proficiencies.[14]

Working with faculty across disciplines and creating a collaborative culture are thoughtful and intellectual aspects of my administrative work. At a time when administrative work is too often focused on accountability for meeting SLOs, the work of developing the IDS degree has brought together initiatives to improve our students' educational experiences and measure students' knowledge.[15] I have witnessed a cultural change within the Humanities Department. Faculty are overcoming the fragmentation between disciplines, articulating how their scholarly and instructional work fits into integrative learning, and engaging in initiatives to improve student development. When these two come together, assessment is not aimed at course completion but at producing students' growth mindset around their acquisition of knowledge and their ability to demonstrate their skills. In guiding the vision for the IDS degree, my administrative work includes exciting opportunities to envision and implement a curriculum based on real-world application and public demonstrations of students' skills and abilities.

Administrators have the capacity to create vibrant intellectual environments for faculty interested in intentional innovation of teaching and student learning. Whether creating new programs in IDS or reenvisioning discipline-specific programs, curriculum development is a means to build community among disparate members of the faculty and cultivate consensus about the purpose and value of the degree. Administrators do this by sustaining a culture based on social experiences and active engagement in the improvement of teaching. One of the most fascinating outcomes of implementing the IDS degree is witnessing how the goals of integrative learning are becoming woven into the department culture, where courses enable discovery and are guided in constructing academic and career pathways. Already, conversations among faculty are emerging regarding adding the ePortfolio in other senior seminar courses, including English and philosophy. For the faculty at Central State, this has become an enriching and empowering experience of delivering an undergraduate education that supports student success in and beyond the classroom.

Change within higher education no longer is a momentary condition or a temporary situation. As faculty and administrators, we are keenly aware that the pandemic has brought a transformative moment to higher education, and we do not know yet what the paradigm shift will mean for higher education at a national and global level. Throughout my work in creating and administering the IDS degree, I had to remain flexible and lead with courage as faculty viewpoints brought new opportunities and perspectives to the initiative. As faculty leaders, we have the positionality to understand the organizational structure of our institutions and can directly implement change in teaching and learning. The types of challenges we will face throughout our careers will be varied and complex, but the tools to motivate others and produce change remain the same. Administrators trained in the humanities can effectively be agents of change by relying on the skills we develop through our disciplines—communicating a vision, listening to various perspectives, cultivating innovation and creativity in a process of cocreation, and providing goals for faculty career enrichment.

NOTES

1. "College Navigator—Central State University," National Center for Educational Statistics, https://nces.ed.gov/collegenavigator/?q=Central+State+University&s=all&id=201690–finaid.

2. I would like to acknowledge the committee members who were integral in developing the course curriculum: Kenneth Hayes, Jonathan Holmes, Anthony Milburn, Bryan Mullins, and Genevieve Ritchie-Ewing.

3. Valerie Strauss, "The Surprising Thing Google Learned about Its Employees—and What It Means for Today's Students," *The Washington Post*, April 5, 2019, https://www.washingtonpost.com/news/answer-sheet/wp/2017/12/20/the-surprising-thing-google-learned-about-its-employees-and-what-it-means-for-todays-students/. "Job Outlook 2019" (Bethlehem, PA: National Association of Colleges and Employers, 2018), https://www.odu.edu/content/dam/odu/offices/cmc/docs/nace/2019-nace-job-outlook-survey.pdf.

4. Benjamin Schimdt, "The Humanities Are in Crisis," *The Atlantic*, August 23, 2018, https://www.theatlantic.com/ideas/archive/2018/08/the-humanities-face-a-crisisof-confidence/567565/.

5. Hart Research Associates, "It Takes More Than a Major: Employer Priorities for College Learning and Student Success" (Washington, DC: Hart

Research Associates, 2013), 6, https://www.aacu.org/sites/default/files/files
/LEAP/2013_EmployerSurvey.pdf.

6. Margaret Pinnell et al., "Leveraging Regional Strengths for STEM Teacher Professional Development: Results from an NSF RET Program Focused on Advanced Manufacturing and Materials," *Research in the Schools* 25, no. 1 (2018): 20–34.

7. "Career Readiness: Competencies for a Career Ready Workforce" (Bethlehem, PA: National Association of Colleges and Employers, March 2021), https://www.nace-career-readiness-competencies-revised-apr-2021.pdf (naceweb.org).

8. Ann S. Ferren and David C. Paris, "Faculty Leadership for Integrative Liberal Learning," (Washington, DC: Association of American Colleges and Universities, 2015), https://www.aacu.org/publications-research/publications/faculty-leadership-integrative-liberal-learning.

9. The curriculum design of the seminars is based on research in interdisciplinary methods, see William Newell, "A Theory of Interdisciplinary Studies," *Issues in Integrative Studies* 19 (2001); 1–25, https://our.oakland.edu/handle/10323/4378; and Julie Kline and William Newell, "Advancing Interdisciplinary Studies," in *Handbook of the Undergraduate Curriculum: A Comprehensive Guide to Purposes, Structures, Practices and Changes*, eds. J. Graff and J. Radcliff (San Francisco: Jossey-Bass, 1997), 393–415.

10. Organizational culture change is a leadership concept in the field of business that has been applied to higher education institutions. See Adrianna Kezar and Peter D. Eckel, "The Effect of Institutional Culture on Change Strategies in Higher Education," *The Journal of Higher Education* 73, no. 4 (2002): 435–60, https://doi.org/10.1080/00221546.2002.11777159; and Colleen Lucas and Theresa Kline, "Understanding the Influence of Organizational Culture and Group Dynamics on Organization Change and Learning," *The Learning Organization* 15, no. 3 (2008): 277–87, https://doi.org/10.1108/09696470810868882.

11. Fred. C. Lunenburg, "Managing Change: The Role of the Change Agent," *International Journal of Management, Business, and Administration* 13, no. 1 (2010): 1. https://naaee.org/sites/default/files/lunenburg_fred_c._managing_change_the_role_of_change_agent_ijmba_v13_n1_2010.pdf.

12. Milton M. Cox, "Introduction to Faculty Learning Communities," in "Build-

ing Faculty Learning Communities," ed. Milton M. Cox and Laurie Richlan, special issue, *New Directions for Teaching and Learning* 97 (Spring 2004): 5–24, https://doi.org/10.1002/tl.129.

13. David Skorton and Ashley Bear, eds., *The Integration of the Humanities and Arts with Science. Engineering, and Medicine in Higher Education: Branches from the Same Tree* (Washington, DC: The National Academies Press, 2018), 66, https://doi.org/10.17226/24988.

14. Bret Eynon, Laura Gambino, and Judit Török, "What Difference Can ePortfolio Make? A Field Report from the Connect to Learning Project," *International Journal of ePortfolio* 4, no.1 (2014): 95–114, https://www.theijep .com/pdf/IJEP127.pdf; George D. Kuh, *High-Impact Educational Practices: What They Are, Who Has Access to Them, and Why They Matter* (Washington, DC: Association of American Colleges and Universities, 2008), https://secure .aacu.org/imis/AACUR.

15. Jeffrey L. Buller, "Academic Leadership 2.0," *Academe* (May–June, 2013), https://www.aaup.org/article/academic-leadership-20#.YKOzoNXwZ8Y.

BIBLIOGRAPHY

Buller, Jeffrey L. "Academic Leadership 2.0." *Academe* (May–June, 2013). https:// www.aaup.org/article/academic-leadership-20#.YKOzoNXwZ8Y.

Cox, Milton M. "Introduction to Faculty Learning Communities." In *Building Faculty Learning Communities*, edited by Milton M. Cox and Laurie Richlan. Special issue, *New Directions for Teaching and Learning* 97 (Spring 2004): 5–24. https://doi.org/10.1002/tl.129.

Eynon, Bret, Laura Gambino, and Judit Török. "What Difference Can ePortfo- lio Make? A Field Report from the Connect to Learning Project." *Interna- tional Journal of ePortfolio* 4, no.1 (2014): 95–114. https://www.theijep.com/pdf /IJEP127.pdf.

Farren, Ann S., and David C. Paris. "Faculty Leadership for Integrative Liberal Learning." Washington, DC: Association of American Colleges and Universi- ties, 2015. https://www.aacu.org/publications-research/publications/faculty -leadership-integrative-liberal-learning.

Hart Research Associates. "It Takes More Than a Major: Employer Priorities for

College Learning and Student Success." Washington, DC: Hart Research Associates, 2013. https://www.aacu.org/sites/default/files/files/LEAP/2013 _EmployerSurvey.pdf.

Kezar, Adrianna, and Peter D. Eckel. "The Effect of Institutional Culture on Change Strategies in Higher Education." *The Journal of Higher Education*, 73, no. 4 (2002): 435–60. https://doi.org/10.1080/00221546.2002.11777159.

Kline, Julie, and William Newell. "Advancing Interdisciplinary Studies." In *Handbook of the Undergraduate Curriculum: A Comprehensive Guide to Purposes, Structures, Practices and Changes*, edited by J. Graff and J. Radcliff, 393–415. San Francisco: Jossey-Bass, 1997.

Kuh, George D. *High-Impact Educational Practices: What They Are, Who Has Access to Them, and Why They Matter.* Washington, DC: Association of American Colleges and Universities, 2008. https://secure.aacu.org/imis/AACUR.

Kuh, George D., Laura M. Gambino, Marilee Bresciani, and Ken O'Donnell. "Using ePortfolio to Document and Deepen the Impact of HIPs on Learning Dispositions." Occasional Paper No. 32. Urbana, IL: University of Illinois and Indiana University, National Institute for Learning Outcomes Assessment (NILOA), 2018. http://learningoutcomesassessment.org/occasionalpaper thirtytwo.html.

Lucas, Colleen, and Theresa Kline. "Understanding the Influence of Organizational Culture and Group Dynamics on Organization Change and Learning." *The Learning Organization*, 15, no. 3 (2008): 277–87. https://doi.org/10.1108 /09696470810868882.

Lunenburg, Fred. C. "Managing Change: The Role of the Change Agent." *International Journal of Management, Business, and Administration* 13, no. 1 (2010): 1–6. https://naaee.org/sites/default/files/lunenburg_fred_c._managing_change _the_role_of_change_agent_ijmba_v13_n1_2010.pdf.

National Association of Colleges and Employers. "Career Readiness: Competencies for a Career Ready Workforce." Revised March 2021. https://www .naceweb.org/uploadedfiles/files/2021/resources/nace-career-readiness -competencies-revised-apr-2021.pdf.

National Association of Colleges and Employers. "Job Outlook 2019." 2018. https:// www.odu.edu/content/dam/odu/offices/cmc/docs/nace/2019-nace-job -outlook-survey.pdf.

National Center for Educational Statistics. "College Navigator—Central State University." https://nces.ed.gov/collegenavigator/?q=Central+State+University &s=all&id=201690-finaid.

Newell, William. "A Theory of Interdisciplinary Studies." *Issues in Integrative Studies* 19 (2001): 1–25. https://our.oakland.edu/handle/10323/4378.

Pinnell, Margaret, M. Suzanne Franco, Leanne Petry, Ahsan Mian, Brett Doudican, and Raghavan Srinivasan. "Leveraging Regional Strengths for STEM Teacher Professional Development: Results from an NSF RET Program Focused on Advanced Manufacturing and Materials." *Research in the Schools* 25, no. 1 (2018): 20–34.

Schimdt, Benjamin. "The Humanities Are in Crisis." *The Atlantic* August 23, 2018, https://www.theatlantic.com/ideas/archive/2018/08/the-humanities-face -a-crisisof-confidence/567565/.

Skorton, David, and Ashley Bear, eds. *The Integration of the Humanities and Arts with Science, Engineering, and Medicine in Higher Education: Branches from the Same Tree.* Washington, DC: The National Academies Press, 2018. https://doi .org/10.17226/24988.

Strauss, Valerie. "The Surprising Thing Google Learned about Its Employees—and What It Means for Today's Students." *The Washington Post*, April 5, 2019. https://www.washingtonpost.com/news/answer-sheet/wp/2017/12/20/the -surprising-thing-google-learned-about-its-employees-and-what-it-means -for-todays-students/.

PART 3

Leadership, Equity, and Social Justice

8

LEADING WHILE YOUNG, BLACK, AND ON THE TENURE TRACK

CHYNA N. CRAWFORD

While the numbers of students and faculty of color in US higher education are increasing, minorities are still significantly underrepresented in senior-level leadership, based on data reported by the US Department of Education.[1] According to the National Center for Education Statistics of the US Department of Education, Black women account for fewer than 3 percent of administrative/tenured faculty positions.[2] African American professors in the United States frequently face barriers that limit their capacity to advance in the academic hierarchy. The tendency of African American teachers to be overburdened with teaching and service commitments, as well as the inflexible expectations of universities and colleges about research and publication, are two major roadblocks.[3] Many African American academics begin their careers in universities that prioritize teaching over scholarship, resulting in heavy teaching loads and few possibilities for research and publishing. As a result, they rarely publish a large body of work and remain outside the academic mainstream for the duration of their careers.[4]

African American women live in a society that devalues both their sex and their race.[5]

Because of the contradictory messages they frequently get, African Americans in higher education, particularly women, are generally unable to anticipate whether their hard work is appreciated or condemned by their colleagues and administrations.[6] This presents an inherent contradiction in the ability to ascribe genuine meaning to situations or anticipate consequences based on past experiences. Differential standards imposed upon African Americans about the same action may be the source of contradictory communications, which is kin to subtle racism.[7] Divergent expectations do a lot of harm to faculty since they may believe that their work is indeed not truly satisfactory, despite good feedback from those in leadership.

Black female faculty, and often administrators, are placed at a unique disadvantage of having to navigate their race, as well as their gender.[8] There is a decrease in Black female faculty entering higher education, and of those hired, they are not being retained, promoted, and tenured.[9] There is a breadth of literature on the experiences of African American females in higher education. However, few researchers address the issues that may occur for tenure-track faculty who are appointed to leadership roles before they are awarded tenure. Faculty who exercise this option often do so at great peril. They may frequently be afraid to discuss their scholarship, struggles, or areas where they need guidance, and they may need to create partnerships with senior faculty to dodge opposition and safeguard themselves. My goal in this chapter is to discuss what I believe are the challenges and rewards of being a Black woman in a leadership role while on tenure track, including my personal experiences, as well as how integral the role of mentorship is for those leading while in pursuit of tenure.

EXPERIENCES OF A YOUNG BLACK TENURE-TRACK LEADER

My educational experiences cultivated my belief that Black female educators are important to the development of Black students in our colleges and universities. It is important as Black female faculty to be able to see that it is possible. If there are few to no Black faculty, no female faculty, and no Black female representation in the faculty, it may be difficult for Black students, both male and female, to visualize the possibilities for themselves.

I was raised in a single-parent home where education was stressed, and going to college was the only option. The undergraduate institution I attended is a regional Predominantly White Institution (PWI). My time as a student at this institution was fraught with various challenges, from the immense feelings of homesickness, and the lack of peer support, to the perceived lack of faculty support. As an undergraduate student, I felt alone. Faculty and staff at PWIs are often unaware of the unique emotional problems that Black women experience.[10] Microaggressions are experienced by both Black male and female students at PWIs, such as being picked out by security staff, being academically dismissed, or being viewed as indistinguishable from other Black individuals.[11] All of these are incidents that I experienced. It wasn't until I began to excel academically, that faculty at my institution began to offer more advice and assistance. Early on, it felt like faculty were willing to let me fail before offering any support. To me, no one cared enough to reach out until they deemed me worthy of the effort.

Mentoring is critical for Black women pursuing degrees to succeed, whether at the undergraduate or graduate level. Unfortunately, mentors who provide formal mentorship for Black women graduate students at PWIs are few and far between. As a result, I found myself seeking assistance and direction from informal mentors such as colleagues, other older students, and relatives. My sisters on campus were a huge source of emotional support and companionship. My other mothers have offered spiritual counsel as well as polite reprimands. My family has assured me that they are only a phone call away, even though I may have been miles away.

My academic background is very similar to Rachel N. Bonaparte-Hagos's.[12] By the age of 29, I had earned two graduate degrees (and a host of graduate credits in counseling, education, and other areas that interested me) and had discovered my place in, and love for, higher education. I was on the job market for about two years prior to graduation in preparation for landing a tenure-track position. I was always aware that the odds were not in my favor and that the recruiting process was far from equitable.

Upon taking my first tenure-track position at a small regional HBCU (historically Black college or university), it was my initial goal to be observant, learn the university structure and institutional culture, and figure out what I needed to do to be successful in this environment. Unfortunately, or fortunately, university administration recognized that I had a certain set of skills: organization, planning, the ability to be forward-thinking, and not only manage tasks but also problem solve when needed. By my second year on tenure track, I was appointed director of summer school, which was before I had reached the age of thirty. I was named assistant department chair the spring before my thirty-first birthday and interim department chair by thirty-two. These administrative changes progressed logically, but at an accelerated pace, which drew the ire of many of my colleagues who believed that there was something wrong with these appointments.

As an untenured chair, I was reminded of a harsh truth in higher education: many professors and staff struggle to navigate their jobs due to a lack of mentorship and openness. Learning the atmosphere and culture of my department was tough my first year. Faculty members who had been at the present institution for five, ten, or fifteen years or more, in my opinion, had absorbed the politics of their institutions and departments and forgotten how bizarre they may appear to a new set of eyes.

For me, it was easy to mistrust my own worth as an early career academic and the value I brought to my position as an individual. I attempted to surround myself with accomplished peers and worked to close the perceived gap in knowledge and experience by filling it with activities that I believed would get recognized by my peers at my home institution, while also alleviating symptoms of impostor syndrome. Though this strategy worked in the short term, it stretched my resources thin over a variety of unrelated disciplines, delaying my ability to establish myself as the go-to expert in a certain sector.

HURDLES TO PROMOTION AND ELEVATION AS A BLACK WOMAN

The outlook for minorities, and Black women specifically, in the academy is bleak.[13] The absence of Black women in tenured professor jobs is a symptom of a far larger systemic breakdown in independent educational institutions. The "pipeline" that leads PhDs to tenure-track jobs is frequently cited as a source of underrepresentation. There is undoubtedly a "crack" in the pipeline for Black women.

African American academics are frequently burdened with a disproportionate amount of advising responsibilities. Officially, all faculty members' advising assignments are the same, regardless of race/ethnicity or gender. Many African American faculty members, on the other hand, find themselves in situations where students' expectations complicate matters. In my experience, there is a lot of informal and unofficial mentoring, as students expect to be supported by their faculty of color when their assigned mentors don't get it or are less approachable. These additional advisory responsibilities can be time and energy consuming, detracting from research and writing. Mentoring, in particular, is a vital activity that most academics practice in some way.[14] Due to a shared feeling of responsibility to their students, many African American faculty members choose to mentor many more students than their White counterparts. Given the history of racial and ethnic inequity in the United States, most African American professors feel bound to embrace this role. Time constraints can be significant once again (e.g., giving social support and assistance to students, producing letters of recommendation, assisting with graduate or professional school selection, and analyzing several versions of employment, grant, and scholarship applications).[15]

Black professors may also be overloaded by departmental, institutional, and community committee responsibilities. In addition to standard committee meetings, African American faculty members are expected to serve on working groups that address minority issues, campus safety, race inequality, recruiting and selection of faculty and students of color, academic relations, and community engagement by their leaderships, faculty, colleagues, students, and sometimes civic leaders. In such situations, higher education academic staff are acutely aware of their responsibilities to their departments, the institution, students, and larger communities. However, they inevitably do so at the expense of curtailing their efforts in other areas.[16]

In addition to the heavy scholarly and advising load, Black faculty are often seen as spokespersons for the Black community in some situations. And, as a result of our country's racial turmoil, it is more widespread than ever. We, as Black Americans, often spend time with people who look like us and develop good friendships with them. I've also encountered instances where instructors inquired about Black conduct to acquire a better understanding of student behavior. I share my viewpoint, provide advice where appropriate, and pose questions. However, because being Black is not a one-size-fits-all experience, I occasionally get it wrong. Being Black means being a part of a complex, multifaceted, and vibrant culture.

As a faculty member, the onus is on you. You must have developed the internal mechanisms and the time to dedicate to scholarship. For women of color, this is often overshadowed by family obligations and the perceived inability to say no to additional workloads that take away from scholarly endeavors. In my case, no matter how well I did, I always felt that I wasn't good enough for the rarefied publishing world. I didn't come from a pedigree; I was just a hard-working Black woman. I felt (and sometimes literally was) unacknowledged in the hallways, and my voice was hardly heard. It wasn't unusual that ideas I presented at meetings got a lukewarm reception, but two meetings later, someone else suggested a similar thought, which was instantly deemed a must-write story. Even though I knew I could do the work, I was riddled with doubt. It was years later that I learned there was a term for what I felt: impostor syndrome. But lack of physical representation is just one of the factors that feed into impostor syndrome.

The struggle for tenure for Black women is about more than just diversity for the sake of diversity. In a White-dominated atmosphere, learning from faculty who share their perspectives promotes the sense that they, too, have significant information to give. In some cases, women of color, especially in a new job or embarking on a career change, temporarily experience symptoms of impostor syndrome. However, if these feelings linger, they can negatively impact job performance. This can spur a self-fulfilling prophecy, externally confirming feelings of self-doubt. In my experiences as a young tenure-track faculty member, I have been name-called and treated as if I did not possess the same levels of knowledge that other tenured faculty may have. It was because of these feelings of being an impostor, and ultimately feelings of inadequacy, that I felt the need to branch out in other areas to show my tenured colleagues that I, too, was capable and worthy of being in the same spaces. It was at this stage that I began to increase my service (I became advisor to two student-led organizations) and look at other leadership roles within the department, namely offering my assistance to an obviously overwhelmed department chair.

Finding methods for leadership to count as institutional service is one of the most important techniques for supporting academics in seeking leadership possibilities. It would be exceedingly difficult to engage as a leader while still fulfilling service obligations by working on appointed committees during the pretenure years. Personally, I discovered creative methods to credit leadership toward tenure and promotion. While it may seem natural to substitute leadership for service, as department chair, I went even further, replacing leadership for teaching. With 50 percent of released time now being utilized for administrative responsibilities, this leadership has taken over the time which would ordinarily be attributed to teaching. Finally, such innovative approaches to promoting faculty leadership benefit both the institution and the individual faculty member and they solve some of the issues raised by the tenure system. In my position, it was easy to utilize my leadership position to advance my teaching. By implementing workshops on effective teaching and including professional development and conference attendance all related to the operation and success of summer school, I was able to duly focus and apply what was learned in one capacity (summer school) in another capacity (regular academic teaching). So, although my teaching load has been reduced from four courses per semester to two courses per semester, I'm able to apply new and inventive teaching techniques to those two new courses, making up for a reduced teaching load.

Trying to exert leadership on campus, especially for pretenure professors, may be highly risky. People may doubt your ability and talents as a result of a poor leadership attempt. Successful faculty leaders frequently hone their skills in low-stakes situations before attempting to lead an effort on campus once they are more confident. For Black female faculty, taking on additional leadership and administrative roles can backfire. Black female faculty are usually the only persons or women of color in their departments, which results in them being solicited to be the on-campus spokesperson for minorities and the advisor for minority students.[17] In many arenas, these faculty may be the *first*. Many students, instructors, and colleagues have never had a Black teacher, colleague, or school leader, and that comes with a lot of responsibility. Students who come from minority households, underrepresented populations, or first-time college attendees

need much more guidance, understanding, and support. All of these require more diverse and available mentoring opportunities not only for students but also for the faculty who are there to support the students. There
should be a group of minority collectives at every institution. These additional responsibilities accompany being a successful Black professor, and
often spare time for other pursuits isn't necessarily as structured.

Entering department leadership marked perhaps the profoundest transition in my academic career. It is the point at which the job description
changed from areas, such as research and teaching, in which my peers were
very quick to point out to me that they had years of training and practice, into an area where I had little to no prior experience and expertise
in higher education leadership. However, I believe my training in the social sciences allowed me to be successful. The social sciences shape leaders
who treat the members of their teams as adults capable of handling statistics (given in an understandable manner), comprehending the signifi-
cance of their decisions, and taking control of their lives. As head of a department, it is possible to keep your finger on the pulse simply by engaging
in casual conversations with staff and students in the hallways. This allowed me to maintain a regular schedule of encounters with groups from
within the university, and this gave me time to consult with one group or
another and to truly understand the culture and how the institution functioned. In my quest to understand the culture of the university, I sought
out many voices. These individuals ultimately became mentors in a sense
and helped to guide me through the process.

MENTORS, MENTEES, AND
GUIDANCE WHILE LEADING

For many women of color in the academy, the establishment of mentoring relationships is minimal at best.[18] Those who have mentors often go beyond their academic area to find such support. There is a direct
link between mentoring African American women in academia and their
achievement in higher education.[19] One of the key benefits of mentoring is professional progression and mobility.[20] African American women
can benefit immensely from mentoring and modeling because they can

observe someone, preferably a person their age, and of similar racial background, who is still striving to make it and is succeeding in this endeavor.
This enables a young faculty member or emerging leader to increase their
self-efficacy by demonstrating that if their mentor can succeed, so can
they.[21] Many African American women in leadership believe that their potential was not developed through mentoring relationships, but rather they
were equipped with knowledge and skills, and that their individual higher
education institutions had not capitalized on their potential. And, while
there is clear evidence that mentoring is beneficial to African American
women's success in gaining leadership positions, there are hurdles to the
number of mentors accessible to match the need for this relational technique among African American women.[22]

African American female administrators have been especially vulnerable in this within the academy due to a lack of sensitivity toward minorities
on most university campuses. Mentoring isn't available to these women
as a means of improving job satisfaction and progress. If academic leaders offer the direction and resources necessary to launch and sustain these
changes, a supportive climate for mentoring will emerge, which is an important component of the initiative to improve overall institutional diversity. Mentoring cannot be dictated or regulated; it must be individually
valued and embraced. The academy can use this resource to support the
development of African American female administrators if they choose
to participate in a mentoring program. Mentoring would increase the role
and responsibility and awareness of African American female administrators, as well as inspire young African Americans to pursue higher education as a vocation. Mentoring would, in the end, not only transform their
perspectives but also help to shift the whole power structure. Mentoring
relationships with female academics and advisors can help to ease feelings
of exclusion, especially in male-dominated fields where it might be difficult for postgraduate women to find mentors.[23]

Aside from supporting growth and other psychosocial benefits, one of
the most significant advantages of mentoring is job advancement.[24] In addition, recent degree holders said they experienced more mentoring that
benefited them in their professions rather than emotional or advisory support. Lori Patton outlines a wide range of topics related to mentorship

and African American women.[25] When individuals in the academy have a high level of value, they are less likely to let harsh comments, racism, or sexism affect their good projected outcome.[26] These qualities can be reinforced by healthy mentoring relations.

Ultimately, having a mentor does not promise that all professional goals will be met, but it is crucial in maintaining and establishing that the mentee is socially conditioned into the institution's implicit and explicit rules and processes.[27] As a new tenure-track faculty member in a very interdisciplinary department composed of history, political science, criminal justice, sociology, and social work, the faculty available to me had varied interests and different mentoring styles. Early on, prior to connecting with my dean, I sought out mentors from various disciplines and was denied for various reasons. Many gave excuses such as time constraints or even noted that research and scholarship across disciplines aren't fruitful (an elitist misconception), and often, no reason was given. These dead ends forced me to find other opportunities to be successful, and other people from whom to seek guidance.

For me, the intersection of mentoring and its importance in my life has come to the surface in the last two years. As a young untenured leader, I was at a crossroads. I did not know whether I could successfully apply for and attain tenure due to the amount of service and time I had spent in my leadership roles. It was at that time that two people showed up for me: the first, an associate professor and longtime colleague within the field, and the second, a full professor within my school and coincidentally my dean, who gave me a set of guidelines and advice to follow. She unofficially became my mentor, whether she realized it or not. Her guidelines were relatively simple and shifted the responsibility to me. As a young faculty member with limited experiences outside of the institution at which I was seeking tenure, her advice and experiences at various institutions (public, private, HBCU, PWI) were tremendously helpful.

Part of this important and necessary mentoring work involved learning to set boundaries between work tasks and making time for self-care and other personal activities. At this stage of my career, and having gone through a period of absolute burnout, I still struggle with saying no. To ensure that I aim for a balanced and happy life (not simply survival), I have a useful set of techniques for me to manage work and enjoy life—and vice versa. I now include time in my weekly calendar for the critical research tasks that I all-too-often neglect when other priorities seem more pressing. I also set aside weekends and after-hours time as work-free time. I need to squeeze everything into the remaining hours. When I receive a request or an invitation, I ask myself certain questions and then take the appropriate actions. I've been doing a lot of expectation management in addition to putting this framework in place. The biggest step and most important for me is that I have created a "No Committee." This committee consists of my two best gal pals (one of whom is in K–12, the other who works in law), my mother, my sisters, my mentor, and my significant other. Their credentials are that they care for me, that they are familiar with the academy, and that they keep track of me so that they know how much is too much for me to bear.

Self-care has become a term in recent years, raising awareness of how important it is to practice. Despite the reality that it is acknowledged as vital by leaders, it is not often given the emphasis it needs, instead receiving only scant attention. Self-care isn't simply for recovering from illness or a disaster; it's also proactive and preventive. It's a method to not just value and love yourself but also to show others that you care about putting your best foot forward for others, both personally and professionally. Self-care is a technique of resilience that helps us get through the tough moments by sustaining our energy and enthusiasm to keep going through life successfully.

I want to emphasize that my advice is based on my experience as an established early career teacher and scholar at a small regional HBCU who has transitioned successfully to leadership and tenure. I aim not to dismiss the experiences of other people at various stages of their careers and/or backgrounds, and I would be interested to hear about others' experiences with leadership, mentoring, and saying no and how it has impacted the way they operate. I also see the hypocrisy of urging academics to take on additional mentoring work, seek out mentors, and lead while simultaneously turning down some committee work for self-care and writing outside of working hours. My colleagues' achievements, on the other hand, are very significant to me. I value academic well-being and want African

American women to be successful in academia. I recognize the efforts we make to help our students, colleagues, and many others succeed—but we can only accomplish this achievement if we do not neglect our own.

NOTES

1. US Department of Education, "Advancing Diversity and Inclusion in Higher Education," Office of Planning, Evaluation and Policy Development and Office of the Under Secretary, 2016, 1–89, https://www2.ed.gov/rschstat/research/pubs/advancing-diversity-inclusion.pdf.

2. National Center for Education Statistics, "Characteristics of Postsecondary Faculty," Condition of Education, 2022, U.S. Department of Education, Institute of Education Sciences, accessed May 30, 2022, https://nces.ed.gov/programs/coe/indicator/csc.

3. Allen, Walter R., Edgar G. Epps, Elizabeth A. Guillory, Susan A. Suh, and Marguerite Bonous-Hammarth, "The Black Academic: Faculty Status Among African Americans in US Higher Education," *Journal of Negro Education* (2000): 112–27.

4. Allen et al., "The Black Academic," 112–27.

5. Claire Alexander, *Aiming Higher: Race, Inequality and Diversity in the Academy* (London: Runnymede Trust, 2015), http://www.runnymedetrust.org/uploads/Aiming%20Higher.pdf.

6. Gail Hackett and Angela M. Byars, "Social Cognitive Theory and the Career Development of African American Women," *Career Development Quarterly* 44, no. 4 (1996): 322–40, https://onlinelibrary.wiley.com/doi/pdf/10.1002/j.2161-0045.1996.tb00449.x.

7. Hackett and Byars, "Social Cognitive Theory," 322–40.

8. Nivischi N. Edwards, Monifa Green Beverly, and Mia Alexander-Snow, "Troubling Success: Interviews with Black Female Faculty," *Florida Journal of Educational Administration & Policy* 5, no. 1 (2011): 14–27.

9. Zawadi Rucks-Ahidiana, "The Systemic Scarcity of Tenured Black Women," *Inside Higher Ed*, July 16, 2021, https://www.insidehighered.com/advice/2021/07/16/black-women-face-many-obstacles-their-efforts-win-tenure-opinion.

10. Christine R. Hannon, Marianne Woodside, Brittany L. Pollard, and Jorge Roman, "The Meaning of African American College Women's Experiences

Attending a Predominantly White Institution: A Phenomenological Study," *Journal of College Student Development* 57, no. 6 (2016): 652–66, https://muse.jhu.edu/article/629810.

11. Elan C. Hope, Micere Keels, and Myles I. Durkee, "Participation in Black Lives Matter and Deferred Action for Childhood Arrivals: Modern Activism Among Black and Latino College Students," *Journal of Diversity in Higher Education* 9, no. 3 (2016): 203, https://files.eric.ed.gov/fulltext/EJ961223.pdf.

12. Rachel N. Bonaparte-Hagos, "Young, Black, Female, and Moving into Campus Leadership," *The Chronicle of Higher Education*, June 30, 2021, https://www.chronicle.com/article/young-black-female-and-moving-into-campus-leadership?cid=gen_sign_in.

13. Rucks-Ahidiana, "The Systemic Scarcity of Tenured Black Women."

14. Allen et al., "The Black Academic," 112–27.

15. Allen et al., 112–27.

16. Allen et al., 112–27.

17. Caroline Sotello Viernes Turner, "Women of Color in Academe: Living with Multiple Marginality," *Journal of Higher Education* 73, no. 1 (2002): 74–93, http://www.jstor.org/stable/1558448.

18. Gloria D. Thomas and Carol Hollenshead, "Resisting from the Margins: The Coping Strategies of Black Women and Other Women of Color Faculty Members at a Research University," *Journal of Negro Education* (2001): 166–75, https://doi.org/10.2307/3211208.

19. Sharon L. Holmes, Lynette Danley Land, and Veronica D. Hinton-Hudson. "Race Still Matters: Considerations for Mentoring Black Women in Academe," *Negro Educational Review* 58, no. 1/2 (2007): 105, https://ecsu1891.idm.oclc.org/login?url=https://www.proquest.com/scholarly-journals/race-still-matters-considerations-mentoring-black/docview/218980397/se-2?accountid=10717.

20. Holmes, Land, and Hinton-Hudson, "Race Still Matters," 105–31.

21. Hackett and Byars, "Social Cognitive Theory," 322–40.

22. Kijana Crawford and Danielle Smith, "The We and the Us: Mentoring African American Women," *Journal of Black Studies* 36, no. 1 (2005.): 52–67, https://www.jstor.org/stable/40027321.

23. Lori D. Patton, "My Sister's Keeper: A Qualitative Examination of Mentoring Experiences Among African American Women in Graduate and Professional

Schools," *Journal of Higher Education* 80, no. 5 (2009), https://doi.org/10.1080/00221546.2009.11779030.

24. Patton, "My Sister's Keeper," 510–37. Patton notes the experiences of recently minted African American PhD recipients in the discipline of sociology were researched and the authors concluded that the vast majority of those surveyed had experienced mentoring. Mentoring opportunities are few and far between when it comes to African American women because this community is underrepresented in educational disciplines. As a result, African American women frequently seek mentoring connections outside of academia through social interactions. Outside mentorship relationships tend to improve African American women's psychosocial development. Black women who create mentoring and support networks reap career rewards and tend to be more willing to serve as mentors to others.

25. Patton, 510–37.

26. Hackett and Byars, "Social Cognitive Theory," 322–40.

27. Crawford and Smith, "The We and the Us," 52–67.

BIBLIOGRAPHY

Adserias, Ryan P., LaVar J. Charleston, and Jerlando F.L. Jackson. "What Style of Leadership Is Best Suited to Direct Organizational Change to Fuel Institutional Diversity in Higher Education?" *Race Ethnicity and Education* 20, no. 3 (2017): 315–31.

Alexander, Claire E., and Jason Arday. *Aiming Higher: Race, Inequality and Diversity in the Academy.* London: Runnymede, 2015.

Allen, Walter R., Edgar G. Epps, Elizabeth A. Guillory, Susan A. Suh, and Marguerite Bonous-Hammarth. "The Black Academic: Faculty Status Among African Americans in U.S. Higher Education." *Journal of Negro Education* 69, no. 1/2 (2000): 112–27. https://www.jstor.org/stable/2696268.

Arday, Jason. "Understanding Race and Educational Leadership in Higher Education: Exploring the Black and Ethnic Minority (BME) Experience." *Management in Education* 32, no. 4 (2018): 192–200. https://doi.org/10.1177/0892020618791002.

Attell, Brandon K., Kiersten Kummerow Brown, and Linda A. Treiber. "Workplace Bullying, Perceived Job Stressors, and Psychological Distress: Gender and Race Differences in the Stress Process." *Social Science Research* 65 (2017): 210–21.

Bonaparte-Hagos, R. N. "Young, Black, Female, and Moving into Campus Leadership." *The Chronicle of Higher Education*, June 30, 2021. https://www.chronicle.com/article/young-black-female-and-moving-into-campus-leadership?cid=gen_sign_in.

Brown, Michael T. "The Career Development of African Americans: Theoretical and Empirical Issues." *Career Development and Vocational Behavior of Racial and Ethnic Minorities* (1995): 7–36.

Crawford, Kijana, and Danielle Smith. "The We and the Us: Mentoring African American Women." *Journal of Black Studies* 36, no. 1 (2005): 52–67.

de Brey, Cristobal, Lauren Musu, Joel McFarland, Sidney Wilkinson-Flicker, Melissa Diliberti, Anlan Zhang, Claire Branstetter, and Xiaolei Wang. "Status and Trends in the Education of Racial and Ethnic Groups 2018. NCES 2019-038." *National Center for Education Statistics* (2019). https://nces.ed.gov/pubs2019/2019038.pdf.

Edwards, Nivischi N., Monifa Green Beverly, and Mia Alexander-Snow. "Troubling Success: Interviews with Black Female Faculty." *Florida Journal of Educational Administration & Policy* 5, no. 1 (2011): 14–27.

Hackett, Gail, and Angela M. Byars. "Social Cognitive Theory and the Career Development of African American Women." *The Career Development Quarterly* 44, no. 4 (1996): 322–40. https://onlinelibrary.wiley.com/doi/pdf/10.1002/j.2161-0045.1996.tb00449.x.

Hannon, Christine R., Marianne Woodside, Brittany L. Pollard, and Jorge Roman, "The Meaning of African American College Women's Experiences Attending a Predominantly White Institution: A Phenomenological Study," *Journal of College Student Development* 57, no. 6 (2016): 652–66. https://muse.jhu.edu/article/629810.

Holmes, Sharon L., Danley Land Lynette, and Veronica Hinton-Hudson. "Race Still Matters: Considerations for Mentoring Black Women in Academe." *Negro Educational Review* 58, no. 1 (2007): 105–31. https://ecsu1891.idm.oclc.org login?url=https://www.proquest.com/scholarly-journals/race-still-matters-considerations-mentoring-black/docview/218980397/se-2?accountid=10717.

Hope, Elan C., Micere Keels, and Myles I. Durkee. "Participation in Black Lives Matter and Deferred Action for Childhood Arrivals: Modern Activism

Among Black and Latino College Students." *Journal of Diversity in Higher Education* 9, no. 3 (2016): 203–15.

Kelly, Bridget Turner, Joy Gaston Gayles, and Cobretti D. Williams. "Recruitment Without Retention: A Critical Case of Black Faculty Unrest." *Journal of Negro Education* 86, no. 3 (2021): 305–17.

National Center for Education Statistics. "Characteristics of Postsecondary Faculty." *Condition of Education*, 2022. U.S. Department of Education, Institute of Education Sciences. https://nces.ed.gov/programs/coe/indicator/csc.

Ogbu, John U. "Minority Coping Responses and School Experience." *The Journal of Psychohistory* 18, no. 4 (1991): 433–56.

Patton, Lori D. "'My Sister's Keeper': A Qualitative Examination of Mentoring Experiences Among African American Women in Graduate and Professional Schools." *The Journal of Higher Education* 80, no. 5 (2009): 510–37.

Perna, Laura W., Danette Gerald, Evan Baum, and Jeffrey Milem. "The Status of Equity for Black Faculty and Administrators in Public Higher Education in the South." *Research in Higher Education* 48, no. 2 (2007): 193–228.

Rucks-Ahidiana, Zawadi. "The Inequities of the Tenure-Track System." *Inside Higher Ed*, June 7, 2019. https://www.insidehighered.com/advice/2019/06/07/nonwhite-faculty-face-significant-disadvantages-tenure-track-opinion.

Rucks-Ahidiana, Zawadi. "The Systemic Scarcity of Tenured Black Women." *Inside Higher Ed*, July 16, 2021. https://www.insidehighered.com/advice/2021/07/16/black-women-face-many-obstacles-their-efforts-win-tenure-opinion.

Thomas, Gloria D., and Carol Hollenshead. "Resisting from the Margins: The Coping Strategies of Black Women and Other Women of Color Faculty Members at a Research University." *Journal of Negro Education* (2001): 166–75.

Turner, Caroline Sotello Viernes. "Women of Color in Academe: Living with Multiple Marginality." *The Journal of Higher Education* 73, no. 1 (2002): 74–93. http://www.jstor.org/stable/1558448.

US Department of Education. "Advancing Diversity and Inclusion in Higher Education." Office of Planning, Evaluation and Policy Development and Office of the Under Secretary, 2016. https://www2.ed.gov/rschstat/research/pubs/advancing-diversity-inclusion.pdf.

Walkington, Lori. "How Far Have We Really Come? Black Women Faculty and Graduate Students' Experiences in Higher Education." *Humboldt Journal of Social Relations* 39 (2017): 51–65. http://www.jstor.org/stable/90007871.

Williams, Damon A. *Strategic Diversity Leadership: Activating Change and Transformation in Higher Education.* Sterling, VA: Stylus Publishing, LLC, 2013.

Whitford, Emma. "'There Are So Few That Have Made Their Way.'" *Inside Higher Ed*, October 28, 2021, https://www.insidehighered.com/news/2020/10/28/black-administrators-are-too-rare-top-ranks-higher-education-it's-not-just-pipeline.

Wood, J. Luke. "5 Ways to Make a Real Improvement in Hiring Black Professors." *The Chronicle of Higher Education*, September 7, 2021. https://www.chronicle.com/article/5-ways-to-make-a-real-improvement-in-hiring-black-professors?cid2=gen_login_refresh&cid=gen_sign_in.

9

LEADING THROUGH PRECARITY

A Tale of (Un)Sustainable Professional Advancement

KRISTINA QUYNN

> *In nova fert animus mutatas dicere formas / corpora.*
> I intend to speak of forms changed into new entities.
>
> OVID, *METAMORPHOSES*[1]

OVID'S TALES OF *METAMORPHOSES* (AD 8) REMIND US THAT OUR PURSUITS RARELY TURN OUT as we plan: our lover may turn into a tree to escape our affections; our true love may become so enamored with their own reflection they cannot see or value us; our magnificently carved stone statues may turn flesh-and-blood, only to expose the limitations of our own imaginations. While the affections and skirmishes between gods, demigods, and humans may seem eons away from the professional relationships and work routines that make up our lives as leaders in higher education, all of us have either experienced or witnessed capricious academic job searches, dismissive or narcissistic colleagues and administrators, and our own inability to affect widespread equitable systemic change.

The most epic battle of all in the humanities, however, has been the most commonplace: the erosion of tenure and the corresponding rise of contingency and job insecurity, affecting generations of faculty and leadership. We might expect a story about the rise of precarity in the humanities to open with explanations of decreased funding for higher education. It would start in the 1970s and feature a brilliant but neurotic academic who had more book sense than street sense but who, thank goodness, seemed to make sense in the college classroom. As the twentieth century passed, the tale would change dramatically to feature throngs of hapless faculty (mostly English and philosophy instructors) who would be pitted against tone-deaf, self-serving administrators—leaders who had long abandoned noble educational causes to manage shrinking budgets as well as the throngs. But this is not that story. Well, not exactly, anyway.

What follows are my tales of fortuitous professional success in the humanities. Altogether, these tales tell of recurring bouts of contingency as an English instructor, the founding director of a writing program at an R1 university, and now an associate professor and associate dean. They afford us a moment to reflect on the oft-hidden (or ignored) and ultimately toxic effects of contingency on leadership in the liberal arts and humanities. Just as we glean lessons from Ovid's tales of transformation, my intention is to share lessons for current and prospective leaders. My hope is that they inspire us to make decisions and enact changes that usher forth greater job security and professional belongingness for all within the humanities. Our transformation is ongoing.

TRANSFORMING LESSON #1:
The stories we tell about the humanities matter.

I have written elsewhere about the *adjunctroman*—narratives of contingency in the academic novel—about the abject characterization of contingent laborers and about the nonprogressing nature of such tales.[2] Suffice it to say, contingency makes for abject protagonists and off-putting stories. For both an employer practice and a narrative figuration, contingency tends to enact motion without progress. Laborers cycle through their appointments and the stories we craft about such lives go nowhere. Of course, we know some temporary faculty do not wish for the security of tenure or have partners who support their teaching habit, but they are the minority.

For most of us, contingency is painful and restrictive. Contingency is a mode of oppression. It keeps us spinning in our place with the effect of scholarly atrophy. Hamster wheels, treadmills, assembly lines, freeway flying—these are common metaphors for the nonprogressing nature of the experience for many of us who teach and, if we are lucky enough, who lead while adjunct. More than a figuration of career drudgery and insecurity in the humanities, these metaphors remind us that contingent employment bars access to the conventional avenues of promotion and advancement in colleges and universities.

I know contingency well. My career has been built on the shifting sands of renewable contracts and, until recently, low-paid employment. From 1998 to 2002, I started as an adjunct instructor of English with a master's degree, teaching full time (36 credit hours per year) at a community college for less than $18,000 with no benefits. As you might expect, during this time I experienced job, food, and housing insecurity. This is an all too familiar tale about "career-building" in the humanities these days. In 2014, my account of selling plasma twice a week to pay for daycare for my daughter was quoted before the US House Education and Workforce Committee. My account was subsequently reported by the American Association of University Professors (AAUP) and referenced in Kevin Birmingham's 2017 Truman Capote Award acceptance speech that was published in the *Chronicle of Higher Education*.[3]

Until now, the identity of that adjunct has remained anonymous—just one of the nameless, shamed, and ever-growing number of contingent faculty in the United States. Here, I share with you: I was the woman who sold her plasma on Tuesdays and Thursdays to pay for her daughter's daycare while teaching English on overload and advising students with disabilities at a community college. By 2012, I had returned to graduate school and earned a doctorate, but eventually, I was once again teaching adjunct—this time at a Carnegie 1 Research Institution (R1) and, this time, with a yearly contract just above the poverty line. Just above.

Where can this story go from here? In my experience, telling our tales of drudgery and woe has done little to foster substantive change or to convey the valuable work we do as teachers, scholars, and leaders in the humanities. Recognizing our expertise and valuing our labor can offer an alternative perspective and conscientious path to a better tale. Broadcasting the nature and importance of the humanities clearly and compellingly beyond the humanities is crucial. And, most importantly, we must seek out and listen to our cross-campus colleagues so that we might better understand the effects of contingency on our campuses. So armed, we can review institutional policies and practices with an openness to traverse the conventional binaries that construct tales of drudgery and woe. Us/them, leader/follower, professor/adjunct—such divisions inform our conventional tales of contingency but do little to reflect its realities.

Since 2017, I have been part of the Colorado Wyoming Network of Women Leaders, a regional branch of the American Council on Education (ACE). Twice I have directed their flagship training program for women leaders, the Academic Management Institute (AMI). Over an academic year, we bring together more than fifty leaders for six all-day trainings. We discuss ACE's models of "Shared Leadership" and "Shared Equity Leadership," which provide essential leadership frameworks and researched strategies about the value of listening to connect with our colleagues and of bringing other voices forward as we make decisions. ACE defines shared leadership "as moving away from the leader/follower binary; capitalizing on the importance of leaders throughout the organization, not just those in positions of authority, and creating an infrastructure so that organizations can benefit from the leadership of multiple people."[4] The most powerful element of the AMI training program is not the curriculum, however. The power resides in the repeated bringing together a cohort of leaders from different colleges, divisions, ranks, titles, backgrounds, and interests who can talk with one another, listen to one another's stories of professional growth and becoming, and practice leadership anew.

For those of us who lead in the humanities, it may help to recognize that contingency is an equity issue on many of our campuses. On our respective campuses—you and I—we must pause, connect, and listen. We must recognize that some of our contingent and underrepresented colleagues may be especially hard to hear. We listen the best we can, and then we step forward to create new opportunities together. This sounds aspirational but, in reality, such cocreating manifests through hours of email, spreadsheets, meetings, and code changes. Ultimately, to shift the tales of contingency from drudgery to collective progress means that we openly acknowledge (rather than turn away from) the pernicious effects of unstable employment among the highly educated in the humanities. Only then can we explore alternative models for shaping our interactions, leadership decisions, and campus policies.

TRANSFORMING LESSON #2:

Leading in the humanities requires working and building relationships beyond the humanities.

My career at Colorado State University (CSU), Fort Collins, speaks to the potential for systemic change and the need for tenured mentors and sponsors to foster alternative pathways to advancement and leadership opportunities for the contingent. It also demonstrates the persistence of contingency across faculty and administrator positions: I started in the English Department with a one-year "special teaching appointment" and then advanced to a senior teaching appointment (three-year contract). The hamster wheel continued to turn, only more slowly.

My options grew in 2015 when I applied for grant funds and started a writing productivity program to support CSU researchers and scholars across the span of their careers. This program, now base funded, launched my gradual move out of the English Department and into the Graduate School, where I have negotiated additional contracts with such titles as "assistant professor and director of CSU Writes" and, later, "assistant dean of professional development programs and director of CSU Writes." In 2021, I navigated the tenure process to earn promotions to "associate professor" and "assistant dean," positions that do not actually carry the contractual securities of tenure because these are contractually *tenure-equivalent* positions. I seem to have left the hamster wheel, but time will tell.

Our tenure equivalency process is new enough that there were no other associate-level contract faculty in the College of Liberal Arts to serve on my department committee. Thus, my committee of peers consisted of a tenured full professor of English and two contract associate professors—one from the College of Health and Human Sciences and one from the School of Public Health. I belabor titles and promotion processes to make a point: my career advancement has taken place simultaneously within the humanities as I am a scholar of literary and writing studies and outside of the humanities as the science, technology, engineering, mathematics, and medicine (STEMM) fields where I have found additional peers, mentors, and sponsors.

My advancement required behind-the-scenes support from my mentors (more than a dozen from across and outside the university) who helped me embrace entrepreneurial-styled approaches to program funding and building within a university. My current dean (a soil scientist)—both a mentor to me and a sponsor of my work—has spent countless hours navigating dense forests of university policies and protocols to clear a path for my position and promotion. It is in her efforts to recognize the value of my work to the university that I glimpse a broader change for recognizing and valuing the labor of the humanities more broadly. I should stress that the building out of my faculty and dean positions was made possible due to changes in the faculty code, long envisioned, considered, negotiated, and compromised upon by department-, college- and university-based faculty committees in conversation with university administration. It takes a village to affect policy change to assure greater stability and valuing of our faculty professionals.

I recognize that my experience is not typical. Most adjunct faculty may be too exhausted, undermentored, and overmanaged to grow much beyond the limitations of their employment status. Michael Bérubé and Jennifer Ruth remind us in *The Humanities, Higher Education, and Academic Freedom: Three Necessary Arguments* that the dual academic freedoms of tenure include both the institutional protection of a scholar to produce risky or politically unpopular research and the protection to speak freely among colleagues and college administrators.[5] Speaking freely among colleagues and supervisors without fear of losing one's job is crucial for the informal professional development of individual faculty and for expanding the pools of advancement. For sure, not every non-tenure-track faculty wishes to become a department chair or a dean (just as not every tenured faculty wishes to lead), but I know several adjuncts who would be excellent administrators if given the opportunity to grow and advance.

From the directorship onward, each position I have held has been created so that my work might better serve our predominantly STEMM-focused university from my entirely humanities-based background. Such advancement, while unusual, is obviously not impossible. Therein lies some hope and a reminder that administrators can and do positively affect individuals and institutions alike. My advancement required the broad sponsorship and, at key moments, the Herculean efforts of two consecutive deans and two associate deans of the Graduate School with backing from the provost and vice president of faculty affairs to build a pathway to promotion and to offer a commensurate salary. More humanities faculty should be so lucky. We need champions at all levels, but particularly in the middle, to sponsor changes to address contingency and heal its effects. Deans, as George Justice recognizes in *How to Be a Dean*, are positioned at the mid-level managerial and leadership heart of university administration.[6] My Graduate School deans' efforts demonstrate that change is possible with support from leaders invested in innovation, even within siloed bureaucratic systems. Our efforts reflect Eric Hayot's claim in *Humanist Reason: A History. An Argument. A Plan* that "the humanities should be found everywhere in a university," and we require unconventional, transdisciplinary methods, discussions, and leaders to renew our disciplines and institutional structures across all ranks and units.[7]

TRANSFORMING LESSON #3:
Collectively, we must acknowledge and grapple with the ongoing effects of contingency — deprofessionalization, shame, and burnout.

I stopped building a career as a literary scholar of contemporary "experimental" fiction and performative criticism to pursue a career in academic writing productivity and support. Within five years of applying for and receiving a grant to improve the work-life of writers at CSU, I began to exhibit classic signs of burnout: stress, fatigue, lack of focus, sadness, sleeplessness, work rumination, and decreased satisfaction with my work. With no little irony, the program I founded, CSU Writes, helps faculty, postdocs, and graduate students develop skills that support life balance so that they might build careers through research writing. I was failing, even as the metrics, awards, leadership training, and offers of advancement suggested otherwise. This is what I know: internalized contingency means that I feel compelled to work ever harder.

My experience of burnout is not unique. Burnout is a factor for workers across higher education these days. And, for many, their feelings of professional exhaustion have been exacerbated by the global pandemic. For me, pandemic-enforced remote work provided some ease of routine stressors. For instance, racing across campus from classroom to meeting became as easy as clicking into a new Zoom session. I stopped commuting over twelve hours a week and could allocate that time to sleep. I am grateful to feel more rested, even as so many of my colleagues do not. Although, I confess I still feel compelled to work just as hard.

Years of acting from a pressure to prove my value to the institution so that I might stay to teach another semester have taken their toll. The workload for the ambitious in higher education is overwhelmingly high. We know it, but it bears hearing some unifying numbers across faculty and administrative ranks: ten- to twelve-hour workdays, six to seven days per week, are common to both freeway-flying, piecemeal instructors and mid-level administrators alike. The effects of worth-proving contingency accrue for individuals and for institutions, and we must take practical and compassionate actions to mitigate distrust, exhaustion, and deprofessionalization among our colleagues and cocreators.

The decline of funding and status for the humanities in higher education started decades before the 2008 economic downturn that resulted in a succession of *worst job markets* in Modern Language Association history. We might think of many of today's problems as issues of budget since then, but we should remember that in 2005, Joe Berry had already called for adjuncts to organize as means for *Reclaiming the Ivory Tower*, and in 2007, Marc Bousquet detailed the capitalist underbelly of *How the University Works: Higher Education and the Low-Wage Nation.*[8] They identified a multi-decade trend of increased hiring of temporary faculty that was eroding the professoriate and creating top-heavy institutions where a select few raked it in, and the majority squabbled over scraps.

Shamed employees tend to say little, stay in their place, maintain the status quo, and rarely move into leadership roles. Birmingham, the first contingent faculty to win the Truman Capote Award for his book *The Most Dangerous Book: The Battle for James Joyce's Ulysses*, acknowledged that the seep of precarity, from the pools of the contingent to the lines of the tenured, has produced a generation of risk-averse faculty. Birmingham spoke, "By now, decades of adjunctification have made the professoriate fearful, insular, and conformist. According to the AAUP, adjunct faculty are about half as likely to undertake risky research projects, and the timidity moves up the ladder."[9] The impact of precarity on scholars, scholarship, and scholarly leadership has been pernicious and widespread. We need noble and visionary risk-takers who can lead us conscientiously within the rapidly changing landscapes of humanities scholarship and higher education in the twenty-first century.

We have role models and historical changemakers from whom we can learn much. In 1972, the United Negro College Fund (UNCF) under the leadership of Vernon Jordan launched their "A mind is terrible thing to waste" campaign to draw attention to a story about how lack of access to a college education was fundamental to maintaining systems of White social, economic, and political dominance in a post-Civil Rights Act America. The campaign has been one of the most compelling, activating, and profitable campaigns in American nonprofit history. Today, the UNCF's goal remains for all Americans to have the opportunity for a college education.[10] The clear and poignant recognition that a lack of access to higher education for a segment of Americans squandered their talents and limited the strength of the nation was a powerful and mobilizing message. As Chyna N. Crawford recognizes in her chapter in this volume, African American females in academe frequently experience contradictory messages about the quality of their work, carry heavy teaching and service loads, and face social and systemic barriers to advancement. We in the humanities will do well to mark the disproportionate number of faculty who are women and faculty of color and to reflect on the formal (code) and informal (social and cultural) barriers to advancement.

The contingently employed may have the privilege of training to become an expert in a field of study, but the process of *deprofessionalizing*, to recall Bérubé and Ruth's argument, begins the moment they sign the contract for employment. Without the expectations, institutional investments, and protections of tenure (or its equivalent), contingent faculty have limited—if any—options for professional development. They have few opportunities to continue both researching *and* teaching (the most powerful and empowering combination for continued professional development), and they have limited access to department or campus decision-making processes. The lack of institutional investment in these faculty often bars access to institutional advancement and erodes opportunities to develop new leadership skills to serve in upper levels of college administration. These are structurally imposed limits on the continual honing of faculty expertise and stymieing of their institutional contributions. A mind is a terrible thing to waste, indeed.

Deprofessionalization is the great, rarely talked about shame of the humanities in higher education. It is widespread and widely unacknowledged. I have yet to hear boards of trustees, governors, or regents wring their hands about the deprofessionalization of faculty at their institutions. Nor, in my experience serving on college and university faculty committees, are the concerns about contingent employee development the focus of many conversations or policy changes. In the instances when they have been at the fore, those conversations have focused on providing development that will also keep the contingent "in their place." An example is the common practice at CSU to offer professional development opportunities to non-tenure-track teaching faculty related almost exclusively to "pedagogy," which ignores the necessity for them to also stay current with and to contribute to field-specific knowledge.

More than wasting the opportunity to develop excellent leaders in our disciplines and institutions, contingency corrodes the relationship workers have with their colleagues, their institutions, and even with themselves as professionals. Studies of job insecurity among workers, regardless of job classification, note that its effects are widespread and often negative: chronic stress and increased psychological morbidity; "exhaustion (burnout), general mental/psychological well-being, self-rated health, and a variety of somatic complaints"; low organizational trust and corresponding poor mental well-being.[11] These studies are not specific to employees of humanities nor of higher education, but, as Genesea M. Carter, Aurora Matzke, and Bonnie Vidrine-Isbell point out in their chapter in this collection, "Navigating Networks and Systems," we need only to look around at our own working conditions to witness the relationship between job insecurity and burnout as true for contingent faculty too. Contingency is *the* epicenter of the policies, practices, and cultures shaping higher education—from temporary staff and adjunct faculty and soft-money researchers who process, instruct, and produce for the university, to the most recent chair, dean, vice president, or president brought in to "fix" problems. All of us—regardless of contract or tenure—know our jobs are expendable in this budget climate.

To be clear, precarity, the feeling of being insecure or uncertain, is the defining feature of employment in academe today. For the past three decades, the humanities have been ground zero. Most opportunities for advancement into campus administration require applicants have tenure or its equivalency for consideration. And for good reason: administrative positions can be short term or precariously held, reflecting the institution's current, but perhaps not long-term, leadership vision. Historically, those who advanced within an institution might serve in an administrative role for a select period or in a part-time capacity before returning to faculty ranks. Their faculty position (presumably tenured) also protected administrators from being fired for taking unpopular but necessary leadership positions and assured confidence in speaking "truth to power," even as those faculty simultaneously held reins of administrative power. Whether we call it tenure or something else, we must find ways to restore job security and sustainable scholarly engagement that serves the needs of our intersecting communities: disciplinary, institutional, civic, familial.

Feeling overworked is also a symptom of institutional reliance on contingent employees and its radiating effects: short-term, nonnegotiable contracts for piecemeal instruction and research; mutual distrust between the rank and file and leadership; feelings of professional exhaustion across all units and ranks; and the risk of burnout. In his 2018 "Pedagogy Unbound" piece on what institutions can do to help faculty avoid burning out, David Gooblar shared a study that correlated institutional loyalty with levels of burnout and mental health challenges among contingent faculty: "The more committed they were to their institution, the more stressed, depressed, and anxious they felt. That result, the report's authors hypothesized, may be the product of faculty members' 'feeling commitment to an organization that fails to reciprocate.'" [12] Faculty and employee burnout rates have increased dramatically across job classifications in higher education over the past decade and surged during the pandemic. [13] Leaving academe may be the only way forward for many of our most engaged scholars of the humanities. "Quit Lit" evidences this trend and is on the rise even among tenured faculty, as longtime *Chronicle of Higher Education* contributor William Pannapacker explained in his column "On Why I'm Leaving Academe." [14] And then, he left.

TRANSFORMING LESSON #4:

Leading sustainable engagement requires a culture shift away from productivity metrics and corporate managerial models to invest resources (attention, time, money) in our people and recognize their contributions to a new humanities landscape.

Academics generally agree that business models are a short-sighted fix for a significant long-term devaluing and defunding of higher education. No matter how hard we squint, we will never see scholarly articles become widgets to be produced on an assembly line, nor will our students become our customers. More than a decade has passed since Ellen Schrecker imagined a grim future for institutions that fail to see beyond their own infighting and fiscal challenges: "More than money is at stake here," she told us, in *The Lost Soul of Higher Education*. "One can envision a dystopic set of institutions, dominated by vocationalism and the bottom line, where the drive for productivity transforms most faculty members into temporary workers with little job security or control over the content of their courses, while scientists and engineers churn out patentable results in industrialized laboratories that service their corporate sponsors." [15] We all have seen these trends on the horizon, at our back door, and in our hallways in higher education. In many departments and institutions, dystopia has arrived. Schrecker was not uniquely prescient, but she clearly laid out the transactional bottom line and long-term effects of capitalist exchange for education.

As the leaders of fields in which scholarship, pedagogy, and instruction have been increasingly devalued and treated as suspect, we in the humanities have the monumental task and opportunity to reassess the needs of multiple and overlapping sectors—public/social, institutional, environmental, even political—and to make the case for the value of the humanities from our own area of expertise. This is a transformation that will require we value the little "h" not big "H" of the humanities, where each of us is empowered to work within our positions to envision and foster incremental, local, and people-grounded change.

To do so, we must examine the decisions we make day-to-day as leaders, and ask, Are we working toward a shared, engaged vision of the long-term (if not always short-term) success of our unit and of those we supervise? Or are we working (overtly or inadvertently) to maintain the status quo and simply *manage* our way to the next fiscal year?

In his survey of the literature of managerial modes and discourses of administrative leadership, Marc Bousquet tracks a turn toward "the notion of administrators 'causing quality'" and "the stressing (or 'continuous improvement') of faculty productivity" from the 1980s to the early twenty-first century. Continuous improvement, whether it be the production of research or the instruction of students, Bousquet interprets as faculty "working harder for lower wages."[16] In the humanities, we see this managerial/labor trend play out most glaringly in departments of writing-centric programs that have hired an ever-higher percentage of their faculty into contingent appointments. These offer few, if any, opportunities for professional development. Under these conditions, leaders risk devolving into managers who oversee the output of their employees (i.e., teaching) with diminishing resources to support high-quality instruction or scholarship.

Other disciplines should observe the downside of managing contingency and beware: the professional precarity that was once a problem of liberal arts also affects the presumably more stable STEMM fields, with a growing reliance on postdoctoral fellows and soft-money researchers who work on short-term contracts as piecemeal technicians, researchers, and instructors. If we look at the hiring, appointment, and promotion practices of our own institutions—regardless of small college or large research university—we can recognize in our home institutions how contingency has undermined the quality of the work environments and campus cultures.

We can recognize in our own departments and across our campuses the lost opportunities for the collegial bonding that takes place through the search and selection processes. For instance, contingent employees are rarely "courted" through search processes on the assumption that they will soon be gone. Thus, the quality of their collegial work relationships is contractually framed. Their contracts often include diminished or no research expectations, along with few or no service expectations—an absence that I have heard described as a blessing by overburdened ladder faculty, but which, ultimately, limits networking and academic community-building, skill development, and opportunities for contingent faculty. In many institutions, contingent faculty have restricted or barred access to professional trainings, conferences, and other development programs. The professional growth and well-being of academics across disciplines are at stake. We in the humanities have countless tales of deprofessionalization.

Let us now, in our various institutions, imagine, articulate, and prioritize stories of the reprofessionalization of our faculty, staff, and administrators.

Stories of reprofessionalization are where we must begin if we are to envision and build a sustainable, engaged, flourishing humanities. What I write is far from Pollyannaish. If we are realistic, developing a sustainable design that supports our personnel will be time-consuming and costly, but we also know that cutting costs is what got us here to begin with. In his recent campaign for the humanities, Eric Hayot recognizes in *Humanist Reason* that "the best way to restore the humanities in whatever form (though ideally in a new form) would be to restore or increase public funding for primary, secondary, and university education."[17] While much of Hayot's plan is beyond the scope of my tale, his point about adequate funding is just—if preaching to the choir. Money does flow to and through our respective institutions. Put another way, the humanities are not in crisis but are flourishing in new and transforming ways; we simply have a crisis of budget. Identifying, lobbying, and diverting adequate funding is essential to our envisioning of sustainable leadership in the humanities. As unseemly as that may seem.

Most importantly for our purposes, Hayot reminds us that the language we use and stories we tell about the humanities matter. He declares, "The gap between the metadiscourse of humanist reason and the practice of humanist scholarship has made it difficult for humanists to (1) properly understand their own work, (2) fight back against stupid characterizations of it, and (3) free the humanities from a set of institutional and intellectual constraints that limit the scope of their attention, their ambition, and their labor."[18] My tale has been a modest and imperfect enactment of Hayot's sentiment that self-reflexive stories about our work in the humanities are important. We must reflect on the short-term and long-term impacts of our budget-minded decisions, and we must think "outside" of the humanities to lead within the humanities.

Of course, my own tale of professional transformation is but a data point in the metrics of a story of institutional and professional change that recognizes the humanities remain in demand but perhaps not in the same forms as they have been. Our tales of leadership in the humanities are of ongoing collaboration and transformations. We are in process, and the decisions we make today will have long-term consequences. We have an obligation to do better than we have done for the past thirty years. As leaders, let us open the humanities to consider unconventional, sustainable, and rewarding pathways that will expand the scope of our focus, our ambition, and our work together.

Now, tell me your tale.

NOTES

1. Roy Arthur Swanson, "Ovid's Theme of Change," *The Classical Journal* 54, no. 5 (1959): 201.

2. See Kristina Quynn, "Drudgery Tales, Abjectified Protagonists, and the *Adjunctroman* of New Academic Fiction," *Genres: Forms of Discourse and Culture* 52, vol. 2 (2019): 85–108; "Farting and Vomiting Through the New Campus Novel," *Endgame: Can Literary Studies Survive? Chronicle Review*, 2020,

https://connect.chronicle.com/rs/931-EKA-218/images/ChronicleReview _Endgame.pdf; and Kristina Quynn, "The Disgusting New Campus Novel," *The Chronicle of Higher Education, December* 16, 2019, https://www.chronicle .com/article/the-disgusting-new-campus-novel/.

3. Kevin Birmingham, "'The Great Shame of Our Profession,'" *The Chronicle of Higher Education,* February 12, 2017, www.chronicle.com/article/the-great -shame-of-our-profession.

4. Adrianna Kezar, Elizabeth Holcombe, Darsella Vigil, and Jude Paul Mathias Dizon, *Shared Equity Leadership: Making Equity Everyone's Work* (Washington, DC: American Council on Education; Los Angeles: University of Southern California, Pullias Center for Higher Education, 2021), 3.

5. Michael Bérubé and Jennifer Ruth, *The Humanities, Higher Education, and Academic Freedom: Three Necessary Arguments* (New York: Palgrave Macmillan, 2015), 109, 117.

6. George Justice, *How to Be a Dean* (Baltimore: Johns Hopkins University Press, 2019), ix.

7. Eric Hayot, *Humanist Reason: A History. An Argument. A Plan.* (New York: Columbia University Press, 2021), 167.

8. Joe Berry, *Reclaiming the Ivory Tower: Organizing Adjuncts to Change Higher Education* (New York: Monthly Review Press, 2005), xiv; Marc Bousquet, *How the University Works: Higher Education and the Low-Wage Nation* (New York: New York University Press, 2007), backmatter, 83, 94.

9. Birmingham, "'The Great Shame.'"

10. UNCF, "'A Mind Is a Terrible Thing to Waste': 40 Years of an Iconic Motto," video, 7:56, March 2, 2021, https://www.youtube.com/watch?v=lNNjcG1AFYk.

11. J. E. Ferrie, "Effects of Chronic Job Insecurity and Change in Job Security on Self-Reported Health, Minor Psychiatric Morbidity, Physiological Measures, and Health Related Behaviours in British Civil Servants: The Whitehall II Study," *Journal of Epidemiology & Community Health* 56, no. 6 (2002): 450–54, https://doi.org/10.1136/jech.56.6.450; Hans De Witte, Jaco Pienaar, and Nele De Cuyper, "Review of 30 Years of Longitudinal Studies on the Association Between Job Insecurity and Health and Well-Being: Is There Causal Evidence?" *Australian Psychologist* 51, no. 1 (2016): 18–31, https://doi .org/10.1111/ap.12176; A. Richter and K. Näswall, "Job Insecurity and Trust: Uncovering a Mechanism Linking Job Insecurity to Well-Being," *Work &*

Stress 33, no. 1 (2019): 22–40, https://doi.org/10.1080/02678373.2018.1461709.

12. David Gooblar, "3 Ways Colleges Can Help Faculty Members Avoid Burnout," *The Chronicle of Higher Education*, July 23, 2020, www.chronicle.com/article /3-ways-colleges-can-help-faculty-members-avoid-burnout/.

13. "On the Verge of Burnout: Covid-19's Impact on Faculty Well-Been and Career Plans," *The Chronicle of Higher Education*, 2021, connect.chronicle.com /rs/931-EKA-218/images/Covid%26FacultyCareerPaths_Fidelity_Research Brief_v3%20%281%29.pdf.

14. William, Pannapacker, "Advice: On Why I'm Leaving Academe," *The Chronicle of Higher Education*, September 22, 2021, https://www.chronicle.com/article /on-why-im-leaving-academe.

15. Ellen W. Schrecker, *The Lost Soul of Higher Education Corporatization, the Assault on Academic Freedom, and the End of the American University* (New York: New Press, 2010), 233.

16. Bousquet, *How the University Works*, 168.

17. Hayot, *Humanist Reason*, 17.

18. Hayot, 17.

BIBLIOGRAPHY

Berry, Joe. *Reclaiming the Ivory Tower: Organizing Adjuncts to Change Higher Education*. New York: Monthly Review Press, 2005.

Bérubé, Michael, and Jennifer Ruth. *The Humanities, Higher Education, and Academic Freedom: Three Necessary Arguments*. New York: Palgrave Macmillan, 2015.

Birmingham, Kevin. "'The Great Shame of Our Profession.'" *The Chronicle of Higher Education*, February 12, 2017. www.chronicle.com/article/the-great -shame-of-our-profession.

Bousquet, Marc. *How the University Works: Higher Education and the Low-Wage Nation*. New York: New York University Press, 2007.

De Witte, Hans, Jaco Pienaar, and Nele De Cuyper. "Review of 30 Years of Longitudinal Studies on the Association Between Job Insecurity and Health and Well-Being: Is There Causal Evidence?" *Australian Psychologist* 51, no. 1 (2016): 18–31. https://doi.org/10.1111/ap.12176.

Ferrie, J., M. Shipley, S. Stansfeld, and M. Marmot. "Effects of Chronic Job Insecurity and Change in Job Security on Self-Reported Health, Minor Psychiatric Morbidity, Physiological Measures, and Health Related Behaviours in British Civil Servants: The Whitehall II Study." *Journal of Epidemiology & Community Health* 56, no. 6 (2002): 450–54. https://doi.org/10.1136/jech.56.6.450.

Gooblar, David. "3 Ways Colleges Can Help Faculty Members Avoid Burnout." *The Chronicle of Higher Education*, 23 (2020). www.chronicle.com/article/3 -ways-colleges-can-help-faculty-members-avid-burnout/.

Hayot, Eric. *Humanist Reason: A History. An Argument. A Plan.* New York: Columbia University Press, 2021.

Justice, George. *How to Be a Dean.* Baltimore, MD: Johns Hopkins University Press, 2019.

Kezar, Adrianna, Elizabeth Holcombe, Darsella Vigil, and Jude Paul Mathias Dizon. *Shared Equity Leadership: Making Equity Everyone's Work.* Washington, DC: American Council on Education; Los Angeles: University of Southern California, Pullias Center for Higher Education, 2021. https://www.acenet .edu/Documents/Shared-Equity-Leadership-Work.pdf.

"On the Verge of Burnout: Covid-19's Impact on Faculty Well-Being and Career Plans." *The Chronicle of Higher Education*, 2021. connect.chronicle.com /rs/931-EKA-218/images/Covid%26FacultyCareerPaths_Fidelity_Research Brief_v3%20%281%29.pdf

Pannapacker, William. "Advice: On Why I'm Leaving Academe." *The Chronicle of Higher Education*, September 22, 2021. https://www.chronicle.com/article /on-why-im-leaving-academe.

Quynn, Kristina. "The Disgusting New Campus Novel." *The Chronicle of Higher Education*, December 2019. https://www.chronicle.com/article/the-disgusting -new-campus-novel/.

Quynn, Kristina. "Drudgery Tales, Abjectified Protagonists, and the adjunctro-man of New Academic Fiction." *Genres: Forms of Discourse and Culture* 52, no. 2 (2019): 85–108.

Quynn, Kristina. "Farting and Vomiting through the New Campus Novel." Endgame: Can Literary Studies Survive? *Chronicle Review*, January 2020. https:// connect.chronicle.com/rs/931-EKA-218/images/ChronicleReview_Endgame .pdf.

Richter, A., and K. Näswall. "Job Insecurity and Trust: Uncovering a Mechanism Linking Job Insecurity to Well-Being," *Work & Stress* 33, no. 1 (2019): 22–40. https://doi.org/10.1080/02678373.2018.1461709.

Schrecker, Ellen W. *The Lost Soul of Higher Education Corporatization, the Assault on Academic Freedom, and the End of the American University*. New York: New Press, 2010.

Swanson, Roy Arthur. "Ovid's Theme of Change." *The Classical Journal* 54, vol. 5 (1959): 201–5. https://www.jstor.org/stable/3295215.

UNCF. "'A Mind Is a Terrible Thing to Waste': 40 Years of an Iconic Motto." March 2, 2021. Educational video, 7:56. https://www.youtube.com/watch?v= lNNjcG1AFYk.

United States House Committee on Education and the Workforce. "The Just-in-Time Professor: A Staff Report Summarizing eForum Responses on the Working Conditions of Contingent Faculty in Higher Education." January 2014. https://edlabor.house.gov/imo/media/doc/1.24.14-AdjunctEforumReport.pdf

10

ITO ANG KWENTO KO[1]

Pinayist Pedagogy/Praxis and Community College Leadership

ROWENA M. TOMANENG

D*id you always want to be a college president? What challenges did you face in your leadership journey and how did you overcome the barriers? What philosophies inform your leadership?* These are only a few of the questions I have been asked since advancing to the presidencies of Berkeley City College (BCC) and San José City College (SJCC).[2]

In the last six years, I have been invited to share my *kwento*, my story, my leadership journey in a variety of venues, from higher education-focused news media, conferences and convenings, leadership institutes, and ethnic-based staff associations. I have been a multicultural educator in the California Community Colleges for over twenty-seven years. Prior to SJCC and BCC, I served in multiple roles at De Anza College in the Foothill-De Anza Community College District as faculty in English, intercultural studies, and women's studies; chair of the English Department; the founding faculty co-director of the Institute of Community and Civic Engagement (ICCE); acting dean of language arts; and associate vice president of instruction. Beyond academia, my experience as a community organizer in the Pilipinx community in Santa Clara County further contributed to my leadership development, growth, and resiliency.

This chapter presents a counter-story of my lived experience as a community college president of color whose leadership, teaching, and service are guided by social justice and equity frameworks. As a method of critical race theory, counter-storytelling is the practice of individuals from minoritized communities sharing stories of their lived experience and knowledge in order to challenge White racial dominance within educational institutions and within the school curriculum.[3] This practice can strengthen resiliency and agency among leaders of color such as myself because it validates intersectional experience in higher education. This narrative offers a nontraditional, non-Western, non-White-male view of leadership and shows that current and aspiring leaders of color can achieve success by maintaining their authentic selves and cultural values.

ON BECOMING A CRITICAL EDUCATOR

Ang kwento ko starts with my early research and teaching interests to expand the humanities from its traditional "Western" roots to a more global, multicultural discipline. This early interest became a professional passion to decolonize the community colleges where I worked, with the goal of transforming them from Eurocentric institutions to multicultural and equity-oriented institutions. During my undergraduate program at the University of California, Irvine, I was introduced to multicultural texts written by Native American, Asian American, African American, and Mexican American writers in my upper-division English literature courses. I became very interested in the cultural and racial histories of people of color in the United States, including the intersectional experiences of women of color. My political consciousness was awakened, and I was angry that none of my prior schooling had exposed me to narratives of the Philippine-American War, US colonialism of the Philippines, Pilipinos and the Farmworkers Movement, the Struggle of Pilipino World War II Veterans, and other historical events connected to the Pilipinx-American experience. I chose to apply to the University of California, Santa Barbara's (UCSB) doctoral program in English because there were professors whose research and teaching focused on ethnic American literature, critical race studies, and Third World feminism. My goal back then was to complete a dissertation on a comparative analysis of Chicana and Pilipina American feminist literary traditions within a postcolonial context.

While teaching in the writing program, I was introduced to critical pedagogy and encouraged to apply this approach in my writing courses. As I advanced into my faculty and administrative leadership roles, I also applied the major tenets of critical pedagogy in my leadership praxis. To Darder et al., "critical pedagogy emerged from a long historical legacy of radical social thought and progressive educational movements, which aspired to link democratic principles of society and transformative social action in the interest of oppressed communities."[4] Critical Pedagogy has its origins in the life and work of Brazilian educator Paulo Freire, who was deeply committed to educating the Brazilian poor working class, so they could politically engage in improving their oppressive social condition. In *Pedagogy of the Oppressed*, Freire argues for a radical transformation of the student-teacher relationship through problem-posing education to increase literacy and critical engagement among the common people. He maintains that the acquisition of knowledge and what we come to understand as the cultural norm must be critically analyzed in relation to socio-historical, cultural, economic, and political contexts. Freire's educational model centered on consciousness-raising, dialogue, reflection, and praxis—that in the expansion of these individual acts, collective action for social transformation can take place.[5] Since these early teaching experiences almost thirty years ago, I continue to embrace the role of critical educator, interrogating and challenging dominant and hegemonic discourses rooted in Eurocentric ideology and White supremacy. I see critical pedagogy as a pedagogy of resistance and myself as a critical educator and institutional leader, an activist for building a more just world.

I left UCSB's doctoral program after I completed my master's degree because of my family's relocation to the San Francisco Bay Area and my dissatisfaction with the English Department's treatment of students of color. After one year of teaching as a part-time lecturer, I was hired into a tenure-track position in English at De Anza College in 1996. My hire was part of a larger diversity, equity, and inclusion (DEI) hiring initiative, and I became the first Asian American faculty member in the English Department and the first Pilipina American faculty member at the college. Being the first in any role comes with great responsibility and stress, especially for faculty and leaders of color. We feel the pressure to be successful in our position responsibilities and in anything we set out to do because we know it will open doors for others to follow. Studies such as Gutiérrez y Muhs et al. explore how women of color in academia persistently deal with questions about their competency and knowledge base instead of being recognized for their accomplishments and potential.[6] Since these early days in my career, I have embraced what I see as my responsibility to pay it forward by coaching and mentoring other educators of color informally and in established leadership programs. Mentoring by educational leaders of color can increase an institution's DEI efforts because they can provide navigational strategies during and after tenure and foster growth and resilience against impostor syndrome, self-doubt, and questioning of one's own achievements.[7]

Because of the limited number of faculty of color at the college, I was encouraged to take on leadership outside of my department, specifically within the Asian Pacific American Staff Association and the district's Minority Staff Association. My mentors told me that I could be successful in these leadership roles because of my strong skills in building authentic relationships with and connecting to diverse groups of people. Colleagues also told me that my background in the humanities and literature coupled with just having left a PhD program with a University of California institution also gave me legitimacy with the elites of the institution. However, I question the need for leaders of color to have an academic pedigree. Being an effective leader or administrator requires a broader range of skills and applied knowledge that most likely are not part of any formal curriculum. From my experience, I don't recall any White faculty or leaders having to market their academic backgrounds in order to get committee and other leadership appointments.

Before I received tenure, I was recruited to join a group of tenured women of color and White women faculty who were involved in student equity efforts and campus organizing for a multicultural transformation of the curriculum. It is with this group of women that I first learned to apply community organizing principles to campus leadership. Together, we worked to develop ally relationships across campus areas, facilitated anti-racism workshops/institutes between women of color and White women who worked across different departments across campus, and provided our equity-oriented perspectives to middle management, executive administration, and participatory governance committees.[8]

Having a genuine interest in collaborative work and actively developing partnerships serves as an entryway into campus leadership. Cultivating this talent also contributes to others' perception that you have an entrepreneurial spirit, a talent sought in leaders across higher education institutions focused on fiscal stability and increasing college/university resources.

By the time I was granted tenure in 2000, I was looked upon as a faculty leader in my home department, English, and in the Language Arts and Intercultural Studies/International Studies Divisions. I worked collaboratively and team-taught with faculty who were critical educators, and I developed trainings in culturally responsive curriculum and pedagogy. For a number of years, I co-taught with other faculty in the humanities and social sciences (arts, women's studies, and political science), where we centered our courses on exploring the cultural histories of marginalized communities using a critical pedagogy approach.

In 2008, I left my tenured faculty position after serving as the founding co-director of De Anza's ICCE for two years. In this work, I had the opportunity to strategically build meaningful community partnerships to advance a critical service learning program, a student leadership program, and human rights-based programming focused on immigrant rights and women's rights. Colleagues in the English Department encouraged me to take on the acting dean of language arts position because they wanted leadership that could advocate for programs and the faculty during a time of budget reduction. When I accepted the position, I didn't anticipate that I would have to navigate two years of budget crisis within the district and a $1.2 million reduction to one of the largest academic divisions.

While painful, and resulting in the elimination of one academic program, two full-time classified professional positions, and over twenty-seven part-time instructional teaching assistant positions, my credibility as an equity-oriented leader remained intact because of the humanizing approach I took in addressing the crisis. I worked with department leaders to brainstorm potential solutions and spent many hours listening to their fears, anxieties, and concerns. I believe that my transparency and caring approach to those whose positions were eliminated and my valuing all voices within the division mitigated additional harm. As a critical educator, I was also able to engage senior leadership in deep dialogues about how the reduction targets did not align with our institutional mission, vision, and values.

Because of my work ethic, commitment to student engagement, student equity, and student success, I was invited to apply for the associate vice president of instruction (AVPI) position in 2010, instead of applying for the permanent dean of language arts position. I made the decision to accept the promotion to AVPI for three reasons: (1) the AVPI supervised the Academic Services Division, which housed the ICCE, Office of Equity, Social Justice, and Multicultural Education, Office of Staff and Professional Development, Learning Communities, Honors Program, and others that I had been involved with as a faculty leader; (2) the AVPI supervised the new Learning Resources Division, which housed the Student Success Centers in Math and Language Arts and Library Services, departments that were critical for students' academic achievement; and (3) the AVPI was a senior staff position, which meant that I would have decision-making authority at the executive cabinet level. Moreover, the AVPI was a newly created position that was designed to bridge Academic Affairs and Student Affairs in support of the institution's student equity goals, which very much aligned with the work I had been doing in and outside of the classroom for over twelve years.

It was also during this time that I began another doctoral program in the International and Multicultural Education Department (IME) at the School of Education, University of San Francisco (USFCA).[9] As a graduate of the IME Department, I joined a network of critical educators who value and actively promote liberatory education. The program provided me with opportunities to reflect and refine my own practice in and outside of the classroom. The preparation and tools I received have helped my leadership response to crises these past years in my role as president of BCC and president of SJCC. These crises include the lack of national leadership and racialized attacks toward immigrant, undocumented, and Black, Indigenous, People of Color (BIPOC) communities since the 2016 election, COVID-19 pandemic, and ongoing racial violence. Unlike my experience at UCSB, my experience at USFCA was affirming, culturally responsive, and nurturing. I especially appreciated the encouragement I received from my professors to integrate my humanities background into my dissertation project, *The Educational Dimensions of Pilipina Workers' Activist Identities*. My qualitative study included the *kwentos* of my family members who were overseas workers, experiences of Pilipina migrant workers affiliated with a Migrant Center and activist organization, literature, and the arts—poetry, drama, and visual arts. My dissertation was grounded in my love for community, and my joy in the research and writing process.

DIWANG PINAY (SPIRIT OF THE PILIPINA)

I am a first-generation immigrant born in the Philippines. My parents immigrated to the United States a few months after then president Ferdinand Marcos declared Martial Law in 1972.[10] To me, an important aspect of being a critical educator of color is the recognition that I stand on the shoulders of those who paved the path before me. I acknowledge the elders in my family who have passed down their generational knowledge and wisdom to my generation. My passion for serving marginalized communities stems from the *kwentos* my mother, Nenita De Joya Tomaneng, would tell me of my Lolo (grandfather) Patricio "Crosby" De Joya, a *Manghihilot*.[11] My Lolo Crosby was a leader in his community, *Abra De Ilog*, in the Occidental region of the island of Mindoro, Philippines. He loved the community and worked to improve people's lives. His life continues to inspire leadership and commitment to service among many members of my family.

When asked about my identity as an educator and leader, I talk about myself as a *Pinay* and Asian American president because to me, these descriptors speak to my political engagement with the social justice issues Pilipinx and Asian Americans continue to face. I am drawn to Pinayist pedagogy/praxis as a leadership framework because of its focus on the empowerment of Pilipina American women and its application of Freire's idea of transformative agency through theory practice and personal reflection. In *Practicing Pinayist Pedagogy*, Tintiangco-Cubales and Sacramento define Pinayist pedagogy/praxis in the following way:

Pinayist praxis is a process, place, and production that aims to connect the global and local to the personal issues and stories of Pinay struggle, survival, service, sisterhood, and strength. It is an individual and communal process of decolonization, humanization, self-determination, and relationship building, ultimately moving toward liberation. Through this process, Pinays create places where their epistemologies are at the center of the discourse/dialogue/conversation and organizing. Pinays also represent Pinayism through critical cultural production of art, performance, and engaged scholarship that expresses their perspectives and counternarratives.[12]

Here, we see that a Pinayist pedagogical/praxis approach is deeply rooted in both critical and ethnic studies pedagogies in addition to transnational feminism. Development of self-agency is grounded in decolonizing praxis for restoration of humanity, Pilipina women's knowledge production, community dialogue, and commitment to action.

My leadership and engaged scholarship reflect Pinayist pedagogical/praxis in my commitment to unearthing individual and group counternarratives of Pilipinx and Asian American communities and finding solutions to issues. My dissertation and current research, for example, include Pilipina migrant stories coupled with my own personal experiences with Pilipinx labor migration. Within the context of Philippine colonial history and globalization, I honor *Diwang Pinay* by continuing to actively research and teach the impact of intersectionality (race, class, and gender oppression) on the lives of Pilipina migrant workers.[13] Equally important, I celebrate the ways in which political activism and a desire to work for social justice and human rights is developed. While challenging because of the time constraints of leading an institution, I have found it meaningful to do research and write because these activities contribute to my ongoing professional learning on a number of topics—humanizing education, gender and globalization, sense of belonging, transfer receptive cultures—that have direct relevance and application to my leadership role within the institution.

From 2001 to 2010, I served as a community organizer for Pilipinx immigrant and migrant workers in Santa Clara County and across the

United States. While at De Anza College, I volunteered as a community organizer for Pilipino Community Support-Silicon Valley (FOCUS-SV), MALAYA (Pinay Activist Organization), and the National Alliance for Pilipino Concerns. I was also invited to be a founding member of the Critical Pilipina and Pilipino Studies Collective (CFFSC), composed of other activist scholars from the humanities and social sciences across community colleges, California State University, and University of California Campuses. CFFSC members used our scholarship to publish and distribute reports on human rights issues impacting the Pilipinx community in the United States, Philippines, and wider Philippine diaspora. With the organizations, I became familiar with developing and providing political education and activist curricula and various skills workshops ranging from digital literacy, public speaking, advocacy letter writing, and community organizing strategies. The executive director of FOCUS-SV sent me to numerous trainings and workshops centered on developing and running advocacy campaigns, building relationships with journalists, community and civic leaders, and local and national foundations. Looking back at these experiences, I developed skills in strategic partnership development, planning and assessment, conflict mediation, fundraising, and donor cultivation, all important skills to have as a college president.

LEADERSHIP REDEFINED BY SOCIAL MOVEMENT THEORY

Social movement theory has shaped my social justice lens and strengthened my commitment to decolonizing the institution through the practice of humanizing education. Robin D. G. Kelley and Grace Lee Boggs, for example, explore the impact of Marxist ideologies, race-based ideologies, and/or humanism on social movements in and outside the United States. In *Freedom Dreams: The Black Radical Imagination*, Kelley argues that sustained political engagement is not rooted in people's misery but instead is rooted in people's hope and dreams; thus, we need to recover activists' ideas and visions and explore how social movements inspire individuals to imagine another world is possible. Black activists' visions manifest in art, literature, song, and other forms; these poetics of struggle/artifacts of social movements "enable participants to imagine something different, to realize things need not always be this way."[14]

Kelley's concept of freedom dreaming and the role that artists and writers play in nurturing hope has influenced the interdisciplinary nature of my research and teaching, and the types of academic and cultural programs the Office of the President supports. In the years that I have been an executive administrator, my offices have sponsored lectures by notable scholars and public intellectuals, poetry and book readings, and workshops by well-known local and national figures. I have brought in human rights scholars, diversity trainers, writers from minoritized communities, local community activities, etc. While some leaders may perceive these activities as outside of a president's responsibilities, I see these activities as both cocreating with and directly supporting students and faculty. The campus also sees the president's commitment to matters of access, equity, and social justice.

Boggs writes about building a movement that values the creative force of people (human solidarity), and she incorporates the major tenets of critical pedagogy into her activist approach. In *The Next American Revolution: Sustainable Activism for the Twenty-First Century*, Boggs writes, "These are the times to grow our souls."[15] She views radical social change as a two-sided transformational process, of ourselves and of our institutions, and she urges us to move away from reductive and divisive thinking by engaging in ongoing dialogue with others. Boggs also argues that we can transform our colleges/universities by engaging in humanizing education, which is central to decolonization of the institution and dismantling White supremacy. In valuing the cultures, lived experiences, and voices of all in the institution, I practice humanizing education, which I consider an outgrowth of global humanities study and an ethical obligation to uphold human rights. I encourage my students and my employees to share *kwentos* with one another to connect, to foster understanding and mutual respect. Having led two institutions that serve predominantly BIPOC communities, my leadership priorities center on humanizing education, creating spaces and opportunities for people to engage with one another through facilitated panel discussions, listening sessions, dialogues, and healing circles for students and employees.

My development of a practice of care, compassion, empathy, and cultural humility I credit to colleagues at De Anza College and USFCA. I am privileged to be part of an extended network of critical educators who model these values in their relations with students, members of their institutions, and external communities. The practice of these values is so urgent right now for educators and leaders across all systems of education. Over the past two years, I witnessed the breakdown of systems and values I have worked to strengthen in community colleges over two decades. My students and their families have lost employment and housing, struggle with food insecurity, and are disproportionately impacted by COVID-19. Many students faced challenges with technology and Wi-Fi access, childcare, and quiet spaces to study. I also witnessed the struggle of my faculty in their pivot from in-person instruction to online modality, with limited training in distance education and equity-minded online practices. Some lacked access to childcare, and members of their households have also lost employment. Campus climate has been challenged due to the ongoing racial violence directed toward Black, Brown, and Asian communities. I have students and employees who are experiencing racial trauma and hopelessness. These conditions have undermined the work I have been trying to do at SJCC to foster a sense of belonging, which educational research has long connected to the retention, persistence, and academic success of minoritized student populations.

FINAL REFLECTIONS

Recently, I've been listening to songs from the movement for Philippine National Democracy to help me reflect on the impacts of the COVID-19 pandemic and #BlackLivesMatter. Participating in this movement for over a decade was a transformative experience in my leadership journey, and I draw inspiration from that experience. One song that deeply resonates with me is "River (Chico Redemption)" by a local San Francisco band, Diskarte Namin, who served as the cultural arm for Bay area Pilipino activists fighting for human rights, immigrant rights, and against the US wars in the Middle East.[16] "River" is a tribute to the victorious struggle of the Butbut tribe and Cordillera people against the Marcos Regime and

World Bank who had planned on installing a massive dam along the Chico River that would have displaced over 100,000 people. I've been holding themes from this song in my heart and mind—ancestral wisdom, hope, commitment, and the power of the collective. These themes also resonate with educators who uphold Freire's idea of liberatory education, the belief that educational praxis can bring about progressive change in oppressive societies. In the times that I feel the weight and fatigue of being a leader in the middle of multiple crises, I step back from, reflect upon, and reframe the conditions under which I'm operating. I also turn to other BIPOC leaders because they help me focus on the strengths, courage, and resilience of our students as they face seemingly insurmountable challenges.

As a first-generation Pilipina immigrant and community college transfer student, I experienced firsthand the failures in our education system: absence of culturally responsive curriculum, pedagogy, and student services, deficit thinking and practices as applied to BIPOC students, women, low-income people, etc. Those of us from minoritized communities learn at an early age that we are rarely invited to the room, and if we do arrive there, we feel the pressure to perform so as to not be looked upon as an impostor. However, institutions that have taken a transformative approach to education instill in minoritized students' confidence, power, and agency. BIPOC students see themselves as welcomed, valued, and cocreators of knowledge. If we, as institutional leaders, truly want to move the needle on educational outcomes for BIPOC and other marginalized students, we need to embrace with joy humanizing education and caring learning environments.

NOTES

1. *Ito Ang Kwento Ko* is the Tagalog (national language of the Philippines) translation of *This Is My Story* in English.
2. Berkeley City College and San José City College are two-year community colleges in California. They are dual designation Minority Serving Institutions: Hispanic Serving and Asian American Native American Pacific Islander Serving. For more information, see www.berkeleycitycollege.edu and www.sjcc.edu.
3. Daniel Solorzano and Tara J. Yosso, "Critical Race Methodology: Counter-

Storytelling as an Analytical Framework for Education Research," *Qualitative Inquiry* 8, no.1 (2002): 23–44.

4. Antonia Darder, Marta P. Baltodano, and Rodolfo D. Torres, eds., *The Critical Pedagogy Reader* (New York: Routledge, 2012), 2.

5. Paulo Freire, *Pedagogy of the Oppressed* (New York: Continuum, 2000).

6. Gabriella Gutiérrez y Muhs, Yolanda Flores Niemann, Carmen G. Gonzalez, and Angela P. Harris, eds., *Presumed Incompetent: The Intersections of Race and Class for Women in Academia* (Boulder: University of Colorado Press, 2012).

7. Isis Settles and David Nguyen, "Mentoring Experiences and Perceptions of Faculty of Color," Faculty Inclusion and Excellence Study, University of Michigan, 2017, https://inclusion.msu.edu/_assets/documents/research /MentoringReportExecutiveSummary-May2017.pdf.

8. Assembly Bill 1725 in 1988 required participatory governance in California's community colleges. The goal of the legislation was to move to a collegial model of governance, where faculty is involved in meaningful ways in college decision-making in faculty-related areas. Governance committees usually include academic affairs/instructional planning, finance and resource allocation, facilities planning, college council, and others.

9. I did not complete my PhD in English at University of California, Santa Barbara, because of leaving the program with my MA in 1995. I received my EdD in 2017 from the University of San Francisco.

10. President Ferdinand Marcos was the president of the Philippines from 1966 to 1986 before fleeing to the United States during the People Power Revolution in February 1986. In establishing Martial Law in 1972, the Philippines was plagued by corruption and human rights violations. For more information, see https://www.biography.com/dictator/ferdinand-marcos.

11. Tagalog word for a faith healer who specializes in healing muscular pain.

12. Allyson Tintiangco-Cubales and Jocelyn Sacramento, "Practicing Pinayist Pedagogy," *Amerasia Journal* 35, no.1 (2009): 179–87.

13. At the University of San Francisco, I started teaching in the IME Department as a part-time lecturer in 2018, and more recently, I started teaching in the Leadership Studies Department. My courses include *Gender and Globalization* and *Campus Environments and Cultures.*

14. Robin D. G. Kelley, *Freedom Dreams: The Black Radical Imagination* (Boston: Beacon Press, 2002), 9.

15. Grace Lee Boggs, *The Next American Revolution: Sustainable Activism for the Twenty-First Century* (Oakland: University of California Press, 2012), 36.
16. For full lyrics to "River," go to https://kulturalguerrillas.bandcamp.com/track /river-chico-redemption. For background on *Diskarte Namin,* go to https:// kulturalguerrillas.bandcamp.com/.

BIBLIOGRAPHY

Boggs, Grace Lee. *The Next American Revolution: Sustainable Activism for the Twenty-First Century.* Oakland: University of California Press, 2012.

Darder, Antonia, Marta P. Baltodano, and Rodolfo D. Torres, eds. *The Critical Pedagogy Reader.* New York: Routledge, 2017.

Freire, Paulo. *Pedagogy Of the Oppressed.* New York: Continuum, 2000.

Gutiérrez y Muhs, Gabriella, Yolanda Flores Niemann, Carmen G. Gonzalez, and Angela P. Harris, eds. *Presumed Incompetent: The Intersections of Race and Class for Women in Academia.* Boulder: University of Colorado Press, 2012.

Kelley, Robin D. G. *Freedom Dreams: The Black Radical Imagination.* Boston: Beacon Press, 2002.

Settles, Isis, and David Nguyen. "Mentoring Experiences and Perceptions of Faculty of Color." Faculty Inclusion and Excellence Study. University of Michigan, 2017. https://inclusion.msu.edu/_assets/documents/research /MentoringReportExecutiveSummary-May2017.pdf.

Solorzano, Daniel, and Yosso, Tara J. "Critical Race Methodology: Counter-Storytelling as an Analytical Framework for Education Research." *Qualitative Inquiry* 8, no.1 (2002): 23–44.

Tintiangco-Cubales, Allyson, and Jocelyn Sacramento. "Practicing Pinayist Pedagogy." *Amerasia Journal* 35, no. 1 (2009): 179–87.

PART 4

Community, Communication, and Calling

11

COLLABORATIVE, INTROVERTED LEADERSHIP

Engaging Your Stakeholders to Move a Program Forward

EMILY J. MORGAN

W hen I announced I had accepted a new position as director of Colorado State University's (CSU) dance program, there was a similar response from friends and colleagues: something to the effect of, "Wow, it'll be your program; you can do whatever you want." While that idea is admittedly tantalizing—ultimate power, the ability to issue decrees that are followed without question—it is not reflective of my beliefs about leading, and it is not the way I have led the program over the past several years. It should be a required task for any leader or potential leader to think about why she wants to lead. I suspect this does not always happen, but one must recognize that no matter how many people one leads, a leadership role is impactful. It merits philosophical and practical consideration, and I hope, a strong desire to be a good leader. Some do want authoritarian power. Power can be appealing. But, for me, the power to affect change and make something already good even better is far more appealing. I was excited to consider, too, how we might, over time, stay current and present in our field. Good leadership and good teaching are not complacent. We must be open to thoughtful, conscious change that responds to the needs of our students and our ever-evolving field. Change, however, at a large, public, Research I university, can be challenging, as even small curricular changes move through a long process of checks and balances. Yet, I still find these challenges, and my job overall, exciting, and I think daily about what it means to be a leader.

When I interviewed for my position, I was told the program utilizes a collaborative leadership model, and I was asked how I would continue that approach. While I had never heard of the method, it made perfect sense and seemed to dovetail with how I wanted to lead. I have long believed the group is more powerful than the individual. The group accomplishes more, and that work can be done thoughtfully with all voices present in the room. Nonetheless, I had to learn exactly what collaborative leadership was. This launched me on a journey of reading, trial and error, some failures, and some successes. Collaborative leadership is working for my program because everyone has a voice, everyone is valued, and we move our program forward together.

There are multiple factors that contribute to how I function as a collaborative leader. I was an external candidate hired to lead a well-established dance program and charged with immediately implementing significant curricular changes decided prior to my arrival. It was easy to get behind these changes, as they made sense for the program. This is not always the case for an incoming leader. One can unknowingly walk into a dysfunctional or toxic department. One might replace an adored and revered leader. I was fortunate to join a program that was appreciative of my predecessor but also ready for change. This is not to say my transition was without challenges. Some were minor; others, particularly strained relationships among faculty, were more substantial, and we are still working on them. Yet, we have accomplished a great deal. In my first three years as director of the program, we wrote a mission and vision statement, identified new program learning outcomes, and designed, passed, and implemented new BFA and BA degrees. We are well on our way to establishing a unique concentration in dance education within our BFA. This has all been done with a collaborative leadership model, and it has arguably yielded positive results. The collaborative leadership approach is applicable to any program, department, or college. By engaging one's stakeholders, collaborative leadership can empower one's community, create a better opportunity for substantial results, and help a program move forward in the best possible direction.

It is important to note that I am an introverted leader. This affects how I lead, as I consider my own personality and the personalities of the faculty, staff, and students with whom I work. Introverts tend to prefer writing to talking, while extroverts are energized by social interaction and external stimulation. External stimulation—from the sound of the traffic that comes in and out of our main office on a daily basis, to too much people watching—often exhausts me. Leaders in particular are often associated with extroverted characteristics: outgoing, enthusiastic, and charismatic, but introverts can be good leaders too. Andrew Spark, Timothy Stansmore, and Peter O'Connor conclude in "The Failure of Introverts to Emerge as Leaders," that introverted leaders are often better at leading a proactive team than extroverted leaders.[1] Introverts are also more effective at improving task proficiency. Because introverted leaders tend to listen more and dominate less, we are good at leading people who take initiative. We are more likely to hear and implement suggestions and then find ways to motivate others to be even more proactive. In contrast, extroverted leaders are more likely to want their name on something, and they may risk losing others' good ideas along the way.[2] In order to be a good leader, I studied introverted leadership in addition to and in tandem with collaborative leadership.

COLLABORATIVE LEADERSHIP

There are a myriad of leadership styles and perhaps an almost infinite number of resources on them. While collaborative leadership aligns with a number of other leadership styles, particularly servant leadership, I focus solely on collaborative leadership to provide a clear definition and approach. In collaborative leadership, a group works together to pursue a common goal. While there is likely a designated leader, that hierarchy is theoretically diluted in order to hear everyone's voices, honor everyone's contributions, and make decisions together. A collaborative leader must foster trust and teamwork and cannot be power hungry. Collaborative leadership is a process. Perhaps most importantly, the leader is a facilitator, leading the process, not the group. It is not about what leaders do; it is about how.

Writers and scholars place community at the heart of collaborative leadership. David Chrislip and Carl Larson define collaborative leadership as "a mutually beneficial relationship between two or more parties who work toward common goals by sharing responsibility, authority, and accountability for achieving results. . . . The purpose of collaboration is to create a shared vision and joint strategies to address concerns that go beyond the purview of any particular party."[3] In academia, our priority is student learning, and we, the faculty, benefit when our students succeed. To achieve that success, though, we must have an established sense of community, and we must work together. We must know each other as individuals, which means our outside lives, to the extent we are comfortable sharing, filter into conversations and meetings. We are not solely our working selves, as that persona is not enough to build a community. The Center for Community Health and Development's Community Tool Box at the University of Kansas offers a similar assertion: "Most of all, [participants] want a sense of community—a sense that all of us are in this together."[4] In writing not explicitly about collaborative leadership but about leading without authority, Keith Ferrazzi notes that "when we lead without authority, we consider *all* the people who may be critical to us achieving our goals. And we enlist them as members of our team."[5] Establishing the team and ensuring everyone is included is a significant task in collaborative leadership.

David Archer and Alex Cameron connect a strong community to good communication: "The essence of good communication in collaborative relationships, then, is to behave as one. All parties have to drop their guard and accept that they're in it together, for better or worse."[6] Good communication skills and the ability to truly listen are key tenets of collaborative leadership. Ferrazzi notes that "real leadership is not about telling others what to do. It's about inviting others, encouraging others, getting others excited about new possibilities."[7] Collaborative leadership requires ongoing dialogue and an ever-present emphasis on the whole. As Archer and Cameron write, "The most effective collaborative leaders are good at expressing the needs of their own organization clearly and succinctly and also good at listening hard to understand the needs of others."[8] This also requires dealing directly and expediently with conflict, a challenging but necessary task in establishing transparent communication.

While collaborative leadership may strike one as a slam dunk in higher education, particularly in the humanities, I do not think it is a common approach. The University of Kansas's Community Tool Box is a departure from the others cited here in that it is a product of the university's Center for Community Health and Development. While it is situated within an academic context, its mission, to provide resources for community development, extends beyond the university's walls. None of the literature speaks specifically to collaborative leadership in academia. I believe it is more often desired than actually implemented, particularly because our institutional hierarchy in higher education is so ingrained. To give marginalized voices—faculty and staff of color, students, not to mention any participating stakeholder—a role in decision-making may make those already in power feel threatened. Recognizing a part-time faculty member as a valued person in a department's governance pushes up against the power and stature frequently associated with a tenured or tenure-track faculty member. Collaborative leadership is not expedient; it requires more time on everyone's part, and time to govern in institutions of higher education is already scarce. I have held full-time positions at three universities and part-time positions at two, and collaborative leadership has never been utilized. In fact, the number of meetings I attended in which the department chair talked for almost the entire time is too great to count. It takes time and energy to engage everyone involved, and it seemed easier for the department chair to lead a meeting. It is hard to seek out and truly listen to other people's ideas, and this is the key tenet of collaborative leadership. This is another area where introverts, who may prefer to listen, excel.

COLLABORATIVE LEADERSHIP IN
DANCE AND THE LIBERAL ARTS

At CSU, the dance program is housed within the School of Music, Theatre, and Dance in the College of Liberal Arts. Dance does not always sit neatly in liberal arts or in academia in general. I have sat next to strangers who, when I said I am a dancer, hinted, directly or indirectly, that I am a stripper. The almost immediate link some make between dance and sexuality is a problematic stereotype, to say the least. Other strangers, seeing me grade papers on a plane and hearing I teach dance, ask with incredulousness, "You write?" Dancers write reflective papers, history papers, position papers, critique; the range of writing we do in dance is significant. I once received an email from a department head at my current institution saying that, in his field, "we think." The clear implication was that dancers do not think. These experiences, though, pushed me to further articulate the ways in which dance *does* fit into higher education and the liberal arts, as well as how my dance training specifically prepared me for a collaborative leadership role.

As I pull up the website for the College of Liberal Arts, one of the rotating images is of two of our dance majors performing a *pas de deux* from the ballet, *Don Quixote*. It is immediately clear that dance belongs in the liberal arts. CSU's College of Liberal Arts mission statement reads, "We create and extend knowledge and artistry that develops reflective citizens and confident leaders."[9] This is in keeping with the general goals of a liberal arts education that joins "the qualities of mind commonly associated with developing wisdom with the responsibilities of citizenship."[10] I will not trouble the use of "citizen," but, beyond the initial image on the website, dance belongs in the liberal arts for a variety of reasons, and the liberal arts and dance are both germane to collaborative leadership.

Dance allows students and graduates to make a positive contribution in the world. Without art, our world would be a colorless place, but dance does more than create visual interest. In particular, at a land grant university like CSU, we create opportunities for students to recognize the value of dance in the world by working with community members, using the same ideas that underpin collaborative leadership. Whether it is rehearsing a dance for a performance or planning a workshop for the community, our dancers work together in pursuit of a common goal. We have a class in which students develop lesson plans around dances they spent the previous semester creating. This process emphasizes group engagement and dialogue. Then, they tour the community, performing and teaching people aged two to ninety. In doing this, they are not only leaders, but they also are facilitators, guiding participants in creating their own dances. They lead the process; they invite, encourage, and get others excited. Dancers engage on a broader scale, too, using their choreography to reflect the world in which we live. At times, this is directly evident as student choreographers create dances that tackle the MeToo or Black Lives Matter movements. Dancers embody collaborative leadership principles in sharing dance with the world beyond our dance studios.

I also look to twenty-first-century skills to explain what dance teaches students, and these ideas coincide with those of the humanities, liberal arts, and collaborative leadership. The four tenets of the twenty-first-century skills are critical thinking, communication, collaboration, and creativity,[11] and dance's connection to these cornerstones is explicit. We engage in creative practices every day. While dance is not always collaborative, our program constantly strives to be. This includes a collaborative pedagogical approach—valuing students' voices and recognizing what they bring into the classroom—as opposed to a more traditional authoritarian approach. Any growth or learning that takes place is the result of the intersection between faculty and student knowledge, practice, and effort. Additionally, dancers collaborate with the choreographer; they make a dance together. Choreographers collaborate with lighting, costume, and set designers and sometimes with composers, musicians, and others. Contrary to what some I have encountered believe, dancers write, we reflect, and we communicate. We communicate on multiple levels—through the written word, through the spoken word, and through the body, both as teachers and students. I dare argue a dancer may have the most developed means of communication of all liberal arts subjects.

My literal lifetime in dance offers a number of qualities that lend themselves to a leadership role. Unlike many academics who pick a major in college and pursue that as a career, many dancers started studying dance as a child. I started dancing at the age of three, paused around age ten due to boredom, and resumed it wholeheartedly at age eleven. After graduating from college, a persistent foot injury forced me to momentarily pursue veterinary school, and then I chose dance again. My years in dance mean I can take criticism; I have been yelled at as a child dancer and as an administrator. I have a thick skin, though it could be thicker. I am certain that the physical skills I possess as a dancer translate to specific abilities as a leader. I can pivot quickly. I can change directions as a situation demands. I am flexible and adaptable. When I fall off balance, I know how to right myself and find equilibrium again. At the opposite end of that spectrum, I can let go, I can release my weight into the floor. I know how to fall, and I know how to get back up again. As a choreographer, I have to consider multiple perspectives, and as a choreographer and a dancer, I am constantly finding creative solutions to problems. I recognize good pain versus bad pain, know when to persist through a temporary situation, and when I need to stop and step back or pause. No matter how difficult a situation is, I can usually recognize its impermanency. I need all these skills as a leader, and my ongoing work as a dancer helps me develop them.

My identity as a dancer also lends itself to collaborative leadership in higher education. As aforementioned, communication is at the heart of collaborative leadership. As a teacher, choreographer, dancer, and leader, I am always communicating, and, perhaps more importantly, I have to consider *how* to communicate. What is the best movement for a particular moment in a dance? What is the best way to discuss a sensitive topic with a faculty member? Good communication necessitates good listening. In taking a dance class each day, I have to listen to my body. I must understand where it is at any given moment. Collaborative leadership requires I apply that same attentiveness to the faculty and students I lead. Of course, I am not perfect, and I do not always lead as well as I could, but I, like collaborative leadership, am a work in progress.

The practices I have forged in dance are applicable to any leader in the humanities. Listen to people. Truly listen. Do not just nod and smile, and do not generate a response while listening to them. When I need to talk—because leaders undoubtedly do—I think and plan first. Particularly when I have to have a more challenging conversation, I make notes, and I practice what I will say. In the same vein as listening, keep your eyes open. Our bodies communicate a great deal. Walk around, say hi to students in the hallways, visit faculty in their offices, and step into classes. Do the latter to be informed, to be able to know and talk about how and what faculty are teaching, not to criticize. When people are frustrated, the leader is the one who often bears the brunt of it, but it is helpful to remember it is not (usually) about the leader. Similarly, it is not the leader's agenda, it is the community's agenda. A collaborative leader must be open, willing to consider a different perspective and change one's mind. Think creatively, take risks, and be willing to make mistakes, but also own up to them. That transparency gives others permission to make mistakes and serves as another way in which trust is built.

BUILDING TRUST AND HEARING EVERYONE

Collaborative leadership requires trust. Immediately upon my arrival at CSU, I conducted a listening tour and met one-on-one with each of our tenured, tenure-track, and part-time faculty. These one-on-one conversations are also my preference as an introvert. While I planned each meeting for an hour, many went well beyond that. I asked faculty to speak in response to four prompts: what they felt was working in the program, what was not working, their research goals and interests, and their pie-in-the-sky desires. The purpose of these meetings was twofold: to learn about the faculty and through them, the program, and to let them know that I was listening. I am inclined to say the latter was more important to me. I made sure to follow up with answers to any questions that arose, and I have an ongoing list of needs and desires from the faculty that I continue to pursue. This practice also assists me in knowing the faculty beyond their working selves. As our conversation sometimes veers beyond work, I start to build a solid relationship with each individual. From the beginning, I wanted the faculty to know they had a voice and that it would be heard.

Collaborative leaders value the whole team, and they must push against the long-established hierarchy in higher education that places a full professor at the top of the food chain and adjunct faculty at the bottom. Making sure our faculty who are not on the tenure track believe they are valued and heard is of the utmost importance. We would not be where we are without them, and their contributions to our program are significant. In my own experiences as an adjunct faculty member at one university, getting access to a printer was unnecessarily difficult and stressful. At another university, I learned one of my classes had been canceled, not via communication from the department chair, but when I received my contract a few weeks before the start of the semester. I am proud and fortunate that CSU has made concerted steps to protect faculty off the tenure track by ensuring a base salary, a minimum amount of work, and an ongoing contract for some of them. But I play a role in including them, too, and that contributes to building trust. In addition to my listening tour, every faculty member is invited to all our faculty meetings. They contribute to the maintenance and development of our program, and they vote on all applicable decisions. I am perhaps more protective of their time than I am of the tenured and tenure-track faculty, as some have no service in their contract, while others have 5–10 percent of their load attributed to service. Admittedly, this is hard to quantify, but I do my best to be mindful of their time. I treat them with respect in all that we do.

Students are also stakeholders in our program, and they must be included in a collaborative leadership model. Their perspectives are important, as they feel a direct impact from our decisions, and their experiences differ from professors and leaders and are necessary to hear. During my first spring, I continued my listening tour with the students. I met with each class—first-year students, sophomores, juniors, and seniors—and asked them the same questions I asked the faculty: what is working, what is not working, and what are your pie-in-the-sky desires? I started each session by assuring them of their anonymity in anything I shared with faculty and explained that, while I was happy to answer any questions, our time together was truly for them to talk and for me to listen. I meet with our first-year students each spring, and I will repeat my listening sessions with each class every four years. While some may feel students come and go, and their opinions are therefore not as valuable, they are at the root of what we do and deserve the opportunity to share their thoughts. Even when the faculty move in a direction counter to the students' wishes, many students have taken the time to let us know that they appreciated the opportunity to weigh in.

Explicit communication is also essential, particularly with students. When I arrived, the then seniors resisted a number of changes. They were quick changes that made the program more efficient, but they were not what the senior students were used to. I explained why we made the changes and acknowledged the simple fact that change can be difficult. I emphasized that they can always challenge any decision I make and that I will always explain my rationale. All leaders will encounter situations in which details or actions taken are confidential, but, again, leaders can still be explicit. I tell students that there are aspects of the situation I cannot share, and it may seem like I am not doing anything. I acknowledge the frustration around that and ask that they trust that I hear their concerns and do not sit and do nothing in response to them. Even when we cannot share details, leaders can communicate, and that goes a long way.

WHAT DO MEETINGS LOOK LIKE?

While aspects of our faculty meetings might resemble facets of any generic faculty meeting, I use strategies informed by collaborative leadership to plan and facilitate our meetings. I am not interested in meetings where we simply go through points on an agenda. Those can be shared via email or on the agenda without discussion. Our time is valuable, and our time together is even more so. I seek to facilitate faculty meetings in which thinking and discussing are prioritized, whether we consider our teaching, our class schedule, or the larger tenets of our program, such as our mission and vision statements, program learning objectives, and curriculum. Some discussion items require advance reading while others do not. I try not to overload the faculty with meeting preparation, which might result in their appearance at a meeting in an already overwhelmed state of mind. Meetings are an opportunity for our hive mind to come together and think together. In the interest of making progress, though, it is also important to use our thinking to produce concrete results.

We continue to build trust during meetings. For a collaboration to be successful, a team must establish norms and ground rules for participation.[12] Particularly for retreats, we review our community guidelines, which emphasize active listening, taking responsibility for one's thoughts and opinions, and a willingness to stretch. In the symbiotic relationship that collaborative leadership necessitates, "building a common set of values and codes of behaviour is always a high priority."[13] To further foster trust, collaborative leadership must acknowledge the whole person. Our faculty meetings can veer from our work lives when participants are willing. Often at the beginning of the meeting, I provide a prompt to which everyone responds verbally. Sometimes it is work-related; other times it is not. This ensures we know each other as human beings, beyond the work we do together. We also move together briefly, retaining and reinforcing our identities as dancers. Any meeting can start this way; take a minute to take a few deep breaths together. Lastly, while this may go without saying, the symbolism of it is too important to omit: if there is a head of the table, I never sit there.

There are a variety of ways in which to "make sure everyone is heard."[14] This is key in making decisions together and leading the program collaboratively. As we move into discussions of ideas and bigger-picture items during our meetings, I often prompt us to write on our own. This, in particular, serves introverted faculty members by giving them some quiet time to process on their own. They are not, then, left in the dust as more extroverted faculty members process verbally and quickly during a meeting. After we write, we pool our ideas. Sometimes we do this in small groups and bring something back to the larger group, and sometimes we process together. While we have had no major disagreements, we hear and respond to each other's critiques of ideas or, when writing something, each other's words. Eventually, we drill down to something we all agree on, and we vote when needed. Our meetings always include open time for questions, comments, and thoughts. While everyone has an opportunity to contribute items to the agenda in advance of the meeting, there is time for questions or concerns to be brought to the fore during the meeting. These strategies ensure everyone has the opportunity to share and discuss. As a result of these approaches, our meetings feel productive, and I dare say, sometimes even enjoyable.

SPEED BUMPS AND SUCCESSES

Collaborative leadership is not for everyone. It is time-consuming, requires facing conflict head-on, and demands that a leader subsume her ego.[15] "Many collaborative efforts fail and many leaders find the personal challenges of sharing control impossible to overcome."[16] I am mindful of the time commitment, and I am learning to manage conflicts quickly and openly. One of my challenges is the opposite of surrendering my ego and sharing control. There are times when any leader, even a collaborative leader, must make a decision. Once, in an effort to get input from everyone on a decision I was already fairly certain about, I caused the faculty to do unnecessary work. I hesitated to share my decision in my desire to hear everyone's opinions. I should have trusted my judgment and shared my thoughts, let faculty respond, and made my decision. Leaders have to lead. Even with a collaborative leadership model, it is the leader's responsibility to keep the program's mission and vision at the forefront and make decisions that connect to them and serve the students. This may mean a short discussion to confirm a decision instead of a longer one that leads to the same outcome. I know the faculty would have appreciated this far more than doing additional work.

Engaging the students in a meaningful way continues to be a challenge, but they are clearly appreciative of the opportunity. When asked for comments, a handful of students always express gratitude for seeking their feedback. Students are most reflective of the moving target academia often encounters. They are with us for two to four years, give or take, so do we take their feedback with a grain of salt, or do we wholeheartedly embrace it? Sometimes, they simply do not respond to requests for comment. When faculty sought responses to a draft of our vision statement, two students commented. We had a written draft hanging on the wall with sticky notes available for comments. Was this too public? The response rate to anonymous Google surveys has been far better, with rates of about 80 percent each time. We are also grappling with whether or not we wish to include a student in our faculty meetings. How involved should they be? Finding the middle ground in a leadership model where we strive to hear all the voices is tricky because we could easily default to an "adults know best" approach. After we wrote our mission statement, one faculty member made an offhand comment about students' thoughts on the new statement. I realized I missed an opportunity to ask for their input and opinions. We deal with these questions through trial and error and ongoing dialogue with each other. Ultimately, I do feel I can do more in involving our students in our work.

Recognizing one's imperfections means recognizing when one needs help and reaching out to ask for it. There have been and will continue to be faculty and student rifts and occasions when trust rests on shaky ground. I do not have all the skills needed to see our stakeholders through each conflict, and so I look beyond myself. CSU is fortunate to have a conflict resolution center, and I have also utilized our human resources manager, our ombudspeople, the Office of Equal Opportunity, and our Office of Inclusive Excellence as resources for dealing with conflict. Some meetings are small, while others occur with our full faculty, and we have resolved some, but not all, conflicts. I am grateful for the resources I have at my disposal, as I could not navigate these challenges alone.

Our successes are notable. In three years, we proposed and received approval to launch a new degree program. We substantially edited an existing degree program, submitted it, and received approval. We developed a mission statement, a vision statement, and learning objectives for our two degree programs. One faculty member led a collective effort to develop a clear and transparent method of assessment for our dance technique classes. We created new policies and procedures that make our program more efficient. These achievements required a great deal of big-picture thinking and attention to detail as we parsed everything out. I am proud of these successes, but I am most proud of the process that led to them. I hear from faculty and students who appreciate being heard and feel they are a part of our dance program. While we can still improve, and while not every single person agrees with all that we do, each change represents the voices of our program and a collective effort to move our program forward.

CONCLUSION

A leader is and should always be a work in progress. While I am beholden to collaborative leadership, I work to embrace the gray area. In leading our dance program, I also draw on ideas from servant leadership, transformational leadership, and situational leadership. We know teaching is leading, too, and my feminist pedagogical approach influences my approach to leadership. As Chrislip and Larson confirm, "there is no 'model' collaborative process that will work on all issues in every community."[17] While I commit to this approach and to the process, I know I will still stumble from time to time, but as a dancer, I know how to pick myself up and keep moving. I have shared my approach here, but it will continue to adapt and evolve to fit the stakeholders and our program. I am certain, though, that there is clear value in a collaborative leadership approach in the humanities in academia. Collaborative leadership engages everyone, empowers the community, and allows a program to not just succeed, but to thrive.

I am a strong proponent of faculty leaders investing in a collaborative leadership model. In seeking opinions and letting everyone have a say in decision-making, one gets buy-in from one's stakeholders. They feel valued and heard, and that results in happier employees and ultimately, less turnover. Student retention may increase as students are more engaged and involved. Collaborative leadership also has the ability to create a well-functioning, thoughtful group of people who have the best interests of the department or school in mind. To draw on a cliché, it is a "we not me" approach. As with most things, those who embark on collaborative leadership will not achieve it overnight. Be patient as you build your community. Start by actively listening to your stakeholders. Create space for them to talk freely and, it bears repeating, truly, actively listen to them. Be curious. Get to know them as people, not just as faculty members or students who chose the major. Build trust and give them reason after reason to trust you. Accept the sometimes-lengthy amount of time it may take to achieve something, but recognize that when it is achieved together, it is a group success, not just your success. Note your stumbles, embrace them, and use them to keep moving forward. Keep your balance and keep putting one foot in front of the other.

NOTES

1. Andrew Spark, Timothy Stansmore, and Peter O'Connor, "The Failure of Introverts to Emerge as Leaders: The Role of Forecasted Affect," *Personality and Individual Differences* 121 (2018): 84–88.

2. Susan Cain, *Quiet: The Power of Introverts in a World That Can't Stop Talking* (New York: Broadway Books, 2012), 57.

3. David D. Chrislip and Carl E. Larson, *Collaborative Leadership: How Citizens and Civic Leaders Can Make a Difference* (San Francisco: Jossey-Bass Publishers, 1994), 5.

4. "Section 11. Collaborative Leadership," Community Tool Box, University of Kansas, accessed February 6, 2021, https://ctb.ku.edu/en/table-of-contents /leadership/leadership-ideas/collaborative-leadership/main.

5. Keith Ferrazzi, *Leading without Authority: How the New Power of Co-Elevation Can Break Down Silos, Transform Teams, and Reinvent Collaboration* (New York: Currency, 2020), 29.

6. David Archer and Alex Cameron, *Collaborative Leadership: Building Relationships, Handling Conflict and Sharing Control*, 2nd ed. (London: Routledge, 2013), 52.
7. Ferrazzi, *Leading without Authority*, 41.
8. Archer and Cameron, *Collaborative Leadership*, 12.
9. "About Us," Colorado State University College of Liberal Arts, accessed May 10, 2021, https://www.libarts.colostate.edu/about/.
10. Patricia M. King, Marie Kendall Brown, Nathan K. Lindsay, and JoNes R. VanHecke, "Liberal Arts Student Learning Outcomes: An Integrated Approach," *About Campus* 12, no. 4 (2007): 3.
11. "Framework for 21st Century Learning Definitions," Partnership for 21st Century Learning, 2019, https://www.battelleforkids.org/networks/p21.
12. Chrislip and Larson, *Collaborative Leadership*, 52.
13. Archer and Cameron, *Collaborative Leadership*, 43.
14. Community Tool Box, "Section 11."
15. Community Tool Box, "Section 11."
16. Archer and Cameron, *Collaborative Leadership*, 12.
17. Chrislip and Larson, *Collaborative Leadership*, 73.

BIBLIOGRAPHY

Archer, David, and Alex Cameron. *Collaborative Leadership: Building Relationships, Handling Conflict and Sharing Control*. 2nd ed. London: Routledge, 2013.

Cain, Susan. *Quiet: The Power of Introverts in a World That Can't Stop Talking*. New York: Broadway Books, 2012.

Chrislip, David D., and Carl E. Larson. *Collaborative Leadership: How Citizens and Civic Leaders Can Make a Difference*. San Francisco: Jossey-Bass Publishers, 1994.

Colorado State University College of Liberal Arts. "About Us." Accessed May 10, 2021. https://www.libarts.colostate.edu/about/.

Community Tool Box. "Section 11. Collaborative Leadership." Accessed February 6, 2021. https://ctb.ku.edu/en/table-of-contents/leadership/leadership-ideas/collaborative-leadership/main.

Ferrazzi, Keith. *Leading without Authority: How the New Power of Co-Elevation Can Break Down Silos, Transform Teams, and Reinvent Collaboration*. New York: Currency, 2020.

Godsey, Michael. "Why Introverted Teachers Are Burning Out." *The Atlantic*, January 25, 2016. https://www.theatlantic.com/education/archive/2016/01 /why-introverted-teachers-are-burning-out/425151/.

Jung, C. G. *Psychological Types*. Edited and translated by Gerald Adler and R.F.C. Hull. Princeton, NJ: Princeton University Press, 1971.

Kahnweiler, Jennifer B. *The Introverted Leader: Building on Your Quiet Strength*. San Francisco: Berrett-Koehler Publishers, Inc, 2009.

King, Patricia M., Marie Kendall Brown, Nathan K. Lindsay, and JoNes R. VanHecke. "Liberal Arts Student Learning Outcomes: An Integrated Approach." *About Campus* 12, no. 4 (2007): 2–9. https://doi-org.ezproxy2.library .colostate.edu/10.1002/abc.222.

LaGasse, Paul, and Columbia University. "Extroversion and Introversion." In *The Columbia Encyclopedia*, 6th ed. New York: Columbia University Press, 2021, 1.

Pannapacker, William. "Screening Out the Introverts." *The Chronicle of Higher Education*, April 15, 2012. https://www.chronicle.com/article/Screening-Out -the-Introverts/131520.

Partnership for 21st Century Learning. "Framework for 21st Century Learning Definitions." 2019. Accessed May 10, 2021. https://static.battelleforkids.org /documents/p21/P21_Framework_DefinitionsBFK.pdf

Spark, Andrew, Timothy Stansmore, and Peter O'Connor. "The Failure of Introverts to Emerge as Leaders: The Role of Forecasted Affect." *Personality and Individual Differences* 121 (2018): 84–88. https://doi.org/10.1016/j.paid.2017 .09.026.

12

COMMUNICATION AND CRISIS MANAGEMENT

A Case Study and a Cautionary Tale

MICHAEL AUSTIN

To secure the desired influence within the institution requires skill in communication as the basic element in the group process. The elementary skills, such as writing and speaking, can be taken for granted, but those involved in achieving effectiveness and high group morale cannot. The utmost skill is needed to deal with the kinds of problems that stand in the way of good relations between administration and faculty.

ALGO D. HENDERSON "THE DESIRED INFLUENCE:
IMPROVING COMMUNICATION BETWEEN
ADMINISTRATION AND FACULTY"[1]

NOTHING IS MORE IMPORTANT FOR ACADEMIC LEADERSHIP THAN LEARNING HOW TO COMmunicate in ways appropriate to any situation. At no time does this become clearer than in a major crisis. Like most higher education administrators, I got my on-the-job training in crisis management in March of 2020, when the COVID-19 pandemic swept across the globe. The pandemic required dramatic changes in excruciatingly short time frames, and it required an extraordinary amount of communication with faculty, staff, students, and other stakeholders of the university—emails, video conferences, telephone calls, and communication through our university website. Like any crisis, however, the pandemic did not cause new problems as much as it revealed problems that had always existed but had been easy to hide in a noncrisis environment. The reverse is also true: embedded in any crisis is the opportunity to fix what has always been broken. What follows is an attempt to do this by treating the pandemic of 2020 as both a case study in crisis communication and a cautionary tale for those who misunderstand the nature of communication—crisis or otherwise—in a university.

I considered myself a good communicator when I left my position teaching English and became the academic vice president and provost of a small private university. Communication was the coin of my realm as a faculty member. I knew how to write and speak clearly, how to collaborate with others, how to make and support arguments, how to isolate important points and direct discussion toward them, and how to build consensus in diverse groups. My education in the humanities, I felt, was the perfect preparation for an administrative career—especially in an environment that values written communication highly. I was fortunate to have entered administration just at the time that email was becoming the preferred method of communication on college campuses. It played to my strengths as a writer and allowed me to turn many administrative problems into writing problems—giving me something of a home-court advantage in debates with other administrators and an easy, comfortable way to communicate with the faculty that I supervise.

In general, it has worked out well. There are a lot of similarities—and not that many differences—between an academic paper and an accreditation self-study. They are both exercises in making assertions and marshaling evidence. And they both require just enough individuality and creative flair to make the result stand apart from the crowd. None of the writing tasks associated with administration (accreditation studies, assessment reports, board communications, etc.) have ever intimidated me. After all, I had to face Reviewer Two; no administrative critique has ever been as devastating. The communication skills I acquired as a student and a professor of English were well suited to the day-to-day demands of academic administration.

But it is in a crisis, when the stakes are high and the consequences of failure are disastrous, that we discover what we are and are not good at. A major crisis exposes all of the things about an institution that aren't functioning well. In normal situations, minor course corrections are relatively simple. Misunderstandings can be ironed out, difficulties can be glossed over, and incomplete procedures can be invented as required and put in place as needed. In most cases, the things that don't work during a crisis were not working very well before the crisis—it was just a lot easier to hide the deficiencies. When a major crisis hits, you tend to be stuck with the processes and competencies already in place.

We were not taken totally by surprise in March of 2020. Reports of the novel coronavirus began to filter out of China late in December of 2019. By the end of January, we had some reason to believe that it might become a global threat, and, in February, most schools started to monitor World Health Organization and Centers for Disease Control and Prevention warnings regularly. At this point, there had not been any cases of what we were then calling the "novel coronavirus" in the state of Indiana, where our university is located, or in Lincolnshire County in the United Kingdom, where many of our students were studying at our Harlaxton center. But we were not prepared for the enormity of the crisis or the extent that it would transform our operations.

On Tuesday, March 3, during the week before our spring break, I sent a brief note to our faculty asking them to "develop a plan to deliver courses to some or all of [their] students in the event of an emergency that prevents [them] or [their] students from coming to campus" and "communicate this plan to [their] students before they leave for spring break." I hastily added this was all being done out of an abundance of caution. "The likelihood of a major outbreak in our area remains small right now," I asserted with confidence. "But we want to be prepared for different ways that the situation could change, and we want to be good citizens of all our communities and protect the most vulnerable among us from even the remotest possibility of exposing them to this disease."

One week and one day later, everything changed. On Wednesday, March 12, at an all-day meeting at the president's house that was supposed to be devoted to long-range planning, we heard that most of the large schools in the area were closing and moving classes online. By noon, it was clear that we were going to have to do the same thing. By the end of the day, we had announced that we were moving all classes online for at least two weeks and that we were closing our UK site and bringing our students home. By the end of the week, nearly every school in the country did the same. The Great Pandemic—and my own forced introduction to the best practices in crisis communication—had begun.

The situation was almost comically dire. Only about 2 percent of our courses were already online. Our students and our faculty were off campus for spring break, and most of the students had left all their materials in their apartments or dorm rooms. Many of our faculty had never taught online before, and some did not have internet access in their homes. And our entire campus had one paid Zoom license. We had five days to become a kind of school that we had never been, and we could not gather in person to discuss any plans. Acting on the maxim that over-communication was impossible, and smugly aware that writing was my strong suit (I was an English major, after all—three times), I began sending out emails to faculty and staff at a furious pace. All my training in writing and rhetoric, I believed, had prepared me for this moment.

It did not go well.

I began with a daily update every evening explaining where we were on the transition process. To this end, I created a Microsoft Teams site for the entire faculty, with a Facebook-like interface that they could use to discuss pandemic issues. I sent out frequent notes about online resources that were becoming available for teachers—electronic textbooks, Zoom accounts, proctoring services—and about cultural opportunities like the free operas being broadcast by the Metropolitan Opera. And, as I reread Camus's *The Plague* at the start of the pandemic, I occasionally added in my thoughts about the existential nature of the crisis we faced.

This went on for several weeks until I began to receive emails in return asking me to please stop sending out so many messages since the faculty were extremely busy trying to figure out how to teach their courses and meet with their students in an unprecedented environment. About two weeks into the pandemic, I received the following email from a part-time faculty member I had never met.

Hi, Michael –

I am a part-time faculty member, but I would just like to bring something to your attention. I think the idea of limiting faculty work hours needs to be addressed. I think that the expectations for faculty need to be moderated in light of everything that is going on. I cannot be spending 24/7 on my computer trying to learn and implement things for the university, nor can I be mentally available for university responsibilities 24/7.

I (along with all the other faculty) am attempting to manage all of the following simultaneously:

1. *Provide for and take care of my family, including my husband, who has been ill, and my daughter, who is dealing with her own school going online*

2. *Convert/modify all my class materials to be available online, plus create new materials that didn't exist previously to fit the new format*

3. *Keep in touch with all my students, some of whom are very slow to respond to my messages!*

4. *Not be completely stressed out by the constant news stream and fears about Coronavirus getting worse every day—the need for rest and some physical activity is important*

5. *Communicate with family and friends as their lives are in turmoil too*

There needs to be a bit of compassion from you regarding the well-being and sanity of the faculty and staff during this extremely difficult situation. I am overwhelmed by the constant barrage of emails offering new software possibilities for online education because they EACH take many hours to figure out and use.[2]

This message succinctly, and devastatingly, showed me just about everything wrong with the way I had been communicating during the pandemic. Most of the specifics were confirmed by an anonymous faculty survey at the end of the semester. My own attempts at crisis communication had not considered the needs of different audiences, had failed to clarify expectations, and had merged with other communications from the institution to create confusion and frustration. And the communication went mainly in one direction, without enough opportunity for input or feedback.

It was not difficult to see that these had always been weaknesses of my communication style. They were just a lot easier to hide among normal operations. Being a good writer and speaker is not the same thing as being an effective communicator, nor can a high volume of communication substitute for a communication plan. These were difficult truths to face, but the pandemic didn't leave much choice. Our communications after the pandemic hit were subject to the unforgiving logic of natural selection. When something worked, we kept it in place; when something didn't work, we heard about it immediately. And eventually, we ended up with a set of practices that got us through the shutdown and the following year of pandemic-influenced education—and that provided a model for effective university communication when it was all over.

THE PANDEMIC AS A CASE STUDY IN EFFECTIVE COMMUNICATION

By chance rather than design, the university hired an exceptionally talented and experienced communication director less than a week before the pandemic shutdown, and she quickly formed an executive team that met every day during the spring semester. As we worked to refine our communication strategy, I began to understand what effective communication really means. The following list is not a comprehensive list of the principles of crisis communication. Rather, it is a deeply personal, highly idiosyncratic list of things that I thought I knew before the pandemic but didn't really understand. In each case, the crisis crystallized a more general principle that is equally important in day-to-day situations. These are, in other words, the things that a major crisis taught me about communication.

Different Audiences Have Different Needs

We quickly identified six constituent groups that we had to tailor messages to, each with their own needs and objectives:

> *Students* needed to know immediately what to do after spring break was over. How would they go to class? How would they turn in assignments and access university resources? What about all the stuff they left in their rooms? What if they didn't have their textbooks at home with them? What could they do if they didn't have internet access? How would they access university services like the library, the writing center, or the registrar's office? And how long was this all going to take?

Parents had most of the concerns that students had, with an additional set of financial concerns: What kinds of equipment did they need to get to enable their children to learn online? What resources existed if they could not afford the necessary tools? Would we refund any portion of tuition, housing, or meal plans? What happened to students' financial aid if one or both parents were laid off or furloughed because of the pandemic? And when would we be back in person?

Faculty were deeply concerned about moving all of their courses online with almost no notice. And they had a lot of questions that I was not sure how to answer. Would we purchase Zoom accounts for all faculty members? What if they wanted to use another program? How were they going to proctor exams online to prevent cheating? Could they come to their offices on campus to teach? Could they take computers and office equipment from their offices to their homes? What if they didn't have internet access? Were all field trips and study abroad sessions canceled? How were they supposed to advise students? What training resources would we provide? And, within the faculty, there were a lot of specialized needs. How would our music students take voice and instrument lessons? How would theatre students perform? What about the engineering students who had to access specialized equipment for their senior projects? What about adjunct and part-time faculty? The list of questions seemed overwhelming.

Staff and administration, unlike the faculty, could not do their jobs without going to campus. Receptionists had to have a place to receive people, and the grounds crew could hardly mow the grass without coming onto campus. Almost every member of our staff had a unique set of work circumstances that we had to address, and no single communication or set of communications could work for even a small fraction of the employees.

The board of trustees at our university, as with most private schools, is a large and highly engaged board whose members have a fiduciary responsibility for the institution. Closing campus and refunding room and board costs had a huge financial impact, as did the need to spend hundreds of thousands of dollars on internet teaching resources, cleaning supplies, personal protective equipment, and other pandemic-related expenses.

We needed to address these kinds of concerns frequently with both individuals and with the full board.

Members of the community regularly came to campus for concerts, plays, lectures, sporting events, and other public functions. And what happens at a local college or university is inherently interesting to local news organizations. Throughout the pandemic, we provided regular updates to media outlets that sometimes gave different information—but could never contradict—communications to the other five groups.

It would be impossible for any one leader—academic or otherwise—to manage the kind of communication flow that a complex institution requires. It takes coordination and collaboration with a team of people with diverse views and responsibilities. During a crisis like the COVID-19 pandemic, the need for such collaboration becomes apparent very quickly. But it always needs to be the cornerstone of effective communication.

Too Much Communication Can Be Overwhelming

Another reason that crisis communications should be strategic and collaborative is that, during a major crisis, most people are getting a lot of messages from different sources. Nobody is *only* a university employee or student. People are also parents and community members and spouses and dozens of other things that they must balance during a crisis. Also, faculty are trying to manage three or four or more classes with students who are scared and confused. People who are trying to negotiate a crisis do not need, and cannot process, multiple messages from different departments of the university they are associated with.

It Is Easy to Confuse Information with Requirement

My messages to the faculty at the start of the pandemic did not draw a clear boundary between information and instruction, and this produced a lot of confusion and frustration that could have been easily avoided. When a senior administrator sends out a message saying something like "you can access free test proctoring services for the rest of the semester at the following site . . . ," some faculty members will perceive this as a university requirement, and others will see it as an interesting fact to file away for future use. The most institutionally vulnerable faculty—adjuncts, part-time instructors, junior professors—are much more likely to perceive an offhand comment as an institutional requirement unless the communication explicitly says otherwise. The power differential between a provost and an adjunct faculty member is enormous, and a folksy, conversational communication tone comes from a place of privilege not always available to those who read the message. After a few weeks of confusing emails, I began to segment messages into a short section of "Things You Have to Read and Do Something With" and a much longer "Stuff to Read If You Have Time"—making it very clear at the outset which items contained institutional assignments and which were merely informational.

You Have to Find Ways to Listen, Even When It Is Hard

In a major crisis, institutional communication tends to become even more top-down and one-way than normal. People are acting quickly, things have to be done, deadlines have to be met, and results have to be achieved quickly. There is no time for debating things in committees. Meaningful two-way communication is hard under such circumstances, which is precisely why it is so important. In a crisis like the recent pandemic, when decision-makers are physically isolated from the university and its communities, it is vitally important that administrators create space for discussion. The view from the top of the org chart in such situations is just as limited, just as incomplete, and just as uncertain as the view from everywhere else. We can't have all the information that we need unless we find ways to listen.

Perhaps the most important thing we did during the first week of the pandemic was to ask the faculty what computer equipment they had at home, what they still needed, and what activities could simply not be done remotely. This required a fairly detailed, web-based questionnaire, but it allowed us to quickly sort faculty into categories:

- Faculty members whose home computer set up and network access were sufficient for online courses

- Faculty who could move courses online if they were allowed to take their office computers and other equipment home
- Faculty members who needed either a laptop computer, a network access point, or both to be able to move courses online
- Faculty members who would need limited access to campus in order to teach courses online. When the city issued a shutdown order, these faculty had to be provided with a formal letter explaining their need to come to work

We also placed a question box on our COVID-19 web page and encouraged everyone to submit any question they had, promising a twenty-four-hour turnaround. The Communications Office immediately routed questions to the person or office best suited to respond. But intake forms are only useful for certain things. We also found that we had to arrange online meetings with all our constituencies in which we just listened to both the concerns and the ideas that they had. To make it through, we had to find ways to listen—really listen—to the individual thoughts and experiences of everybody who was experiencing the same crisis in different ways.

There Is No Substitute for Individual Communication

Throughout the spring semester, I answered somewhere around 100 email messages a day, plus phone calls, Zoom conferences, and other forms of individual communication. This wasn't my plan, but it quickly became apparent that it was the only way to respond to the profoundly different experiences that everybody was having with the pandemic. The more I reflect, the more I realize that the one-on-one conversations were much more important than the regular communication blasts to different constituent groups. To do this effectively, I had to spend a lot of my own time talking to people, and I had to make sure that deans, directors, and department chairs were empowered to have these conversations with their areas. In the end, communication occurs within individual relationships between human beings and not between institutional categories following a script. And there is no substitute for talking to people about their individual perspectives and concerns.

DOES A HUMANITIES DEGREE HELP?

In the end, I found my training in the humanities invaluable, but not for the reasons I thought it would be when the pandemic began. If I had taken a few more basic undergraduate communication classes, I would have been better suited to a lot of the communication challenges I faced when the crisis began. But the things I kept coming back to during the crisis were the things behind the lessons—the pith and marrow of my humanities education, which is, at its core, the study of how human beings relate to other human beings. How do we deal with pain and loss and anger and fear? What gives us hope? All the woo-woo stuff that we like to hide behind more respectable phrases like "critical thinking," "team building," and "problem-solving." A humanitarian is someone who helps people, and a humanist is someone who believes in people. Communication strategies that treat people transactionally—as problems to be solved—are never going to help an institution get through a major crisis.

When I look at where our institutional communications broke down during the pandemic, I find that my own communication was worst when I interacted transactionally with people in institutional categories. It was at its best when I was interacting with actual humans who were, at different times, angry, scared, frustrated, and hopeful. Certainly, one need not read classical poetry or study religion and philosophy to treat people well, but I believe that these disciplines dramatically increase our ability to understand, and hopefully to empathize with, human beings in all their glorious, messed up, and deeply contradictory diversity. Without genuine empathy and understanding as the motives for communication, the strategies don't matter much. People know when they are being treated as problems.

In a major crisis, the temptation to revert to transactional communication can be overwhelming. Things just have to get done, and they have to get done quickly. The great value of training in the humanities is the understanding that human interaction becomes even more important in such situations than it is when things are going well. Good communication during a crisis requires an understanding of multiple audiences with multiple perspectives and complex needs. Education in the humanities is vital to understanding these kinds of complexities because they emerge naturally out of the human beings at the center of humanistic study. As universities become more corporate, and communication becomes more instrumental, it is just possible that the humanities will save us by keeping the humans in the equation.

NOTES

1. Algo D. Henderson, "The Desired Influence: Improving Communication Between Administration and Faculty," *The Journal of Higher Education* 38, no. 6 (1967): 304–11.
2. Anonymous faculty member, email message to author, March 18, 2020.

BIBLIOGRAPHY

Henderson, Algo D. "The Desired Influence: Improving Communication Between Administration and Faculty." *The Journal of Higher Education* 38, no. 6 (1967): 304–11.

13

VOCATION AND THE DRUDGERY I LOVE

SEAN BENSON

The prospect of going into academic leadership, much like that of a man who "knows he is to be hanged in a fortnight . . . concentrates [the] mind wonderfully."[1] One can approach it with such trepidation, as Roze Hentschell and Catherine E. Thomas observe in the introduction, or with a sense of excitement as to where such a professional life might lead. In addition to new challenges and opportunities, leadership positions offer ancillary benefits—increased pay and stature—though they can equally entail more meetings and less flexible schedules as compared to those of full-time faculty. In my own administrative experience, I learned that the work is not bad (most days), but however one wishes to style it, choosing to pursue such a position involves trade-offs that potential leaders are wise to consider closely before taking the plunge. Having dipped my toes in the water, so to speak, I decided that pursuing higher leadership is not—for now, at least—for me.

Yet my account of not pursuing that path is an important one to tell, as not everyone who enters a role of higher leadership will find it rewarding, or precisely what they had envisioned. My foray into a leadership role, I hasten to add, was not wholly negative: there were multiple aspects I enjoyed, and I would consider taking on such a role in the future. Moreover, considering being a provost clarified what it is I am good at—"called" to do—and directed me to a professorship where my skills and abilities are an ideal match for the job requirements. Finding such a happy confluence in your own life and career is what this chapter is all about. The academy is largely secular, though there are those of us who teach at faith-based institutions, and my journey involves less a story of personal fulfillment and career satisfaction (though I value both as instrumental goods) than of finding a vocation wherein one can love one's neighbors, be they students, faculty, or staff.

I have worked at three different private liberal arts colleges. At the second of these institutions, I was approached in 2016 by the vice president for academic affairs (VPAA), the chief academic officer, who informed me that, in consultation with the president of the college and the executive board, he had been tasked with identifying a potential successor. What he informed me of was that the productivity and quality of my scholarship, the respect I had among colleagues in and outside my department, and my commitment to the mission of the university, made me a good candidate to be his successor—though he made it clear there would also be a wide-open search for the VPAA at the time of his retirement. I was surprised, too, because I knew the VPAA was interested in hiring people in administration from underrepresented groups (to which I did not belong). Moreover, I had not sought the position, in part because paper and book ideas always emerge from my teaching, and in part because I have always cherished the opportunity to shape both mind and character in the classroom.[2]

Still, I was humbled that he and others thought enough of my professional and interpersonal skills to approach me about the prospect. The suggestion made me admin-curious, too, but I was cautious to ask if I could test the waters first to see if becoming a candidate for chief academic officer was the right move for me. I knew that if I could juxtapose my teaching and research with this new leadership possibility, I would be able to make a more informed decision as to which suited me—and the university—best. With the VPAA's blessing, then, but without an additional title, I began splitting my time equally between teaching two courses each semester and working on two special projects that were administrative in nature but outside the usual role of the VPAA.

In this newfound capacity, I first became the liaison and mentor to a group of colleagues completing their doctorates. While a few of these PhD students were in traditional programs, a cohort of a dozen or so was completing a program in leadership by way of National Louis University. What was innovative about National Louis's program is that it offered in-house education; that is, professors from National Louis came to our campus every third weekend for in-person, intensive coursework. In between, students were completing their work and corresponding with their faculty (and each other) online. Because my colleagues were already full-time faculty and staff at our university, National Louis's hybrid model accommodated their busy schedules.

For my part in all this, I met with my colleagues individually when they had questions, and we also gathered monthly for "Coffee Talk," an hour-long conversation where we discussed their hopes, concerns, and worries. As Chyna N. Crawford remarks in her chapter in this volume, serving as mentor to newer, untenured faculty is a crucial role that those in leadership can and should play. I remember telling one of the candidates just starting the program that grit and perseverance were probably the two most important qualities necessary for the successful completion of a PhD program—not, surprisingly enough, intelligence. She had been worried that she was not smart enough, and I did my best to allay those concerns, as she had both the drive and intelligence to complete her doctorate—and eventually did so. I was able to lend my colleagues insight not only into the beginning of their doctoral program but also into what their careers might look like once they completed their dissertations. Helping faculty navigate the hurdles of their programs and realize their dream of earning a doctorate was rewarding work, and it offered a crucial support system for these colleagues.

Second, I served as campus liaison with the Network for Vocation in Undergraduate Education (NetVUE), a nationwide network of colleges and universities formed to assist students in discerning their callings in life. Sponsored by the Council for Independent Colleges, NetVUE has already produced three volumes on vocation and higher education.[3] In my leadership capacity, I attended, sometimes alone, both regional and national NetVUE conferences where I learned the gap that exists in many students' undergraduate education: we teach them how to think and apply their skill sets to various professions, but as a faculty, we were not doing the good and necessary work of helping students to think about the meaning of it all.[4] To what end, other than perhaps a material one—making a living—are they putting their skills? As an administration, we wanted our students to think more intentionally about such broad existential questions. One of my duties included applying for a NetVUE grant to train faculty members to talk about vocation in the classroom. We wanted students, religious and secular, to understand first what a calling is, and then how in their lifework they can realize it in service to others. We were especially keen on introducing vocation into our courses, particularly into the "Senior Seminar" capstone courses that all of our majors were required to take at the end of their respective programs of studies.

Toward that end, in the fall of 2019, I took the lead role in a faculty discussion group where we read a number of works on vocation.[5] As one of my colleagues noted, she hadn't quite decided what she wanted to do when she grew up, but these books were helping her—and would help her students—find their calling. Indeed, as David Cunningham remarks, "the process of vocational exploration and discernment is something that all students need to undertake [not only] *throughout* their undergraduate careers" but also "*throughout* their lives."[6] The experience certainly shaped me. Although our university welcomed students of all religious persuasions, including those who identify as "nones," we were a Presbyterian school rooted in the Judeo-Christian tradition, and that was reinforced both by our president and by our chaplain. Still, our culture has almost lost a sense of vocation as "[t]he action on the part of God or Christ of calling a person to undertake a particular occupation [or] way of life," but that acceptation was widespread for centuries and is still embraced by many religious denominations.[7] Since that is also part of my own faith tradition, I started to think about my calling to higher leadership at this institution.

As the VPAA cautioned me at the time, it is challenging in academic leadership to find the right balance, if one wants to maintain it, between teaching, administrating, and writing. While some may find doing all three possible—my colleagues in this volume are exemplary in that regard—I found it hard to do all three well, and in fact, my teaching and administrative responsibilities crowded out research and writing. As much as I was enjoying mentoring PhD candidates and leading our campus

NetVUE work, I did not really find that those activities engaged my analytical or creative abilities. I also found a few aspects of leadership mundane, particularly the many meetings, because they took time away from the more rewarding aspects of my daily work. In short, I do not think I was being prepared particularly well for a prospective position as VPAA; I was, instead, doing jobs that a middle manager would do. Hentschell and Thomas underscore in their introduction this necessary but undervalued training for higher leadership.

The current VPAA told me that what he liked about me, and about people from the humanities in general, was that we had good ideas and could think through problems, but I was tasked with preassigned duties that didn't really draw upon those skills. I enjoyed mentoring doctoral candidates and serving as a NetVUE liaison, but neither of those positions allowed me to rethink the curriculum; or to reenvision work schedules, say, for staff members who often found themselves sitting around with nothing to do; or to imagine how we might improve the lives and education of our students. Those strike me as more central to what a VPAA does. Since I was reading voluminously about vocation at the time, I began to think carefully about my own calling. I was reminded, too, that vocation for the apostle Paul is the use to which God puts our work: "We know that all things work together for the best unto them that love God, even to them that are *called* of his purpose."[8] To what purpose was I called? I had not thought about this question as much as I should have, even though I had often talked to students about a vocation involving the abilities and interests they have. As Roze Hentschell shared with me, "Academics in general are assumed to have found their calling (why else would you pursue a PhD, right?). But longevity and flourishing, and an examination of one's developing career—especially if one is going to pursue leadership—is critical."[9]

As I began to engage in this process of self-reflection, I realized I preferred teaching and writing to the mid-level administration I was doing. As Kevin Dettmar has observed, academic leadership positions at all levels are true and necessary vocations in their own right[10]—a good academic leader makes the life of those around her less onerous and more enjoyable. My task, though, was one of vocational discernment: I had to weigh the enjoyment of some parts of mid-level management and the prospect that

I might (or might not) someday be selected for executive leadership as VPAA against the joy I took in teaching and writing. I also came to understand better that one can still lead as a faculty member—teaching, mentoring, chairing a department or program—all of which, I should note, I did. Leadership at any level involves the good and the bad, and the truth is that it invariably entails an admixture of both and more.

Discerning one's calling for higher leadership is a matter of weighing its benefits and costs against those involved in other forms of leadership, including roles that involve teaching and researching. Given each person's abilities and interests, we reach different conclusions as to where we can best serve others and still flourish ourselves, and this is as it should be. What settled the matter for me, or at least nudged me in one direction, was a curious incident in a British literature survey course I taught.

Midway through one semester at a previous institution, a student objected to my teaching Alexander Pope's *The Rape of the Lock* (1712). Even though the student, by his own admission, had never read the poem, he objected to Pope's use of the word "rape" in his title, which triggered the student's objection. He asserted that any teaching of a work with "rape" in the title would "support rape culture." He based his comment solely on the poem's title, an interpretive move for which I give him credit—titles indicate "generic conceptions" of a text's meaning.[11] Yet I respectfully disagreed that the poem should not be taught, even though Pope's narrator is perhaps too dismissive of Belinda's (the historical Isabella Fermor) indignation at having a lock of her hair cut off by Lord Petre. Such an act was a clear violation of her wishes, and indeed of her person. Because Pope thought both sides of the scandal blew the incident out of all proportion, he refers to it, in his mock-heroic style, as a "rape." As Pope knew, rape could denote either a (mere) theft or actual sexual assault, and with his verbal facility, he no doubt wished to invoke both senses of the word.

Although the term "rape culture" remains "of uncertain definition,"[12] one can think of any number of early pagan cultures that normalized sexual violence or even of modern subcultures such as that embodied by USA gymnastics and the horrific abuse they allowed a team doctor, Larry Nasser, to visit upon hundreds of female athletes.[13] The question that arises, and that makes Pope's poem relevant today, is whether Lord Petre's cutting of the lock also constitutes an instance of rape culture? It was a question worthy of open and free discussion—ideal, in my view, for a classroom setting—but the student simply asserted without evidence that the use of the word "rape" in the title somehow supported rape culture. Moreover, a colleague shared with me that for a student to suggest Lord Petre's cutting of a lock of hair is akin to rape is in fact to trivialize the sexual violence that actual rape entails. And while I tried to explain to the student why I couldn't allow him to censor Pope's poem on such dubious grounds, he decided to approach a dean in order to complain about the poem and my intention to teach it.

What I expected, if not a quick dismissal of the student's attempt to censor the poem, was at least a hearing on the merits of both the complaint and the poem, and perhaps a lesson in intellectual openness and tolerance of ideas other than one's own. The dean opted for a path of lesser resistance. The student was simply removed from the course and allowed to complete it online with another instructor so that he would have to read neither *The Rape of the Lock* nor engage with the issue he had raised of its alleged complicity with rape culture. I am confident students are not so fragile they need to be removed from exposure to ideas other than their own, and the decision missed a teachable moment. Because this student also threatened to take the matter directly to the board of trustees, the dean and VPAA readily accommodated his request not to have to read a poem to which he so objected, and asked me to affirm his value as a person. I had no qualms with the latter request because I consider every person to be created in the image of God. And if the decision of senior leadership appeased the student, it also catalyzed my own thinking. The incident underscored important philosophical differences about the purpose of education, especially whether removing the student from my course was in his best interests. I also wondered if leadership at this university was part of my calling. The answer, I realized after long and sober reflection, was no.

I share with many theists the belief that we live in a sacramental universe: God's love and grace, if one is attentive to look for them—if we have eyes to see—abound in all aspects of the universe, and certainly in our lives. Such "faith," as Kierkegaard remarks, "is convinced that God troubles himself about the smallest thing."[14] To put it in terms of philosophical theology, the transcendent routinely supervenes on the natural, day-to-day world that God has actualized on this planet. Not only do faith and reason inform believers of God's creation and sustenance of the universe but also of his ability to direct our paths. What I recognized is that teaching is also a leadership role, one in which people of good character need to model what it means to be tolerant of others' views even while holding to one's own. My humanities background, not to mention my Lutheranism, had taught me to ask questions because in asking them we deepen our understanding of issues even if we don't always resolve them or find a neat solution. *The Rape of the Lock* is an eminently worthy poem to teach in an undergraduate English survey course, and if I allowed a student to determine what other students in my class could read, I would have served neither him nor them.

In addition, as I reflected on my abilities, I thought more about the initial caution I had taken to split my time between teaching/research and administration. I recognized in that hesitancy to embrace a full-time move into higher leadership, the misgivings I had about the distance such duties would place between me and my love of ideas, books, and writing. I enjoy the minutiae of scholarship—tracking down sources, writing footnotes, and writing prose that I strive to make both lucid and engaging. Try as I might, I found myself bored to tears by the minutiae of some of my administrative tasks: grade challenges, the many meetings, checking a student's grade-point average to see if she's satisfied the requirements of a degree program, and so on. There are of course more exciting aspects of higher leadership: visioning, strategizing, making hires in relation to the university's mission, and so on. Yet "the test of a vocation," the essayist Logan Pearsall Smith once wrote, "is the love of the drudgery it involves."[15] What an apt statement. I had seen some of the duties of higher leadership, and while I enjoyed aspects of it, I found other parts of it tedious. At the same time, I wondered if God was not using the experience to nudge me toward what I love even in the midst of its drudgery.

It is often easy to advise students disinterestedly, but it can be more challenging to be objective about our own gifts, talents, and inclinations—especially if more money is on the table. It is tempting to equate monetary rewards with career success, but I knew that I had to give serious consideration as to whether material success is the same as vocation. I knew I could still pursue higher leadership in the academy, but I began to recognize in my skills and interests a greater—more insistent—calling for the classroom and for the scholarship I love to write. It is not that one has to give up research and writing in higher leadership. The question for me was not the prospect of doing both, which is possible, but the love of the drudgery I felt in teaching, research, and writing. By way of contrast, when it came to moments of drudgery in mid-level administration, I did not experience that same level of enjoyment. That was telling.

In our NetVUE reading group on vocation, we were reading Gustaf Wingren's superlative work on Martin Luther's treatment of vocation. Luther helped me to think more and more about my own calling. The essence of his teaching on calling is simple: "Love for others is *eo ipso* the fulfillment of my vocation."[16] The Reformers undertook the reordering and reconceptualization of vocation, removing it from the exclusive province of the religious—priests, monks, and nuns—and dignifying the lifework of all people. "A cobbler, smith, peasant—each has the work and office of his trade, and yet they are all alike consecrated priests and bishops."[17] The Reformation "brought with it," as Jaroslav Pelikan notes, "a new respect for what has been called 'the sacredness of the secular,'" and this is largely the work of "the Reformer," Calvin's term of respect for Luther.[18] Again, neither Calvin nor Luther cared particularly which occupation one had; a calling is for our good so that we can help others, be it teaching, administrating, feeding the hungry, sheltering the homeless, giving alms, and so on.

A vocation, as its root (*vocare*) suggests, is not self-chosen; rather, a call comes from outside the self. Vocation chooses us, so to speak, based on our place in life, background, interests, inclinations, and other circumstances that present themselves to us frequently as givens.[19] It is tempting to think, then, because a higher leadership—or any other— position becomes open, one necessarily ought to fill it. Of course one can serve others as an administrator: my coauthors in this volume attest to that, as do the senior leaders where I work at the University of Mary Hardin-Baylor, President Randy O'Rear and Provost John Vassar, both of whom model servant leadership. Nonetheless, not everyone is called to higher leadership, and declining that opportunity as it presented itself in my life freed me to serve others with the gifts and skills I have. I know the drudgery I love, and the drudgery I don't; knowing the distinction between the two is a way of correctly following one's vocation. As Proust remarks of those disenchanted with their jobs, "they imagine that the life they are leading is not the one that really suits them and they bring to their actual occupations either an indifference mingled with whimsy, or an application that is sustained and haughty, scornful, bitter."[20] To be ill-suited for an occupation is to invite disenchantment, and I trusted that my absence from administration at this institution would be filled by someone more suited to the work.

As a scholar of the early modern era, I am also aware of Calvin's belief that God lays upon us the "burden" of vocation: "each man will bear and swallow the discomforts, vexations, weariness, and anxieties in his way of life."[21] To Calvin, even if a woman is ill-equipped for the demands of a particular call, she must still do it ungrudgingly.[22] Calvinist vocation is about duty, and as such, I personally find it uncongenial, a focus on the letter rather than the spirit of vocational service to others. The more I thought about higher leadership, at least at the middle level, it felt uncongenial to my interests, whereas I do feel made to teach and write in service to others. It may well be the case that one should go into higher leadership, but whatever career path opens before one, it would be wise to look first and foremost at one's particular gifts and inclinations, the amalgam of which helps to constitute a calling.

In addition, it seems crucial to ask one's family and friends about their perceptions of one's abilities. From a religious perspective, a vocation is that "to which we are called," and God often "extends His call through other people" who recognize sometimes better than we do ourselves how our abilities should be put to use for others.[23] And one need not be religious to understand a calling in one's life; all one has to do is to look at what one is good at and what one loves doing. When I advise my students, I often see their abilities and inclinations with greater clarity than they do. I do wonder when I see a student who wants to be a teacher but routinely comes late to class: How will she get up punctually every morning? And yet, I suspect she can change, as we all do. Luther was careful to note that one has multiple callings in life—mother, wife, daughter, teacher, and so on—and we know that those callings can change and shift as one grows, develops, and ages.

In my case, my good friend and closest colleague in our department told me privately and gently that he wondered if being a provost really fit my skill set. He himself had faced that same possibility a few years earlier and had politely declined the opportunity. As he put it, "I will never be jealous of an administrator making more money doing a job they couldn't pay me enough to do." That's a point worth pondering, especially when one is in a meeting listening to a dean tell a story about thwarting attempts to cheat on online exams when one would rather (in my case) be reading and discussing Shakespeare. I recalled another colleague with whom I once served on a curriculum committee, and she was fantastic at it. She loved reading the minutes as well as delving into the minutiae of new course proposals. Seeing her in action, I wondered why anyone would or even could love what for me was mere drudgery. Yet at the same time, her attention to detail in curricular matters made me feel—and rightly so—inferior to her in this necessary administrative skill. I am not constituted, I now realize, to revel in that form of work. But that same colleague found the minutiae of scholarly footnotes I enjoy working on mere painful drudgery. We were both called, but to different ends and lifework; both vocations are equally valuable.

Given the time to think about vocation with my colleagues, and to consider Luther's exhortation to use our gifts in "self-giving love" to others, I was able to regard my departure from the VPAA's office as a blessing on both sides.[24] I began to consider the possibility of God's using others, both in and out of administration, to direct me toward his goodness as well as my own and others' good. I had no regrets about the move, and I began to focus more on my attraction to reading and writing, a calling that has only deepened over the course of my life. Situations seldom change overnight, and this was no exception. I knew that if I wanted to write more, and still have time to teach some, I would have to find a position that could accommodate my interests, if there were one. I redoubled my teaching and scholarship, writing summers and every chance I had. After a few years, with multiple articles and a fourth book on the way, I noticed an endowed professorship open at the University of Mary Hardin-Baylor. Even though the teaching description was slightly outside my area, the two-course per semester teaching load, mission of the school, and location appealed to me. I applied, was fortunate enough to make it through both online and campus interviews, and eventually found, God willing, what I am confident is a calling. In this new vocation, I still teach, but I devote the remainder of my professional life to reading, research, and writing, the three activities I love, even in moments of drudgery.

Given the contingency of our lives as human beings, a calling can be subject to change; at times, we see a vocation quite clearly, at others, "we see through a glass darkly."[25] A professorship elsewhere was certainly not the career path of moving into higher leadership I had envisioned several years ago. In some ways, too, I suppose my story in and out of higher leadership may sound like a reverse academic rags-to-riches tale, and I will say that preparing for higher leadership and then leaving that path brings its share of bumps and tumult with it, and people who do not see the reason for leaving academic leadership may often regard it as career failure. It is not. It may equally seem to outsiders as if mine was a "soft landing" into an endowed professorship, but if so, it was one paved with soul-searching and years of hard work that made the move possible.

Moreover, any serious theological understanding of calling has to involve an acknowledgment that "every good gift and every perfect gift is from above" (James 1:17). It would be a form of intellectual dishonesty to talk about *my* accomplishments without acknowledging that everything I have is a gift bestowed on me for a time and a place. And while I feel blessed to have landed where I am, I am far from propounding a prosperity gospel in academia or anywhere else. For Luther (and unlike Calvin), calling is all about loving others so that "a person is ready and glad to do good to everyone, to serve everyone, to suffer everything out of love."[26] A true calling is about the self only insofar as one's talents can be used to help others flourish. What was crucial for me was to be open to other possibilities beyond the usual career path that leads from teaching to higher leadership, though that certainly works for the good of my colleagues in this volume and for the good of those whom they serve. But I also came to see that one can lead where one is, especially if that role equips one to use one's talents for others. What vocation meant for me, and what I hope it means for you, is that you will let your desires and interests guide you in pursuing not just a career but a calling in which you serve those around you. If you do that, I am confident you will find a proper and fitting vocation (or vocations, as Luther would say), your life's work, whether in higher leadership or elsewhere.[27]

NOTES

1. James Boswell, *Life of Johnson* (London & New York: Oxford University Press, 1953), 849.

2. See Mark Schwehn, "Good Teaching: Character Formation and Vocational Discernment," in *Vocation across the Academy: A New Vocabulary for Higher Education*, ed. David S. Cunningham (New York: Oxford University Press, 2017), 294–314.

3. David S. Cunningham, ed., *At This Time and in This Place: Vocation and Higher Education* (Oxford: Oxford University Press, 2015); David S. Cunningham, ed., *Vocation across the Academy: A New Vocabulary for Higher Education* (New York: Oxford University Press, 2017); and David S. Cunningham, ed., *Hearing Vocation Differently: Meaning, Purpose, and Identity in the Multi-Faith Academy* (New York: Oxford University Press, 2019).

4. See David S. Cunningham, "Introduction: Language That Works," in *Vocation across the Academy: A New Vocabulary for Higher Education*, ed. David S. Cunningham (New York: Oxford University Press, 2017), 11.

5. See Gustaf Wingren, *Luther on Vocation*, trans. Carl C. Rasmussen (Eugene, OR: Wipf & Stock, 2004); William C. Placher, ed., *Callings: Twenty Centuries of Christian Wisdom on Vocation* (Grand Rapids, MI: Eerdmans, 2005); Gene Edward Veith Jr., *God at Work: Your Christian Vocation in All of Life* (Wheaton, IL: Crossway, 2011); Kaethe Schwehn and L. DeAne Lagerquist, eds., *Claiming Our Callings: Toward a New Understanding of Vocation in the Liberal Arts* (New York: Oxford University Press, 2014); and Karen Swallow Prior and Leland Ryken, *On Reading Well: Finding the Good Life through Great Books* (Grand Rapids, MI: Brazos Press, 2018).

6. Cunningham, "Introduction," 11, italics his.

7. *Oxford English Dictionary*, s.v. "vocation," 2a, www.oed.com.

8. Lloyd E. Berry and William Whittingham, eds., *The Geneva Bible: A Facsimile*

of the 1560 Edition (Madison: University of Wisconsin Press, 1969), Romans 8:28, italics mine.

9. Roze Hentschell, "E-mail to the Author," February 28, 2022.

10. Kevin J. H. Dettmar, "Don't Cry for Me, Academia!," *The Chronicle of Higher Education*, June 27, 2016, https://www.chronicle.com/article/dont-cry-for-me -academia/.

11. E. D. Hirsch, *Validity in Interpretation* (New Haven: Yale University Press, 1967), 75.

12. Joyce E. Williams, "Rape Culture," in *The Blackwell Encyclopedia of Sociology*, ed. George Ritzer (Malden, MA: Wiley-Blackwell, 2007), 3791.

13. For an example of rape culture in classical antiquity, see Sarah Ruden, *Paul Among the People: The Apostle Reinterpreted and Reimagined in His Own Time* (Pantheon Books, 2010), chapt. 3.

14. Søren Kierkegaard, *Fear and Trembling*, trans. Alastair Hannay (New York: Penguin Classics, 1986), 64.

15. Quoted in Richard Daniel Altick and John J. Fenstermaker, "Vocation," in *The Art of Literary Research*, 4th ed. (New York: Norton, 1993), 18.

16. Wingren, *Luther on Vocation*, 120.

17. Martin Luther, *The Judgment of Martin Luther on Monastic Vows (De Votis Monasticis)*, ed. and trans. James Atkinson, vol. 44, Luther's Works (Philadelphia: Fortress Press, 1966), 130. See also Roland Herbert Bainton, *Here I Stand: A Life of Martin Luther* (New York: Abingdon-Cokesbury Press, 1950), 233.

18. Jaroslav Pelikan, ed., *Selected Psalms II*, trans. Alfred von Rohr Sauer, vol. 13, Luther's Works (St. Louis: Concordia, 1956), 146n.1; William James Bouwsma, *John Calvin: A Sixteenth-Century Portrait* (New York: Oxford University Press, 1988), 12–13.

19. Douglas James Schuurman, *Vocation: Discerning Our Callings in Life* (Grand Rapids, MI: Eerdmans, 2004), 127; Martin Luther, *Lectures on Galatians (1535)*, ed. Jaroslav Pelikan and Walter A. Hansen, trans. Jaroslav Pelikan, vol. 26, Luther's Works (St. Louis: Concordia, 1963), 17–19.

20. Marcel Proust, *In Search of Lost Time: Swann's Way*, trans. Lydia Davis, vol. 1 (Simon & Brown, 2018), 68–69.

21. John Calvin, *Institutes of the Christian Religion*, ed. John T. McNeill, trans. Ford Lewis Battles, vol. 1 (Louisville: Westminster John Knox Press, 2006), sec. 3.10.6.

22. Bouwsma, *John Calvin*, 181.

23. Gene Edward Veith Jr., *God at Work: Your Christian Vocation in All of Life* (Wheaton, IL: Crossway, 2011), 47, 55. The calling proper, however, is ultimately from God.

24. Wingren, *Luther on Vocation*, 6.

25. *King James Bible* (Nashville: Thomas Nelson, 1990), 1 Cor. 13:12.

26. Martin Luther, *Word and Sacrament I*, ed. and trans. E. Theodore Bachmann, vol. 35, Luther's Works (Philadelphia: Fortress Press, 1960), 371. Also quoted in Eric Metaxas, *Martin Luther: The Man Who Rediscovered God and Changed the World* (New York: Viking, 2017), 296. I am grateful to my colleague William Carrell for having pointed out this fundamental distinction between Calvin's and Luther's thoughts on vocation.

27. Martin Luther, *Sermons on the Gospel of St. John*, Chapters 14–16, ed. Jaroslav Pelikan, trans. Martin H. Bertram, vol. 24, Luther's Works (St. Louis: Concordia, 1961), 220; Martin Luther, *Church Postil I*, ed. Benjamin T. G. Mayes and James L. Langebartels, trans. John Nicholas Lenker, vol. 75, Luther's Works (St. Louis: Concordia, 2013), 44.

BIBLIOGRAPHY

Altick, Richard D., and John J. Fenstermaker. "Vocation." In *The Art of Literary Research*, 4th edition, edited by Richard D. Atlick and John J. Fenstermaker, 1–21. New York: Norton, 1993.

Bainton, Roland Herbert. *Here I Stand: A Life of Martin Luther*. New York: Abingdon-Cokesbury Press, 1950.

Berry, Lloyd E., and William Whittingham, eds. *The Geneva Bible: A Facsimile of the 1560 Edition*. Madison: University of Wisconsin Press, 1969.

Boswell, James. *Life of Johnson*. London & New York: Oxford University Press, 1953.

Bouwsma, William James. *John Calvin: A Sixteenth-Century Portrait*. New York: Oxford University Press, 1988.

Calvin, John. *Institutes of the Christian Religion*. Edited by John T. McNeill. Translated by Ford Lewis Battles. Vol. 1. Louisville: Westminster John Knox Press, 2006.

Cunningham, David S., ed. *At This Time and in This Place: Vocation and Higher Education*. Oxford: Oxford University Press, 2015.

Cunningham, David S., ed. *Hearing Vocation Differently: Meaning, Purpose, and Identity in the Multi-Faith Academy*. New York: Oxford University Press, 2019.

Cunningham, David S., "Introduction: Language That Works." In *Vocation across the Academy: A New Vocabulary for Higher Education*, edited by David S. Cunningham, 1–18. New York: Oxford University Press, 2017.

Cunningham, David S., ed. *Vocation across the Academy: A New Vocabulary for Higher Education*. New York: Oxford University Press, 2017.

Dettmar, Kevin J. H. "Don't Cry for Me, Academia!" *The Chronicle of Higher Education*, June 27, 2016. https://www.chronicle.com/article/dont-cry-for-me-academia/.

Hirsch, E. D. *Validity in Interpretation*. New Haven: Yale University Press, 1967.

Kierkegaard, Søren. *Fear and Trembling*. Translated by Alastair Hannay. New York: Penguin Classics, 1986.

King James Bible. Nashville: Thomas Nelson, 1990.

Luther, Martin. *Church Postil I*. Edited by Benjamin T. G. Mayes and James L. Langebartels. Translated by John Nicholas Lenker. Vol. 75. Luther's Works. St. Louis: Concordia, 2013.

Luther, Martin. *The Judgment of Martin Luther on Monastic Vows (De Votis Monasticis)*. Edited and translated by James Atkinson. Vol. 44. Luther's Works. Philadelphia: Fortress Press, 1966.

Luther, Martin. *Lectures on Galatians (1535)*. Edited by Jaroslav Pelikan and Walter A. Hansen. Translated by Jaroslav Pelikan. Vol. 26. Luther's Works. St. Louis: Concordia, 1963.

Luther, Martin. *Sermons on the Gospel of St. John, Chapters 14–16*. Edited by Jaroslav Pelikan. Translated by Martin H. Bertram. Vol. 24. Luther's Works. St. Louis: Concordia, 1961.

Luther, Martin. *Word and Sacrament I*. Edited and translated by E. Theodore Bachmann. Vol. 35. Luther's Works. Philadelphia: Fortress Press, 1960.

Metaxas, Eric. *Martin Luther: The Man Who Rediscovered God and Changed the World*. New York: Viking, 2017.

New American Standard Bible. Nashville: Thomas Nelson, 1977.

Pelikan, Jaroslav, ed. *Selected Psalms II*. Translated by Alfred von Rohr Sauer. Vol. 13. Luther's Works. St. Louis: Concordia, 1956.

Placher, William C., ed. *Callings: Twenty Centuries of Christian Wisdom on Vocation*. Grand Rapids, MI: Eerdmans, 2005.

Prior, Karen Swallow, and Leland Ryken. *On Reading Well: Finding the Good Life through Great Books*. Grand Rapids, MI: Brazos Press, 2018.

Proust, Marcel. *In Search of Lost Time: Swann's Way*. Translated by Lydia Davis. Vol. 1. Simon & Brown, 2018.

Ruden, Sarah. *Paul Among the People: The Apostle Reinterpreted and Reimagined in His Own Time*. Pantheon Books, 2010.

Schuurman, Douglas James. *Vocation: Discerning Our Callings in Life*. Grand Rapids, MI: Eerdmans, 2004.

Schwehn, Kaethe, and L. DeAne Lagerquist, eds. *Claiming Our Callings: Toward a New Understanding of Vocation in the Liberal Arts*. New York: Oxford University Press, 2014.

Schwehn, Mark. "Good Teaching: Character Formation and Vocational Discernment." In *Vocation across the Academy: A New Vocabulary for Higher Education*, edited by David S. Cunningham, 294–314. New York: Oxford University Press, 2017.

Veith, Jr., Gene Edward. *God at Work: Your Christian Vocation in All of Life*. Wheaton, Ill: Crossway, 2011.

Williams, Joyce E. "Rape Culture." In *The Blackwell Encyclopedia of Sociology*, edited by George Ritzer, 3791–95. Malden, MA: Wiley-Blackwell, 2007.

Wingren, Gustaf. *Luther on Vocation*. Translated by Carl C. Rasmussen. Eugene, OR: Wipf & Stock, 2004.

CODA

Leaning in to Twenty-First-Century Leadership

ROZE HENTSCHELL AND CATHERINE E. THOMAS

I n 2021, the American Council on Education (ACE) published a study, *Shared Equity Leadership*, noting the increased need for more inclusive, equitable, and shared models of higher education leadership. In the opening letter, ACE president Ted Mitchell asserts that "true institutional transformation . . . cannot take place without emphasizing the critical role leadership plays in centering equity as a priority, and connecting policy to practice, especially during uncertain times."[1] Changing student demographics, diverse social and cultural values in America, and global challenges such as the COVID-19 pandemic have thrown into relief how current institutional structures are not sufficient to support the needs of students, faculty, staff, and local communities. Budget challenges, particularly drastic decreases in support for public state colleges and universities, and public discourse critical of intellectuals and the work they do have led to increasing devaluation of the professoriate and continued inequitable, and at times unjust, treatment of colleagues in contingent positions.[2] The demands of the twenty-first century are shifting the landscape of higher education in America. This calls for the kind of critical reflection on leadership approaches that our contributors have done in this volume. As individuals employed in higher education and as a collective engaged in the important educational, research innovation, and service endeavors our institutions provide to the community, equity work belongs to us all.

The COVID-19 pandemic that began in 2020 highlighted many already-present cracks in higher education. As Michael Austin comments in his chapter, while the practices and procedures that were well-grounded at an institution likely held up, existing unaddressed problems or less effective practices crumbled under pressure and scrutiny from the demands of pandemic operations. The politics of power were exposed even more distinctively with the contentious positions held by some state governors, local officials, boards of trustees, and boards of regents that seemed at odds with faculty senates' and unions' requests for mask and vaccine mandates to keep them and their students safe. The fiscal aspects and some public opinions decrying the pandemic as a hoax or downplaying its risks appeared to be privileged over the health and well-being of those workers engaging in the labor to keep the doors of the institutions open. Political pressures meant that leadership teams in states with more relaxed public health policies were left with very limited options for how to manage the pandemic on their campuses. Those universities that did address the pandemic by implementing testing protocols and ramping up classroom technology were doing so at their financial peril (to the tune of $24 billion nationally), at a time of a 3.6 percent decrease in enrollment driven largely by a huge drop in first-year and international matriculation. Faculty and staff burnout and student mental health issues—already present on most campuses—increased dramatically.[3] These circumstances have led to further erosion of the trust faculty and staff may have with their upper-level administrators, as well as with system offices around the country. Before any real change can be effected, trust will need to be rebuilt.

Three actions in particular seem critical if higher education is to be sustainable and thrive in the face of this changing environment. Institutions should (1) work with their state and private governing agencies to advocate more powerfully for the contributions and value of the professoriate and the work they do, deflating mischaracterized representations of faculty as overpaid elites and impressing upon them the diversity of positions, perspectives, and compensations at institutions; (2) evaluate policies that impact hiring, evaluation, and shared governance, and work toward more inclusive practices; (3) develop infrastructures that equitably recruit, train, and support leaders from faculty and staff. While faculty involvement and support are integral to these processes, it is not their primary job to show that their work is relevant or that academic programs are directly tied to clear career pathways. However, campus leaders at all levels must collectively and strategically move toward these goals; they cannot only happen at the executive level if systemic cultural change is to occur.

As Laurie Ellinghausen's chapter urges, innovation in higher education need not, should not, be relegated to technology improvements, research entrepreneurism, and new degree and certificate programs. We need to revolutionize the ways leadership recruitment, training, support, and integration happen in higher education and are understood by the public. Committing to and building robust shared equity leadership structures throughout colleges and universities in the United States is key to institutional success, sustainability, and service to students, faculty, staff, and communities. Further, as both Emily J. Morgan's essay suggests and the ACE study argues, this work must be highly collaborative at all levels of the institution to ensure key voices are not only heard but integrated into the plans in which everyone will be expected to participate.[4] Humanities leaders, with their backgrounds in intensely analyzing the history and dynamics of human culture, are well equipped for this work, keeping the focus on the diverse humans involved and the complex ways in which societies produce and consume knowledge.

Of the three proposed actions to move in this direction, the first action is the foundation from which the other two can build. The political and cultural environments in which institutions of higher education operate increasingly seem fraught and oppositional. Rather than seeing colleges and universities as partners in bettering society through cultivating informed citizens and offering upward mobility via education and career opportunities, many politicians, business, and media outlets have embroiled them in the culture wars. Stories about higher education now tend to fixate on free speech controversies, what theories and ideas are or are not present in coursework, (false) accounts of the "indoctrination" of young people, and speculations about the value of teaching and/or researching highly specific topics. While encouraging free thought and pointed curiosity about the inner workings of higher education is healthy and useful, the blatant skepticism and outright hostility of those not understanding the work done there is damaging to higher education as a bedrock of learning. Instead of asking thoughtful, sincere questions of those doing the on-the-ground work, assumptions are made and not all views are considered carefully; other priorities prevail, which can erode goodwill and do real harm to students, faculty, and staff. Decision-making has greater stakes when it is done by people who do not have the background or in some cases, the care to respectfully consider what happens or doesn't happen in the classroom. To be sure, schools have a business side of things that must be considered and managed, but acting like colleges and universities are like any other business is to misunderstand the mission and academic community entirely.

If higher education is to be sustainable through the twenty-first century as an intellectual learning community versus solely a transactional business, rebuilding trust between all stakeholders and improving higher education's status in public forums are necessary. Leaders need to reclaim and amplify the vision of institutions as partners in the work of improving communities. Colleges and universities then need to work to be seen as transparent, authentic leaders, not antagonists putting up barriers to creativity and innovation. The model of shared equity leadership outlined by ACE brings back the human elements so often left out of decision-making and governance discussions, "particularly love, vulnerability, humility, transparency, and being comfortable with being uncomfortable."[5] In many ways, this humanities-inflected work will require both higher education and community members to rethink the language of leadership spoken in conference rooms and Zoom meetings alike. It calls on individuals to reflect deeply on themselves, their communication practices, and the ways in which their decisions impact others, regardless of intent. Following the slow teaching philosophy, might we practice—whenever possible—slow leadership, inculcating a culture of thoughtful, deliberate decision-making over giving into the crisis of the urgent?[6] Within this different orientation to governance, we might further consider the diversity not only of individual identities and groups but also leadership styles and institution types that will inform the pathways to more desirable, just, and equitable practices nationwide.

The second action builds on the first, calling on higher education leaders at all levels to think creatively and conscientiously about inclusivity in all its forms. As Carter et al. urge in this collection, we must not shy away from the difficult process of examining, unpacking, and disrupting the systems and structures of power that can invisibly discriminate and erect insurmountable barriers to those seeking progression and success (be they faculty, staff, or students). Often these power structures are embedded in campus policies, from student admissions and transfer articulations, to expectations around technology access and use, to staff leave and compensation for extra teaching and service work, to faculty evaluation and promotion guidelines. They are written into manuals, codes, and governance documents, some of which haven't been revised in a generation. If we are to lean into an equity-minded leadership model, we must start with our practices, policies, and procedures and always remain mindful of their impact on the more marginalized of our people.

The third action goes far beyond creating diversity, equity, and inclusion (DEI) leadership appointments, creating committees and task forces, publicly stating support for related initiatives, and embracing equal opportunity employment. These are very good first steps, but we must be mindful that words are not enough. Equality is not enough. Equity and justice in higher education leadership should be the goals if we are to effect real change. Admittedly, those are ambitious goals, but they are necessary ones. What does that look like? To begin, there needs to be more accountability in recognizing and actively addressing gaps of representation in leadership roles, whether they be on the ground level of departments and programs or at the top of institutional hierarchies. Representation is an important first step in having multiple perspectives, backgrounds, and voices at the table when decisions are being made about the direction an institution is going and how it treats its students, faculty, and staff.

Additionally, as many institutions elevate or institute the role of chief diversity officer (or vice president for DEI), they must understand that investing in one person's salary is not enough. An ample budget and staff support for that position are necessary to be able to move toward meaningful campus change. Further, DEI work should not be the sole responsibility of one unit on campus. We all need to address and own the work and ask the hard questions. How will the institution not only include but also welcome, affirm, and support all individuals, accounting for embedded, systemic biases, while amplifying their strengths and helping them develop in areas for growth? Recursive and frequent accountability of how all campus units' operations support and are enacting the shared goals of Diversity, Equity, Inclusion, and Justice, accountability that is vocally and visibly endorsed by senior leadership, will make a tremendous difference.

Expanding the web of professional mentors for the admin-curious and leaders at all levels in a more purposeful and systematic way is one intervention that can move institutions in the direction of shared equity leadership. As Darryl Dickson-Carr, Rowena M. Tomaneng, and Chyna N. Crawford discuss, having mentors and mentoring others are powerful ways to share knowledge, skills, experience, and academic culture-specific expertise. Mentors are also invaluable for helping junior faculty and administrators network and navigate politically complex waters, increasing their professional capital, and providing buffering when necessary. While mentorship has often been an ad hoc or informal arrangement between colleagues or relegated to the space of professional organizations, institutions that invest the time, space, and energy to create more accessible forms of mentoring will likely see the pay-off in more informed and well-connected leaders available to serve the college or university.

Another intervention, as Kristina Quynn's essay highlights, is to enact just and equitable practices around contingent faculty and staff. At many institutions, these academic professionals teach most of the introductory level classes—in effect underwriting general education programs—and have lower pay, fewer (if any) benefits, fewer opportunities for professional development, and little to no job security. These critical faculty members may or may not be welcomed by full-time and/or tenure-track colleagues and administrators, and they may not always be ensured a representative voice at the tables of shared governance. Equity issues abound in higher education, and twenty-first-century leadership calls for more attention to solving those around supporting underrepresented or marginalized groups: contingent faculty, women, people of color, members of the LGBTQ+ community, and especially people with intersectional identities.

If higher education administrators at all levels, as well as community and state leaders, undertake the actions outlined in this chapter, we will be in effect redefining what leadership—and the relationships that structure it—looks like. This new leadership for the twenty-first century is much more aware of and attentive to the needs of the people it serves: our students. They are our "why?" Students who identify as part of Gen Z expect more from us who have come before. Higher education leaders must lean into both the expectations and realities of this ever-changing, diverse, cyber-rich global world, innovating leadership models and practices, rather than clinging to outdated structures that no longer serve us. As Arundahti Roy wrote in the early days of the COVID-19 pandemic, inflection points present to us a choice:

> Historically, pandemics have forced humans to break with the past and imagine their world anew. This one is no different. It is a portal, a gateway between one world and the next. We can choose to walk through it, dragging the carcasses of our prejudice and hatred, our avarice, our data banks and dead ideas, our dead rivers and smoky skies behind us. Or we can walk through lightly, with little luggage, ready to imagine another world. And ready to fight for it.[7]

Mapping this to our higher education equity landscape, we must change to avoid being left behind and rendered inconsequential to our students and the public eye, with their new visions of what education and the world should look like, and what communities will look like.

Shared equity leadership is one model that provides professional promise.[8] But it calls on us to do the difficult work of transforming ourselves and our institutions, and to hold each other accountable, no matter how hard or unsettling. We must acknowledge and reckon with the past as well as our current mistakes, and learn from those. We must make hard and sometimes unpopular choices as leaders to do right by more. In ACE's *Shared Equity Leadership* report, one campus leader reflected on the advice she would provide fellow campus leaders wishing to practice shared equity leadership. She stated, "It's really important to be aware of this notion of transformation, because this is transformational work, but really to understand who you're transforming, and you really have to start with yourself."[9] We must first acknowledge our privileges, biases, and identities and accept that we are all at our own stage of learning, and we must continue to learn and grow from there. In some sense, this is what the humanities disciplines have ingrained in us, the habit of noticing patterns of language, behavior, culture, history; the desire to understand them and to produce meaning from them; to endeavor to avoid repeating critical errors and wrongs of the past; to work toward a more complete embrace of the incredible diversity of humanity.

As we reflect on our own leadership transformations, and how better to support others in pursuing theirs, we should keep asking these hard questions, to sit with the productive discomfort that comes with real growth and authentic analysis. Whom are we serving and how? In what ways can we prepare ourselves and others to be more inclusive, effective leaders at our schools and in our communities? How do we realize inclusion and support of our marginalized colleagues and students through our decision-making? As the contributors to this collection have shown, we have begun to do that important work. Let us commit to taking those next steps, together.

NOTES

1. Ted Mitchell, "Letter from the American Council on Education," in *Shared Equity Leadership: Making Equity Everyone's Work*, eds. Adrianna Kezar, Elizabeth Holcombe, Darsella Vigil, and Jude Paul Mathias Dizon (Washington, DC: American Council on Education; Los Angeles: University of Southern California, Pullias Center for Higher Education, 2021), vi.

2. See, for example, the controversy over University of Florida professors testifying in lawsuits involving the state: Greg Allen, "Some Professors Are Blocked from Testifying in Suits Against the State," *NPR*, November 3, 2021, https://www.npr.org/2021/11/03/1051773738/some-florida-professors-are-blocked-from-testifying-in-suits-against-the-state.

3. Audrey Williams June and Jacquelyn Elias, "What Higher Education Has Endured for the Past Year," *The Chronicle of Higher Education*, March 11, 2021, https://www.chronicle.com/article/what-higher-education-has-endured-for-the-past-year.

4. Adrianna Kezar, Elizabeth Holcombe, Darsella Vigil, and Jude Paul Mathias Dizon, *Shared Equity Leadership: Making Equity Everyone's Work* (Washington, DC: American Council on Education; Los Angeles: University of Southern California, Pullias Center for Higher Education, 2021).

5. Kezar et. al., *Shared Equity Leadership*, 16.
6. For more on this idea of bringing the slow movement into higher education, see Hendrik van der Sluis, "Slow Higher Education," *New Vistas*, 2021, https://uwlpress.uwl.ac.uk/newvistas/article/id/105/.
7. Arundhati Roy, "The Pandemic Is a Portal," *Financial Times*, April 3, 2020, https://www.ft.com/content/10d8f5e8-74eb-11ea-95fe-fcd274e920ca.
8. For more detailed reflections on the promise of this leadership model, we recommend the essays in Adrianna Kezar and Julie Posselt, eds., *Higher Education Administration for Social Justice and Equity: Critical Perspectives for Leadership* (New York and London: Routledge, 2020).
9. Kezar et. al., *Shared Equity Leadership*, 9.

BIBLIOGRAPHY

Allen, Greg. "Some Professors Are Blocked from Testifying in Suits Against the State." *NPR*, November 3, 2021. https://www.npr.org/2021/11/03/1051773738/some-florida-professors-are-blocked-from-testifying-in-suits-against-the-state.

June, Audrey Williams, and Jacquelyn Elias. "What Higher Education Has Endured for the Past Year." *The Chronicle of Higher Education*, March 11, 2021. https://www.chronicle.com/article/what-higher-education-has-endured-for-the-past-year.

Kezar, Adrianna, Elizabeth Holcombe, Darsella Vigil, and Jude Paul Mathias Dizon. *Shared Equity Leadership: Making Equity Everyone's Work.* Washington, DC: American Council on Education; Los Angeles: University of Southern California, Pullias Center for Higher Education, 2021.

Kezar, Adrianna, and Julie Posselt, eds. *Higher Education Administration for Social Justice and Equity: Critical Perspectives for Leadership* (New York and London: Routledge, 2020).

Mitchell, Ted. "Letter from the American Council on Education." In *Shared Equity Leadership: Making Equity Everyone's Work*, edited by Adrianna Kezar, Elizabeth Holcombe, Darsella Vigil, and Jude Paul Mathias Dizon, xi, Washington, DC: American Council on Education; Los Angeles: University of Southern California, Pullias Center for Higher Education, 2021.

Roy, Arundhati. "The Pandemic Is a Portal." *Financial Times*, April 3, 2020. https://www.ft.com/content/10d8f5e8-74eb-11ea-95fe-fcd274e920ca.

Van der Sluis, Hendrik. "Slow Higher Education." *New Vistas* 6, no. 1 (2020): 4–9. https://uwlpress.uwl.ac.uk/newvistas/article/id/105/.

CONTRIBUTORS

MICHAEL AUSTIN is executive vice president for academic affairs and provost at the University of Evansville in Evansville, Indiana. He holds a PhD in English from the University of California at Santa Barbara and taught English and world literature for eleven years before becoming a full-time administrator. He has written several books on literary topics and is the editor of the Norton textbook *Reading the World: Ideas That Matter*. His most recent book, *We Must Not Be Enemies: Restoring America's Civic Tradition*, explores the possibility of productive disagreement and civic friendship in a divided and polarized political sphere.

SEAN BENSON holds an endowed professorship, the Frank W. Mayborn Chair of Arts and Sciences, at the University of Mary Hardin-Baylor in Belton, Texas. A literary scholar of the English Renaissance (PhD Saint Louis University), he is the author of numerous articles and three books on the religious dynamics of Shakespeare's plays. With the philosopher Paul Jensen, he coauthored *Fantasy Land: Anti-Realism in America* (2022), which documents the attempt of establishment elites in academia, the judiciary, and the media to determine the acceptability of political and social views, moral beliefs—even the language we use—and to suppress competing views. Sean lives in Temple, Texas, with his wife and two children.

GENESEA M. CARTER is associate director of composition and a special assistant professor of rhetoric and composition at Colorado State University, where she teaches rhetoric and composition and codirects programmatic curriculum design, professional development, and graduate student training. Her work has appeared in *Composition Studies*, *Journal of Teaching Writing*, *Open Words: Access and English Studies*, *Teaching History: A Journal of Methods*, *Writers: Craft and Context*, and *Academic Labor: Research and Artistry*. She is the coeditor of *Class in the Composition Classroom: Pedagogy and the Working Class* (2017) and is currently editing a collection on network theory, social justice, and writing program administration. She lives in Fort Collins, Colorado, with her husband and two muted tortoiseshell cats, Alice and Florence.

RYAN CLAYCOMB is professor of English and theater at Colorado State University and associate dean in the College of Liberal Arts. He teaches courses in modern dramatic literature, gender studies, dramaturgy, and critical theory; his scholarly work on nonfiction drama and performance has appeared in several journals and books, including *In the Lurch: Verbatim Theatre and the Crisis of Democratic Deliberation* (University of Michigan Press, 2023). He is also coeditor, with Randi Gray Kristensen, of *Writing against the Curriculum: Antidisciplinarity in the Writing and Cultural Studies Classroom* (Lexington, 2009). As an administrator, he has served in leadership roles in honors education, interdisciplinary humanities research, faculty development, and student success initiatives.

CHYNA N. CRAWFORD is associate professor of criminal justice and chair of the Department of Social Sciences at Elizabeth City State University. Born and raised in Charlottesville, Virginia, Dr. Crawford was the first in her family to earn a doctoral degree. With a PhD in juvenile justice from Prairie View A&M University, Dr. Crawford's academic research interests lie in the areas of media, juvenile justice, victimology, women, minorities, social justice, and criminal justice reform. Outside of academia, Dr. Crawford can be found engaging in genealogical research and enjoying the hobby of photography.

DARRYL DICKSON-CARR is professor of English at Southern Methodist University, where he served a six-year tenure as department chair. He teaches courses in twentieth-century American literature, African American literature, and satire. His researches focus primarily on African American rhetoric, the "New Negro" or Harlem Renaissance, and African American satirical works in the twentieth and twenty-first centuries. He is the author of *Spoofing the Modern: Satire in the Harlem Renaissance* (University of South Carolina Press, 2015), *The Columbia Guide to Contemporary African American Fiction* (Columbia University Press, 2005), and *African American Satire: The Sacredly Profane Novel* (University of Missouri Press, 2001). He has published essays in such collections as *Editing the Harlem Renaissance* (Clemson University Press, 2021), *Post-Soul Satire* (University Press of Mississippi, 2014), *Contemporary African American Literature: The Living Canon* (Indiana University Press, 2013), and *Literary Expressions of African Spirituality* (Lexington, 2013). He has also published articles in *Studies in American Humor*, *American Literary History*, *Studies in the Novel*, and *CLA Journal*. His current research focuses on African American political rhetoric.

LAURIE ELLINGHAUSEN is professor of English and associate vice provost for Academic Innovation at the University of Missouri–Kansas City. She is the author of *Pirates, Traitors, and Apostates: Renegade Identities in Early Modern English Writing* (University of Toronto Press, 2018) and *Labor and Writing in Early Modern England, 1567–1667* (Ashgate, 2008). She is also the editor of *Approaches to Teaching Shakespeare's English History Plays* (MLA Publications, 2017). In her administrative role, she oversees the development and approval of new academic programs across units on campus.

ROZE HENTSCHELL is senior associate dean for academic programs at Colorado State University. In that role, she helps develop and oversees all undergraduate and graduate programs, curriculum, education abroad, and experiential learning for the College of Liberal Arts. She works with faculty and staff to create innovative academic experiences and promote and foster student success and is committed to enhancing access and success for underrepresented and minoritized students. She has been a leader in strategic planning efforts and is involved in the work of the campus's Academic Master Plan. She was a 2021–2022 American Council on Education Fellow with a placement at the University of California San Diego in the Office of the Executive Vice Chancellor for Academic Affairs. She is a professor of English with a specialization in early modern literature and cultural studies. Her latest book, *St Paul's Cathedral Precinct in Early Modern Literature and Culture: Spatial Practices*, was published in 2020 by Oxford University Press.

EMILY RUTH ISAACSON is associate professor of English, chair of the English Department, and director of the Integrated Studies General Education Program and the Life of the Mind Honors Program at Heidelberg University in Tiffin, Ohio. Prior to her work there, she was on faculty at Chowan University in rural North Carolina, where she served as the coordinator of the Chowan Critical Thinking Program. Trained initially as an early modernist, she studied at Augustana College and the University of Missouri, Columbia. Her scholarly interests include early modern city comedy, as well as the intersection of the humanities and honors education, and her work has appeared in such places as the *Ben Jonson Journal* and *Journal of the Midwest Modern Language Association*. In addition to her work teaching and researching, she has been known to write poetry and dabble in photography.

AURORA MATZKE is senior associate provost at Azusa Pacific University, where she oversees operations and strategic planning. She also teaches in the fields of education and rhetoric and composition and has directed and worked in multiple writing centers and programs. Her recent publications focus on feminist administrative models and promoting inclusivity through higher education systems reform.

EMILY J. MORGAN is director of dance and associate professor at Colorado State University. She is interested in community-based dance and participatory dance in traditional and nontraditional spaces. Emily has performed and presented her work throughout the United States, and in Norway, Austria, Barbados, and Mexico. She has taught at Winthrop University, the University of Texas, El Paso, El Paso Community College, University of North Carolina, Greensboro, Elon University, the North Carolina Governor's School, and at a public magnet arts high school in Winston-Salem, North Carolina. Emily holds an MFA in dance from the University of North Carolina, Greensboro, and a BA in dance from Denison University in Ohio. She is a doctoral candidate in dance at Texas Woman's University, completing her dissertation on community dance practices in the United States.

KRISTINA QUYNN is an assistant dean in the Graduate School and director of CSU Writes at Colorado State University, Fort Collins. Trained as a literary scholar, she has published on experimental fiction and criticism in *Genre*, *Journal of Midwest Modern Language Association*, *MLA Teaching Approaches*, and elsewhere. Quynn coedited a collection on performative criticism with

Robin Silbergleid titled *Reading and Writing Experimental Texts: Innovative Criticism* (Palgrave 2017). She brazenly declares herself to be the only scholar to have a piece published in the *Chronicle of Higher Education* that includes references to "feces, vomit, blood, amputated limbs, corpses" to describe the abject status and characterization of contingent faculty in contemporary academic fiction. After teaching and researching for nearly a decade off the tenure track, Quynn has had the great fortune to work with two leader mentors and sponsors who helped her navigate a path to tenure equivalency and career advancement. Quynn is an active member on the board of the Colorado Wyoming Network of Women Leaders and the director of their Academic Management Institute through which she helps facilitate the professional development of women leaders in higher education. She believes in engaged scholarship, meaningful and shared leadership, and the practical value of the humanities.

PHILIP ROBINSON-SELF is associate professor of learning and teaching at BPP University, United Kingdom, where he teaches curriculum development and leadership. His research and teaching interests span English literature and culture of the late medieval and early modern periods, critical pedagogical theory and practice, and the intellectual history of universities. He is the author of *Early Modern Britain's Relationship to Its Past: The Historiographical Fortunes of the Legends of Brute, Albina, and Scota* (Medieval Institute Publications, 2019), which focuses on the reception of gendered national origin myths in early modern Britain. His current book project is a cultural history of the power relations between universities and states.

CATHERINE E. THOMAS is associate director of Undergraduate Transition Seminars and senior academic professional at the Georgia Institute of Technology. She oversees the first-year and transfer seminar program and supports other high-impact learning initiatives. Thomas is a 2023 Georgia Association for Women in Higher Education (GAWHE) Leadership Program Fellow and participant in the 2023 ACE Women's Leadership Mentoring Program. She is passionate about providing equitable and inclusive access for all students to succeed in higher education, as well as supporting faculty development toward that goal. Thomas has additional research interests in Shakespeare and the comic arts and has published articles, book chapters, and a coedited essay collection on early modern gender, sexuality, and violence.

ROWENA M. TOMANENG has been a multicultural educator in the California Community Colleges for over twenty-seven years and currently serves as the president of San José City College (SJCC), California. Prior to SJCC, she served as the president of Berkeley City College, California, and in multiple roles at De Anza College, California, including faculty in English, intercultural studies, and women's studies. Her research and publications explore human rights, social movements, transnational feminism, and racial equity in education for Asian American and Pacific Islander students.

BONNIE VIDRINE-ISBELL is associate professor and English language program director at Biola University in Southern California. She enjoys multidisciplinary research on second language (L2) composition, social neuroscience in education, and L2 pedagogy. She has taught English as a second and foreign language for over fifteen years in California, Washington, Louisiana, Thailand, Spain, and Belize. She is currently exploring language attachment theory, a multidisciplinary theory linking social bonding to language acquisition and pedagogy.

ANNE-MARIE E. WALKOWICZ is associate professor of English and coordinator of interdisciplinary studies at Central State University. She has previously held administrative positions as the director of teaching and learning and interim director of writing. She is currently working on a monograph entitled *The Drama of Counsel: Staging History in Early Modern Theatre.* Her work analyzes the intersection of early modern drama, history, and political theory. In addition to her work in English studies, she also researches the role of faculty learning communities in providing professional development opportunities for faculty. This work has been presented at the American Association of Colleges and Universities Summer Institute, American Association of State Colleges and Universities Academic Affairs Meeting, and the Air Force Institute of Technology. Her distinction in academic leadership has been acknowledged by the Southwestern Ohio Council of Higher Education, where she was a recipient of the Faculty Excellence Award for three years.

INDEX

Page number in italics indicates figure.